W9-CTW-459

DATE DUE

DEMCO 38-296

Laughlin McDonald is a graduate of Columbia University and the University of Virginia Law School. He has been director of the Southern Regional Office of the American Civil Liberties Union in Atlanta, Georgia, since 1972. He has represented minorities in numerous discrimination cases, testified frequently before Congress, and has written extensively for scholarly and popular publications on constitutional and civil liberties issues.

john a. powell is presently a professor at the University of Minnesota Law School and director of the Institute on Race and Poverty. He is also a consultant on minority and consumer rights in Africa. He previously served as national legal director of the American Civil Liberties Union. Before coming to the ACLU, powell taught law at the University of San Francisco Law School and practiced housing law.

Also in this series

AN AMERICAN CIVIL LIBERTIES UNION HANDBOOK

THE RIGHTS OF RACIAL MINORITIES

THE BASIC ACLU GUIDE TO RACIAL MINORITY RIGHTS

SECOND EDITION
Completely Revised and Updated

Laughlin McDonald
john a. powell

General Editor of the Handbook Series
Norman Dorsen, President, ACLU 1976–1991

SOUTHERN ILLINOIS UNIVERSITY PRESS
CARBONDALE AND EDWARDSVILLE

Copyright © 1993 by the American Civil Liberties Union
All rights reserved
Printed in the United States of America
Production supervised by Natalia Nadraga

96   95   94   93   4   3   2   1

Library of Congress Cataloging-in-Publication Data

McDonald, Laughlin.
    The rights of racial minorities / Laughlin McDonald. john a.
powell. — 2nd ed., completely rev. and updated.
        p.   cm. — (An American Civil Liberties Union handbook)
    Rev. ed. of: The rights of racial minorities / E. Richard Larson,
Laughlin McDonald. c1980.
    1. Race discrimination—Law and legislation—United States.
2. Minorities—Legal status, laws, etc.—United States. 3. Afro-
Americans—Legal status, laws, etc.   I. powell, john a. (john
anthony).   II. Larson, E. Richard. Rights of racial minorities.
III. Title.   IV. Series.
KF4755.Z9L37   1993
342.73′0873—dc20
[347.302873]   93-15756
ISBN 0-8093-1899-7   CIP
ISBN 0-8093-1888-1 (pbk.)

The paper used in this publication meets the minimum requirements of
American National Standard for Information Sciences—Permanence of
Paper for Printed Library Materials, ANSI Z39.48-1984. ∞

Contents

Preface

This guide sets forth your rights under present law and offers suggestions on how they can be protected. It is one of a continuing series of handbooks published in cooperation with the American Civil Liberties Union (ACLU).

Surrounding these publications is the hope that Americans, informed of their rights, will be encouraged to exercise them. Through their exercise, rights are given life. If they are rarely used, they may be forgotten and violations may become routine.

This guide offers no assurances that your rights will be respected. The laws may change, and in some of the subjects covered in these pages, they change quite rapidly. An effort has been made to note those parts of the law where movement is taking place, but it is not always possible to predict accurately when the law *will* change.

Even if laws remain the same, their interpretation by courts and administrative officials often varies. In a federal system such as ours there is a built-in problem since state and federal laws differ, not to speak of the variations among states. In addition, there is much diversity in the ways in which particular courts and administrative officials interpret the same law at any given moment.

If you encounter what you consider to be a specific abuse of your rights, you should seek legal assistance. There are a number of agencies that may help you, among them ACLU affiliate offices, but bear in mind that the ACLU is a limited-purpose organization. In many communities there are federally funded legal service offices that provide assistance to persons who cannot afford the costs of legal representation.

In general, the rights that the ACLU defends are freedom of inquiry and expression; due process of law; equal protection of the laws; and privacy. The authors in this series have discussed other rights (even though they sometimes fall outside the ACLU's usual concern) in order to provide as much guidance as possible.

These books have been planned as guides for the people directly affected: thus the question-and-answer format. (In some areas there are more detailed works available for experts.) These guides seek to raise the major issues and inform the nonspecialist of the basic law on the subject. The authors of these books are themselves specialists who understand the need for information at "street level."

If you encounter a specific legal problem in an area discussed in one of these handbooks, show the book to your attorney. Of course, he or she will not be able to rely exclusively on the handbook to provide you with adequate representation. But if your attorney hasn't had a great deal of experience in the specific area, the handbook can provide helpful suggestions on how to proceed.

Norman Dorsen, General Editor
Stokes Professor of Law
New York University School of Law

Acknowledgments

For their work in helping to prepare the following chapters, we would like to thank Nathan Courtney, who worked on chapter 4 ("Education"); Elizabeth Benjamin, chapter 5 ("Housing"); and Helena Shin, chapter 10 ("Race Conscious Remedies"). We would also like to thank Art Eisenberg for his comments on the housing chapter, Isabelle Katz Pinzler for her comments on the chapter on race conscious remedies, and Chris Hansen for his comments on the education chapter. In addition, we would like to acknowledge the work of Topaz Lennard and Zachary Nightingale in preparing and producing much of the manuscript.

THE RIGHTS OF
RACIAL MINORITIES

I

Introduction and Overview

American democracy was founded on a contradiction—that all people were equal but that human slavery was tolerable. The nation's belief in equality was written into the Declaration of Independence, which claimed that "all men are created equal." Its tolerance of slavery was contained in three original provisions of the Constitution of 1787, which counted a slave as only three-fifths of a person for purposes of apportionment of the House of Representatives, prohibited Congress from abolishing the slave trade prior to the year 1808, and provided for the return of fugitive slaves. The subsequent history of this nation has been in large measure the story—often violent, sometimes heroic, and always traumatic—of its attempts to reconcile its stated beliefs with its actual racial practices.

In 1857 the Supreme Court squarely confronted the issue of whether slavery was lawful in the infamous case of *Dred Scott v. Sanford.*[1] The court held that slaves were not citizens and thus had no access to the federal courts, that temporary residence in a free state or territory did not make a slave free, and that the Missouri Compromise of 1820 abolishing slavery in portions of the Louisiana Territory was unconstitutional since it violated the property rights of slave owners. *Dred Scott* further divided a nation already torn on the issue of slavery and foreshadowed the Civil War, which erupted four years later. Out of that war, in 1866, came the Thirteenth Amendment and the eventual end of "the peculiar institution" of human slavery.[2] The Thirteenth Amendment did not, however, bring to fulfillment the national commitment to equality.

Many of the states responded to abolition by enacting laws known as *black codes*, which imposed upon blacks a status different from slavery in name only. The black codes contained crippling restrictions on the rights of freedmen to own, purchase, inherit, or convey property, to have access to the courts, and to contract and pursue employment. Partly in response to the black codes, the Congress enacted in 1866 a sweeping civil rights act designed to confer full and equal citizenship upon blacks. Then, on 9 July 1868, the Fourteenth Amendment was ratified, which among other things guarantees to all persons without regard to race the equal protection of the laws. The last of the great post–Civil War constitutional amendments was the Fifteenth Amendment, ratified on 3 March 1870, guaranteeing the equal right to vote.

The Civil War amendments were implemented by a number of congressional acts which essentially sought to wipe out racial discrimination, whether supported by local legislation, the courts, or custom and practice. Had the amendments and implementing legislation been effectively enforced, some of the racial division and injustice that ensued over the next hundred years may have been avoided. But Reconstruction, as far as racial minorities are concerned, was a failure. Within only a few years after its passage, much of the legislation designed to enforce the Civil War amendments was declared unconstitutional by the Supreme Court. The Court also severely limited the application of the amendments themselves. Civil rights legislation was further weakened by the Congress, which eventually repealed major portions of the remaining Reconstruction laws.

Following the Compromise of 1877, and the withdrawal of federal troops from the confederate states, Reconstruction ended. The states were left free to adopt their own "local" solutions to race relations. Many states opted for separate-but-equal laws, known as *Jim Crow* legislation. A necessary condition for Jim Crow was political disfranchisement of minority voters. Accordingly, the years following Reconstruction saw the systematic elimination of blacks from the electorate by state legislatures through such discriminatory devices as literacy tests and the poll tax for registering and voting.

The inevitable result of Jim Crow and racial discrimination was injustice, bitterness, and violence. There were some five thousand reported lynchings in the United States after 1859 and full-blown race riots across the nation—in New York in 1900; in Springfield, Ohio, in 1904; in Statesboro and Atlanta in 1906; in Greensburg, Indiana, in 1906; and in Brownsville, Texas, and Springfield, Illinois, in 1908. But the forces for racial change in the United States were never entirely stilled.

In 1905, responding to black lynchings and other forms of racial discrimination, W. E. B. DuBois and others, many of whom were former abolitionists, met at Niagara Falls, New

York, and founded the Niagara Movement. Later, in 1909 and 1910, the group formed the National Association for the Advancement of Colored People (NAACP) and adopted an agenda for racial reform that served as a blueprint during the next fifty years. The Supreme Court was also beginning slowly and sporadically to chip away at Jim Crow in a series of cases declaring a number of laws and practices unconstitutional: a city ordinance requiring racial segregation in neighborhood housing, the enforcement by state courts of racially discriminatory covenants in deeds to real estate, and racial segregation in interstate transportation.

The most dramatic modern breakthrough in racial reform came in 1954 when the Supreme Court handed down its decision in *Brown v. Board of Education*,[3] involving separate but equal public schools. The Court concluded that separate educational facilities were "inherently unequal" and ruled that Jim Crow schools deprived blacks of equal protection of the laws guaranteed by the Fourteenth Amendment. The *Brown* decision marked the beginning of the end of the formal aspects of Jim Crow. The decade following *Brown*, with its renewed promise of racial equality, has aptly been called the second Reconstruction. But if *Brown* held out hope, it also drew intense resistance from states that stood to be most affected by it. School desegregation was not in fact significantly implemented until the 1970s, more than fifteen years after the historic *Brown* opinion.

In response to the growing demand for equal rights of blacks and the relentless pressure being mounted by the Civil Rights Movement, Congress enacted major pieces of modern civil rights legislation during the 1960s that have taken the country an enormous step closer to realizing the promises of the first Reconstruction. These modern statutes, discussed in detail in this book, protect racial minorities against most forms of public and private discrimination in employment, housing, accommodations, federally assisted programs, education, voting, and the administration of civil and criminal laws.

The existence of extensive federal protection does not mean that the law has been translated into nondiscriminatory behavior. Such was the lesson of the first Reconstruction. Actual enforcement of the right of racial minorities is crucial to realizing equality. Unfortunately, enforcement, even in the modern era, has been markedly slow and uneven. In 1968, a century after adoption of the Fourteenth Amendment, the Kerner Commission reported on our lack of progress: "Our nation is moving toward two societies, one black, one white—separate but unequal."[4]

Our constitutional and statutory scheme provides the means to ensure equality and eradicate the continuing effects of past discrimination accumulated over more than two centuries. The challenge to the nation is to make the Constitution and the federal statutes work in order to bring to reality, at long last, the declaration of principle that all persons are created equal.

THE RECONSTRUCTION
CONSTITUTIONAL AMENDMENTS

The first basis for the rights of racial minorities was provided by three constitutional amendments adopted after the Civil War during Reconstruction: the Thirteenth Amendment, which outlaws slavery and involuntary servitude; the Fourteenth Amendment, which prohibits states from denying to any person "equal protection of the laws"; and the Fifteenth Amendment, which prohibits denial or abridgment of the right to vote.

What are the Thirteenth Amendment's prohibitions against discrimination and how are they enforced?
The Thirteenth Amendment, with its narrow prohibition only of "slavery" and "involuntary servitude," was not widely used in civil rights enforcement until the Supreme Court's 1968 decision in *Jones v. Alfred H. Mayer Co.*, where the Court indicated that the amendment was intended to prohibit not just slavery but also the "badges and incidents of slavery."[5] The amendment's prohibitions are directed not only against governments but also against private entities and private persons.[6] The amendment, however, probably prohibits only practices which are intentionally discriminatory rather than unintentional practices which have a discriminatory effect.[7]

The Thirteenth Amendment is mainly enforced through private lawsuits based on the Civil Rights Act of 1866 (the act is discussed further below). In these lawsuits, people discriminated against can obtain court orders ending the prohibited activity and awarding damages to those whose rights were violated.[8] There are no administrative procedures that must be complied with before filing a lawsuit to enforce the Thirteenth Amendment. However, the lawsuit must be filed within the time specified by the applicable state statute of limitations (usually within several years of the discriminatory activity).[9]

What are the Fourteenth Amendment's prohibitions and how are they enforced?

The Fourteenth Amendment broadly prohibits states from intentionally denying to any person the "equal protection of the laws." Although the amendment is directed primarily at the actions of state and local governments, it also prohibits intentional private discrimination if it is closely tied to actions of the government or of government officials. For example, racial segregation of a private lunch counter is prohibited where that segregation is enforced by the local police.[10] Similarly, racial discrimination in a private restaurant is prohibited where the property is leased by the restaurant from the state.[11]

A major limitation on Fourteenth Amendment coverage is that it prohibits only intentional discrimination and not unintentional discrimination that has a discriminatory effect. For example, a government employment test that screens out a disproportionate number of minority applicants but which is not used with an intent to discriminate is not prohibited by the Fourteenth Amendment.[12] Similarly, suburban exclusionary zoning that has a discriminatory impact against potential minority residents but which was not adopted with an intent to discriminate is not prohibited by the Fourteenth Amendment.[13]

Where intentional discrimination is practiced, however, it almost always will be found to be unconstitutional. Such discrimination will be allowed only if it is justified by a "compelling state interest."[14] It is virtually impossible for any discriminator to meet this standard of *compelling* state interest. According to Chief Justice Warren Burger of the U.S. Supreme Court, no discriminator "has ever satisfied this seemingly unsurmountable standard."[15]

The main method of enforcing the Fourteenth Amendment is through private lawsuits based on the Civil Rights Act of 1871 (discussed below). In these lawsuits, people discriminated against can obtain court orders ending the intentional discrimination and awarding damages to those whose rights were violated.[16]

As with the Thirteenth Amendment, there are no administrative procedures that must be complied with before filing a lawsuit to enforce the Fourteenth Amendment.[17] However, the lawsuit must be filed within the time specified by the applicable state statute of limitations (usually within several years of the discriminatory act).[18]

What does the Fifteenth Amendment prohibit? How is it enforced?

The Fifteenth Amendment prohibits denial or abridgment of the right to vote at all levels of the political process by federal, state, and local officials on the basis of race, color, or previous condition of servitude. The amendment was enacted as a limitation on public officials, but the acts of private individuals have been held unconstitutional under it where they perpetuate or act as a substitute for official discrimination.[19] Like the Fourteenth Amendment, a showing of *intentional* racial discrimination is required for a violation of the Fifteenth Amendment.[20]

The Fifteenth Amendment is enforced through lawsuits brought by private individuals or by the Department of Justice pursuant to implementing legislation such as the Voting Rights Act of 1965, through administrative proceedings before the Department of Justice, and through prosecutions under criminal statutes protecting the equal right to vote. As with the Thirteenth and Fourteenth Amendments, there are no administrative procedures which must be exhausted before filing a lawsuit to enforce the Fifteenth Amendment.[21] Remedies include court orders ending the discrimination and awarding damages.[22]

THE SURVIVING RECONSTRUCTION CIVIL RIGHTS ACTS

Each of the Reconstruction amendments, besides prohibiting various forms of discrimination, authorized Congress to enforce the amendments "by appropriate legislation." Congress did so immediately and on a number of occasions. The most important of the Reconstruction laws were the Civil Rights Act of 1866, the Civil Rights Act of 1871, and the Civil Rights Act of 1875.[23] Major portions of the first two have survived. The third, the nation's first prohibition against discrimination in public and private accommodations, was declared unconstitutional by the Supreme Court in 1883.[24]

What is the Civil Rights Act of 1866 and how is it enforced?

The Civil Rights Act of 1866, dormant for nearly a century, was long thought to apply only to state enforced discrimination. In 1968, however, in *Jones v. Alfred H. Mayer Co.*,[25] the Supreme Court revived the 1866 act by declaring that it prohibits private discrimination as well as public discrimination.

The act is divided into two parts, sections 1981 and 1982.[26] Each section prohibits specific acts of discrimination. It is not yet clear whether the sections prohibit all specified forms of discrimination or just specified forms of *intentional* discrimination.[27]

Section 1981 provides that all persons shall have the same right to "make and enforce contracts . . . as is enjoyed by white citizens."[28] This guarantee has been most widely used to prohibit discrimination in employment.[29] It also has been used to prohibit discrimination in the use of recreational facilities[30] and in admissions to private schools.[31]

Section 1982 provides that all citizens shall have the same right as is enjoyed by white citizens "to inherit, purchase, lease, sell, hold and convey real and personal property."[32] This guarantee has been used to prohibit most forms of housing discrimination against racial minorities.[33]

Sections 1981 and 1982, like the Thirteenth Amendment on which they are based, are enforceable through private lawsuits. The remedies in such lawsuits include court orders terminating the discrimination,[34] awarding damages, and awarding attorneys' fees to the prevailing party.[35]

There are no administrative procedures to complete before filing a lawsuit to enforce sections 1981 and 1982.[36] The lawsuit, however, must be filed soon after the discrimination action in order to be filed within the applicable state statute of limitations.[37]

What is the Civil Rights Act of 1871 and how is it enforced?

The central provision of the Civil Rights Act of 1871 is known as section 1983.[38] It is a statutory parallel to the Fourteenth

Amendment. Section 1983 makes liable any "person" acting under color of state law who causes another person to be deprived "of any rights . . . secured by the Constitution and laws" of the United States.[39] The word "person" includes not only government officials and persons and entities acting in concert with them[40] but also municipalities, states, and their agencies.[41]

Since section 1983 parallels the Fourteenth Amendment, it shares the limitation of prohibiting only intentional discrimination rather than also prohibiting unintentional discrimination which has a discriminatory effect.[42] Similarly, it permits such intentional discrimination only in the very rare situation where it can be justified by a compelling state interest.[43]

Like the Fourteenth Amendment, section 1983 is enforced only through private lawsuits. The remedies in such lawsuits include court orders ending the discrimination, awarding damages,[44] and awarding attorneys' fees to the prevailing party.[45] There are no administrative procedures which must be complied with before filing a lawsuit,[46] but the lawsuit must be filed within the time period specified by the state statute of limitations.[47]

Another part of the Civil Rights Act of 1871, section 1985(3), prohibits conspiracies to deprive others of equal protection of the laws.[48] Enforcement of section 1985(3) does not depend upon the involvement of state officials or agencies; the Supreme Court has held that section 1983(3) prohibits purely private conspiracies that deprive others of their civil rights.[49] For example, private persons who conspire to deny employment to minorities are in violation of section 1985(3).[50]

Although private persons need not necessarily engage in intentional discrimination in order to violate section 1985(3), such persons must have intentionally conspired to violate the civil rights of others.[51]

Section 1985(3) is enforced in the same way that section 1983 is enforced (by private lawsuits, etc.).[52]

THE MODERN CIVIL RIGHTS ACT

The Civil Rights Movement of the 1960s reflected the glaring reality that neither the Reconstruction amendments nor the surviving Reconstruction civil rights acts were being enforced well enough to protect the rights of racial minorities. Responding in part to this reality, Congress enacted and thereafter amended a number of significant civil rights acts. Most civil rights enforcement in recent years has been under these modern laws.

Since the acts resulted from legislative compromise, they contain many exceptions and frequently include complicated administrative procedures. They are significant, however, in two ways. First, they do not rely principally upon private lawsuits for enforcement; instead, they also authorize federal enforcement, both through administrative procedures and through lawsuits. Second, they have been interpreted by the federal courts as prohibiting not only intentionally discriminatory practices but also those practices which have a discriminatory effect.

Does Title II of the Civil Rights Act of 1964 prohibit discrimination in accommodations? How is it enforced?

In the Civil Rights Act of 1875, Congress, pursuant to its powers to enforce the Thirteenth and Fourteenth Amendments, prohibited discrimination in public and private accommodations.[53] Eight years later, the Supreme Court voided the act by declaring it unconstitutional.[54] In Title II of the Civil Rights Act of 1964, Congress again prohibited discrimination in public and private accommodations, this time pursuant to its powers under the Commerce Clause of the Constitution.[55] The same year, Congress upheld Title II as constitutional.[56] The difference to the Supreme Court was not simply that the Commerce Clause as a matter of statutory construction was interpreted differently by them from the Thirteenth and Fourteenth Amendments, but that eighty years of racial experience had shown that segregation was intolerable under a system of equality before the law.

Title II prohibits discrimination in the enjoyment of services, facilities, privileges, etc., in any place of public accommodation.[57] Covered establishments that provide accommodations open to the public, and hence are prohibited from engaging in discrimination, include inns, hotels, and motels; restaurants and lunch counters; and theaters, sports arenas, and other places of entertainment.[58] Specifically exempted from Title II, and hence not prohibited from engaging in discrimination by Title II, are private clubs.[59]

Title II is enforced by three methods. First, administrative enforcement may be undertaken by the federal Community Relations Service (CRS).[60] Second, the Department of Justice is authorized to sue violators of Title II.[61] Third, private individuals are authorized to sue violators of Title II.[62]

There is only one administrative prerequisite to a private lawsuit under Title II. If the discrimination occurred in a place where there is a state or local agency that is authorized to seek relief from such discrimination—and there is such an agency in nearly every state—the individual must give written notice of the discrimination to the state or local agency thirty days before filing the lawsuit.[63] No other administrative requirement must be met.[64]

In a private lawsuit, the individual may obtain termination of the discrimination but no damages.[65] Attorneys' fees, authorized for the prevailing party, ordinarily must be awarded to a prevailing plaintiff.[66]

Does Title VII of the Civil Rights Act of 1964 prohibit employment discrimination? How is it enforced?

Title VII of the Civil Rights Act of 1964, as initially enacted, prohibited discrimination only in private employment. In 1972 and 1991, Congress amended Title VII to prohibit discrimination also in local, state, and federal employment.[67]

Title VII contains a number of exemptions. For instance, it covers only employers with fifteen or more employees, and unions with fifteen or more members.[68] Covered employers and unions, however, are prohibited from engaging in a wide variety of specific discriminatory practices, such as discrimination in hiring, promotion, transfers, discharge, or payment of compensation, as well as discrimination in any other terms, conditions, or privileges of employment.[69]

Most significantly, Title VII prohibits not only practices that are intentionally discriminatory but also practices that have a discriminatory effect and are not job related. For example, the Supreme Court has found unlawful under Title VII an employer's good faith use of a standardized written test and of a high school diploma requirement where these criteria discriminated against minorities and were not manifestly related to job performance.[70] Similarly, the Supreme Court has found unlawful under Title VII the use of a height requirement that had a discriminatory effect and that was not related to job performance.[71]

Title VII is enforced by three methods. First, administrative enforcement through investigation and conciliation is pursued by a federal agency, the Equal Employment Opportunity Commission (EEOC).[72] Second, the EEOC and the Department of Justice are authorized to sue violators of Title VII.[73] Third, private individuals may sue violators of Title VII.[74]

Private individuals may sue, however, only after going through several administrative procedures. Most importantly, the individuals must file administrative charges of discrimination with the EEOC within 180 days of the discriminatory action; and, after the EEOC has had an opportunity to investigate the charges, the individuals must sue within 90 days after receiving a "right-to-sue" letter from the EEOC.[75]

Remedies under Title VII include ending the discrimination and awarding backpay from two years before the administrative charges were filed with the EEOC.[76] Damage awards are available under some circumstances, and attorneys' fees may be recovered by the prevailing party.[77]

What are the major provisions of the Voting Rights Act of 1965 and how are they enforced?

The Voting Rights Act of 1965, amended in 1970, 1975, and 1982,[78] contains several major provisions. It suspended tests or devices for voting that had been used in the past to disfranchise racial minorities.[79] *Tests or devices* include literacy tests, educational requirements, good-character tests, and exclusively English language registration procedures or elections where a linguistic minority comprises more than 5 percent of the voting age population of the jurisdiction. A second provision, Section 5, requires jurisdictions that have used a test or device and in which voter registration is disproportionately low to gain approval or preclearance from either the Department of Justice or the federal courts before making changes in voting laws or procedures.[80] The purpose of preclearance is to make certain that the changes do not have the purpose or effect of abridging the right to vote on account of race, color, or membership in a language minority. Other important sections of the act provide for federal voter registrars and observers, absentee balloting in presidential elections, and bilingual ballots for linguistic minorities.[81] The act has been held constitutional by the Supreme Court.[82]

The Voting Rights Act is enforced through administrative preclearance procedures before the Department of Justice,[83] by lawsuits brought by the Department of Justice or by private individuals,[84] and by criminal prosecutions instituted by the federal government (of which there have been none reported, despite frequent violations of the preclearance and other provisions of the act).[85] There are no administrative requirements with which an individual must comply before bringing suit.[86] Remedies include orders requiring compliance with the Voting Rights Act and payment of attorneys' fees to the prevailing party.[87] Damages are not authorized.

Does Title VIII of the Civil Rights Act of 1968 prohibit discrimination in housing? How is it enforced?

Three months before the Supreme Court revived the Civil Rights Act of 1866 by declaring that it prohibits discrimination in private housing transactions, Congress enacted Title VIII of the Civil Rights Act of 1968, amended in 1988 (also known as the Fair Housing Act).[88]

Title VIII contains a number of exemptions, such as not prohibiting discrimination in the sale of a single family dwelling by an owner not using commercial real estate services.[89] But most housing transactions are covered by Title VIII's prohibitions against discrimination. Specifically prohibited are refusals to sell, to rent, or even to negotiate for the sale or rental of a dwelling;[90] representations that a dwelling is not available when it in fact is available;[91] and notices and advertisements indicating a racial preference.[92]

Like the other modern civil rights acts, Title VIII has been interpreted by the courts to prohibit not merely intentionally discriminatory practices but also practices that have a discriminatory effect. For example, suburban exclusionary zoning practices that might not be intentionally discriminatory, and hence are constitutional under the Fourteenth Amendment and section 1983,[93] nonetheless are unlawful under Title VIII if they have a discriminatory impact upon racial minorities.[94]

Title VIII is enforced by three methods. First, administrative enforcement through investigation and conciliation is pursued by the federal Department of Housing and Urban Development (HUD).[95] Second, the Department of Justice is authorized to sue violators of Title VIII.[96] Third, private individuals may sue violators of Title VIII.[97]

There are two methods of private enforcement under Title VIII. Under one method, private individuals must comply with many complicated procedural prerequisites; in lawsuits pursued under this method, individuals may obtain a court order terminating the unlawful discrimination.[98]

Under the second and preferred method of private enforcement under Title VIII, individuals must comply with only one procedural requirement: they must file their lawsuits within 180 days of the discriminatory housing practice.[99] In such lawsuits, the individuals may obtain court orders not only terminating the discrimination but also awarding actual damages, awarding punitive damages up to $1,000 and awarding attorneys' fees.[100]

Do monetary penalties help stop prohibited discrimination?
Yes. It has been hard to enforce many federal civil rights laws effectively because the penalties for practicing illegal discrimination were not sufficiently severe. All too often, illegal discrimination is halted only after long and tedious lawsuits that result in no more than a court ordered end to discrimination. Without severe monetary penalties, there too often is little incentive for violators to change their ways.

In recent years, monetary remedies have been viewed as an important incentive for violators not to discriminate. As the Supreme Court stated in a lawsuit against private employment discrimination under Title VII: "It is the reasonably certain prospect of a backpay award that provides the spur or catalyst which causes employers and unions to self-examine and to self-evaluate their employment practices and to endeavor to eliminate, so far as possible, the last vestiges of an unfortunate and ignominious page in this country's history."[101] The certainty of having to pay attorneys' fees to prevailing plaintiffs in private civil rights lawsuits is also strong incentive for civil rights compliance.[102]

Another remedy is the threatened or real termination of federal financial assistance. As one judge has recognized: "Stop-

ping the flow of lifeblood to a body is certainly more fatal than
enjoining that body from certain activity."[103]

What federal laws authorize cutting off federal assistance to discriminatory recipients?

The most important federal statute authorizing the cutoff of
federal assistance to discriminatory recipients either through
administrative enforcement or through litigation is Title VI of
the Civil Rights Act of 1964, as amended.[104] Title VI applies to
all federal agencies that make grants (approximately thirty).
Title VI is enforced by the various agencies against their individual recipients, and is coordinated overall by the Department
of Justice. In addition to being covered by Title VI, some
agencies and programs are also covered by separate fund termination provisions. The Justice System Improvement Act of 1984
(JSIA),[105] for example, also authorizes the cutoff of federal grants
under the act to discriminatory state and local law enforcement
agencies. The statute is enforced by the Office of Justice Programs (OJP), a coordinating agency created by the JSIA.

These laws are significant in enforcing the rights of racial
minorities because they usually prohibit practices that have a
discriminatory effect. Second, they can be enforced by filing
administrative charges of discrimination with the appropriate
federal agencies. Third, they can cause civil rights compliance
through the threatened or real cutoff of federal assistance. And
fourth, other remedies, such as lawsuits, can be pursued at the
same time to enforce the rights of racial minorities.

Can a victim of discrimination seek remedies under more than one of the foregoing laws?

Yes. Persons who have been discriminated against may pursue their rights under as many laws as are relevant. Sometimes
choices have to be made, but in general a person should try to
use as many options as are available.

NOTES

1. 60 U.S. (19 How.) 393 (1857).
2. Kenneth M. Stampp, *The Peculiar Institution* (New York: Alfred A. Knopf, 1969).

3. 347 U.S. 473 (1954).
4. *Report of the National Advisory Commission on Civil Disorders* 1 (New York: Bantam, 1968).
5. 392 U.S. 409, 441 (1968).
6. *E.g., Johnson v. Railway Express Agency*, 421 U.S. 454 (1975).
7. *See* note 27, *infra*.
8. *E.g., Sullivan v. Little Hunting Park*, 396 U.S. 229 (1969).
9. *Cf. Johnson v. Railway Express Agency*, 421 U.S. 454 (1975), applying a state statute of limitations to a case brought to enforce part of § 1 of the Civil Rights Act of 1866, now codified as 42 U.S.C. § 1981.
10. *Adickes v. S. H. Kress & Co.*, 398 U.S. 144 (1970).
11. *Burton v. Wilmington Parking Authority*, 365 U.S. 715 (1961).
12. *Washington v. Davis*, 426 U.S. 229 (1976).
13. *Village of Arlington Heights v. Metropolitan Housing Development Corp.*, 429 U.S. 252 (1977).
14. *See* notes 12 and 13, *supra*.
15. *Dunn v. Blumstein*, 405 U.S. 330, 363–64 (1972) (Burger, C.J., dissenting). Chief Justice Burger is not entirely correct in that the compelling state interest standard has been met on two occasions. During World War II, the Supreme Court upheld discrimination against Japanese Americans in the context of "gravest, imminent danger to the public safety," *Korematsu v. United States*, 323 U.S. 214, 218 (1944), and in "conditions of great emergency," *Hirabayashi v. United States*, 320 U.S. 81, 111 (1943) (Murphy, J., concurring).
16. *Monell v. Department of Social Services*, 436 U.S. 658 (1978).
17. Part of *Monroe v. Pape*, 365 U.S. 167 (1961), holding that administrative remedies need not be exhausted, was not affected by the overruling of another part of *Monroe* in *Monell v. Department of Social Services*, 436 U.S. 658 (1978).
18. *Cf. O'Sullivan v. Felix*, 233 U.S. 318 (1914), applying a state statute of limitations to a case brought under part of the Civil Rights Act of 1871 now codified as 42 U.S.C. § 1985. *See also* note 9, *supra*.
19. *Terry v. Adams*, 345 U.S. 461 (1953).
20. *City of Mobile v. Bolden*, 446 U.S. 55 (1980).
21. *Reddix v. Lucky*, 252 F.2d 930 (5th Cir. 1958).
22. *Lane v. Wilson*, 307 U.S. 268 (1939).
23. The Civil Rights Act of 1866 is the act of April 9, 1866, ch. 31, § 1, 14 Stat. 27, now codified in part as 42 U.S.C. §§ 1981 and 1982. The Civil Rights Act of 1871 is the act of April 20, 1871, ch. 22, § 1 and § 2, 17 Stat. 13, now codified in part as 42 U.S.C. §§ 1983 and 1985, and as 28 U.S.C. § 1343(3). The Civil Rights Act of 1875 is found at 18 Stat. 335.
24. *The Civil Rights Cases*, 109 U.S. 3 (1883). A nearly identical statute,

Title II of the Civil Rights Act of 1964, similarly prohibiting discrimination in public and private accommodations, was upheld as constitutional in *Heart of Atlanta Motel v. United States*, 379 U.S. 241 (1964). *See* chapter 6, Public Accommodations.

25. 392 U.S. 409 (1968). *See also Runyon v. McCrary*, 427 U.S. 160 (1976); *Johnson v. Railway Express Agency*, 421 U.S. 454 (1975); *Tillman v. Wheaton-Haven Recreational Association, Inc.*, 410 U.S. 431 (1973); *Sullivan v. Little Hunting Park*, 396 U.S. 229 (1969).

26. *See* note 23, *supra*.

27. The issue of whether proof of discriminatory intent is necessary under 42 U.S.C. § 1981 could have been but was not decided by the Supreme Court in 1979 in *County of Los Angeles v. Davis*, 440 U.S. 625 (1979), *vacating* 566 F.2d 1334 (9th Cir. 1978).

28. 42 U.S.C. § 1981.

29. *See Johnson v. Railway Express Agency*, 421 U.S. 454 (1975) and cases cited therein at 459 n.6.

30. *Tillman v. Wheaton-Haven Recreational Association, Inc.*, 410 U.S. 431 (1973); *Scott v. Young*, 421 F.2d 143 (4th Cir.), *cert. denied*, 398 U.S. 929 (1970).

31. *Runyon v. McCrary*, 427 U.S. 160 (1976).

32. 42 U.S.C. § 1982.

33. *Sullivan v. Little Hunting Park*, 396 U.S. 229 (1969); *Jones v. Alfred H. Mayer Co.*, 392 U.S. 409 (1968); *cf. Tillman v. Wheaton-Haven Recreational Association, Inc.*, 410 U.S. 431 (1973).

34. *See* cases cited in note 25, *supra*.

35. 42 U.S.C. § 1988, as amended by the Civil Rights Attorney Fees Awards Act of 1976, Pub. L. No. 94-559, 90 Stat. 2641 (Oct. 19, 1976).

36. *Johnson v. Railway Express Agency*, 421 U.S. 454 (1975).

37. *Id.*

38. 42 U.S.C. § 1983. *See* note 23, *supra*.

39. *Id.*

40. *See* notes 10 and 11, *supra*, and accompanying text.

41. *Monell v. Department of Social Services*, 436 U.S. 658 (1978).

42. *See* notes 12 and 13, *supra*, and accompanying text.

43. *Id.*

44. *See* note 16, *supra*.

45. *See* note 35, *supra*.

46. *See* note 17, *supra*.

47. *See* note 18, *supra*.

48. 42 U.S.C. § 1985(3). *See* note 23, *supra*.

49. *Griffin v. Breckenridge*, 403 U.S. 88 (1971).

50. *E.g., Richardson v. Miller*, 446 F.2d 1247 (3d Cir. 1971); *Pennsylvania*

v. Local 542, Operating Engineers, 347 F. Supp. 268, 290–97 (E.D. Pa. 1972).

51. *See* notes 49 and 50, *supra.*
52. *See* notes 16–18 and 44–47, *supra.*
53. *See* note 23, *supra,* and accompanying text.
54. *The Civil Rights Cases,* 109 U.S. 3 (1883).
55. 42 U.S.C. §§ 2000a, *et seq.*
56. *Heart of Atlanta Motel v. United States,* 379 U.S. 241 (1964).
57. 42 U.S.C. § 2000a(a).
58. 42 U.S.C. §§ 2000a(b) (1), (2), and (3), respectively.
59. 42 U.S.C. § 2000a(e). This exception has been interpreted very narrowly. *See, e.g., Tillman v. Wheaton-Haven Recreational Association, Inc.,* 410 U.S. 431 (1973).
60. 42 U.S.C. § 2000a04.
61. 42 U.S.C. § 2000a-5.
62. 42 U.S.C. § 2000a-3.
63. 42 U.S.C. § 2000a-3(c). *See Harris v. Ericson,* 457 F.2d 765 (10th Cir. 1972).
64. 42 U.S.C. § 2000a-6.
65. 42 U.S.C. § 2000a-3(a).
66. 42 U.S.C. § 2000a-3(b). *Newman v. Piggie Park Enterprises,* 390 U.S. 400 (1968).
67. 42 U.S.C. §§ 2000e *et seq.*
68. 42 U.S.C. §§ 2000e(b) and (e), respectively.
69. 42 U.S.C. §§ 2000e-2(a)–(d).
70. *Griggs v. Duke Power Co.,* 401 U.S. 424 (1971); *see also Albemarle Paper Co. v. Moody,* 422 U.S. 405 (1975).
71. *Dothard v. Rawlinson,* 433 U.S. 321 (1977).
72. 42 U.S.C. § 2000e-4 and § 2000e-5.
73. 42 U.S.C. § 2000e-5 and § 2000e-6.
74. 42 U.S.C. § 2000e-5.
75. 42 U.S.C. § 2000e-5. *See McDonnell-Douglas Corp. v. Green,* 411 U.S. 792, 798 (1973); *Love v. Pullman Co.,* 404 U.S. 522, 523 (1972).
76. 42 U.S.C. § 2000e-5(g). Backpay is awardable not only to the individuals bringing a lawsuit but to all minorities discriminated against. *Albemarle Paper Co. v. Moody,* 422 U.S. 405 (1975).
77. 42 U.S.C. § 2000e-5(k). Prevailing plaintiffs are awarded fees as a matter of course whereas prevailing defendants may recover fees only if the lawsuit was frivolous. *Christiansburg Garment Co. v. EEOC,* 434 U.S. 412 (1978).
78. *See generally,* 42 U.S.C. §§ 1973 *et seq.*
79. 42 U.S.C. § 1973aa.

18 *The Rights of Racial Minorities*

80. 42 U.S.C. § 1973c.
81. 42 U.S.C. §§ 1973d, 1973f, 1973cc, and 1973aa–la.
82. *South Carolina v. Katzenbach*, 383 U.S. 301 (1966); *Katzenbach v. Morgan*, 384 U.S. 641 (1966).
83. 42 U.S.C. § 1973c.
84. 42 U.S.C. § 1973j(d); *Allen v. State Board of Elections*, 393 U.S. 544 (1969).
85. 42 U.S.C. §§ 1973j(a), (b), and (c).
86. 42 U.S.C. § 1973j(f).
87. 42 U.S.C. §§ 1973j(d) and 1973 1(e).
88. 42 U.S.C. §§ 3601 *et seq.*
89. 42 U.S.C. § 3606(b)(1).
90. 42 U.S.C. § 3604(a).
91. 42 U.S.C. § 3604(d).
92. 42 U.S.C. § 3604(c).
93. *Village of Arlington Heights v. Metropolitan Housing Development Corp.*, 429 U.S. 252 (1977).
94. *Metropolitan Housing Development Corp. v. Village of Arlington Heights*, 558 F.2d 1283, 1286–90 (7th Cir. 1977), *cert. denied*, 434 U.S. 1025 (1978), *on remand from* 429 U.S. 252 (1977).
95. 42 U.S.C. § 3610 and § 3611.
96. 42 U.S.C. § 3613.
97. 42 U.S.C. § 3610 and § 3612.
98. 42 U.S.C. § 3610.
99. 42 U.S.C. § 3612.
100. *Id.*
101. *Albemarle Paper Co. v. Moody*, 422 U.S. 405, 417–18 (1975).
102. *Christiansburg Garment Co. v. EEOC*, 434 U.S. 412 (1978); *cf. Newman v. Piggie Park Enterprises*, 390 U.S. 400 (1968).
103. *United States v. Chicago*, 549 F.2d 415, 448 (7th Cir. 1977) (Pell, J., dissenting), *cert. denied*, 434 U.S. 875 (1978).
104. 42 U.S.C. § 2000d *et seq.*
105. 42 U.S.C. § 3789d(c).

II
Voting

During the early history of the United States, voting was typically limited to white male property owners over the age of twenty-one. After the Civil War, the Confederate states were required to guarantee universal male suffrage without regard to race as a condition for reentry into the Union. With the adoption in 1870 of the Fifteenth Amendment, the equal right to vote without regard to race was guaranteed nationwide, at least in theory.[1]

What federal prohibitions against racial discrimination in voting exist today?

Aside from the Fifteenth Amendment, which guarantees the equal right to vote without regard to race, color, or previous condition of servitude, the basic federal prohibitions against discrimination in voting are (1) the Fourteenth Amendment, which prohibits intentional discrimination by public officials; (2) Reconstruction-era statutes imposing civil and criminal penalties upon those who interfere with voting rights;[2] and (3) the modern Voting Rights Acts of 1957, 1960, 1964, and 1965 (amended in 1970, 1975, 1982, and 1992).[3] Of these statutory prohibitions, by far the most important is the Voting Rights Act of 1965, which prohibits literacy and other tests for voting, provides for the appointment of federal voter registrars and examiners, requires federal approval of changes in voting in those jurisdictions that have a history of voting discrimination and low voter registration and turnout, and provides that voting practices that result in discrimination are unlawful whether or not they were enacted or are being maintained with a racially discriminatory purpose.

GENERAL PROTECTION OF VOTING RIGHTS

What kind of discrimination in voting is prohibited by the Fifteenth Amendment?

The Fifteenth Amendment prohibits purposeful discrimination in voting at all levels of the political process by federal, state, and local officials on the basis of race, color, or previous condition of servitude. The amendment, in the words of the Supreme Court, "nullifies sophisticated as well as simple-minded modes of discrimination" and makes unlawful "onerous procedural requirements which effectively handicap exercise of the franchise by the colored race."[4] While the Fifteenth Amendment was enacted as a limitation on public officials, the acts of private individuals have been held unconstitutional under it where they perpetuate or act as a substitute for official discrimination.[5]

Was the Fifteenth Amendment effectively enforced after its ratification in 1870?

Far from it. The good intentions of the Reconstruction Congress were nullified by the other branches of the federal government. By section 2 of the Fifteenth Amendment, Congress was authorized to enact consistent legislation. In due course a variety of voting laws were enacted during Reconstruction, requiring election officials to give all citizens the same opportunity to vote, and making it a federal crime to violate state laws governing the election of federal officials, to interfere privately or officially with a citizen's right to vote, or to commit fraudulent acts in connection with registering voters or counting ballots.[6] Congress also established a system of federal supervisors of elections.[7] None of these laws was adequately enforced, however, and some of them were declared unconstitutional by the Supreme Court.[8] Then, in 1894, after Reconstruction, Congress itself repealed many of the post-Civil War voting laws, including those dealing with federal supervision of state elections.[9]

What was the consequence of the lack of enforcement?

Predictably, the consequence was the disfranchisement of African Americans. After the Civil War, despite widespread intimidation and violence by whites, blacks registered and voted in substantial numbers in the states where they had formerly been disfranchised, and many were elected to office. But minority participation in the elective process was generally possible only because of the presence of federal troops dispatched under various Reconstruction laws.

After Reconstruction ended in 1877, and federal troops were withdrawn from the South, the disfranchisement of blacks began in earnest and the promise of equal voting rights held out by the Fifteenth Amendment faded. A common method of discouraging blacks from voting was to make the elective process more complicated. During this period, white legislators gave free rein to their imaginations in burdening the franchise with onerous requirements.

The main work of disfranchisement was accomplished through a series of state constitutional conventions, the first of which was held in Mississippi in 1890. The avowed purpose of these conventions, in the words of United States Senator "Pitchfork" Ben Tillman, who addressed the South Carolina Disfranchising Convention of 1895, was "to take from [the 'ignorant blacks'] every ballot that we can under the laws of our national government."[10] One generally adopted method of excluding minorities from voting was to impose a literacy test. Typically, the test required the voter to be able to read and write a portion of the Constitution as a condition to register to vote. The literacy test was racially neutral on its face, but it was administered in a way that excluded blacks, but not whites, from registering. To make sure that illiterate whites were not disfranchised, alternatives to literacy were provided if the registrant could "understand and interpret" the Constitution, owned property, or was "of good character." Many states also enacted "grandfather clauses" which excused persons registered on or prior to 1 January 1866, and their descendants, from having to comply with any literacy or property requirement for registration. By definition, few blacks could qualify for registration under the grandfather clauses, since blacks were almost never allowed to vote prior to 1 January 1866. The poll tax was another way of limiting the franchise. The tax was, in essence, a fee for the privilege of voting and fell with disproportionate impact upon poor blacks.

One of the most effective ways of denying political participation to minorities was through the use of the "all-white" primary, established either through political party rule or statute, which restricted party membership and voting to whites. Since political parties were groups of private individuals, not governmentally controlled groups, they appeared to be beyond the reach of the Fifteenth Amendment. And because nomination in the primary was tantamount to election to office in the states that used the all-white primary, African Americans, even those who were registered, were effectively shut out from the elective process.

Voter registration figures reveal the effectiveness of post-Reconstruction disfranchisement. In Louisiana in 1896 there were 130,334 blacks registered to vote. In 1900 there were only 5,320. In Mississippi 70 percent of the black voting age population was registered to vote in 1867. By 1899 the figure had plummeted to 9 percent.[11] Registration statistics from other states are much the same. It is no exaggeration to say that at the turn of the century, after the end of Reconstruction and after judicial and legislative repeal of laws supporting the Fifteenth Amendment, blacks and other racial minorities no longer participated in a meaningful way in the political life of the United States.

Did any of the laws designed to implement the Fifteenth Amendment survive Reconstruction?

Yes. Some of the Reconstruction voting laws have survived, including a statute protecting the right to vote without regard to race or color;[12] two laws making those who interfere with protected rights (e.g., the right to vote) liable for civil damages;[13] and two statutes imposing criminal penalties on persons who hinder others in their attempts to vote.[14] Even these surviving laws were limited in their scope and, until recently, were infrequently used. The criminal provisions for denial of the equal right to vote were used to prevent election fraud but rarely to protect against racial discrimination in exercise of the franchise.[15] The surviving civil remedies were occasionally used effectively in banning all-white primaries[16] but seldom to attack other forms of discrimination in the administration of voting laws.

Was the Fifteenth Amendment eventually revived?

Yes, but only gradually. It was not until 1915, forty-five years after its ratification, that the amendment was actually used by the Supreme Court to invalidate a discriminatory election procedure. In the case of *Guinn v. United States*,[17] the Court declared the grandfather clause unconstitutional on the ground that its only purpose was to exclude blacks from voting in violation of the Fifteenth Amendment's guarantee of the equal right to vote. But in the same case the Court approved the use of discriminatory literacy tests for voting, because, in the Court's view, the use of literacy tests was an "exercise of the state of a lawful power vested in it, not subject to our supervision."[18]

Has Congress taken any action since Reconstruction to protect the voting rights of minorities?

Yes. In 1957, Congress passed the first civil rights act since the Civil War.[19] The act established the six member bipartisan Commission on Civil Rights and gave it the duty of gathering information on discrimination in voting. It also prohibited interference with voting in federal elections, authorized the attorney general to bring lawsuits to protect voting rights, and set out procedures for holding in criminal contempt those who disobeyed court orders ending discrimination. The act was amended in 1960 to authorize federal referees to investigate voting discrimination and to register qualified voters.[20] Four years later Congress enacted the Civil Rights Act of 1964. It provided, among other things, that black registration be based upon the same voter qualifications that traditionally had been applied to whites; that any literacy or other test for voting be given entirely in writing; that immaterial errors in answering test questions not be made the basis for denying registration; and that a sixth-grade education was rebuttable evidence of literacy.[21] These various statues, although they were often used effectively to deal with particular voting rights infringements, did not result in the enfranchisement of any appreciable number of racial minorities.

Then in 1965, Congress adopted an entirely new approach to voter legislation. Instead of relying primarily on lawsuits to ensure fair administration of state voting standards and procedures—as it had done in the 1957, 1960, and 1964 acts—Congress passed the Voting Rights Act of 1965, which suspended the standards responsible for the exclusion of minorities from registration and placed supervision of new procedures in the hands of federal officials.[22] Because of the importance of this act, it is discussed in more detail below.

Can political parties still discriminate or exclude racial minorities from membership or voting in primaries?

No. The Supreme Court, reflecting a thaw in racial attitudes in the country, began an assault on discrimination by political parties in 1927, when it struck down a Texas law declaring Negroes ineligible to participate in Democratic party elections.[23] Subsequently, some states, in an effort to remove the conduct of primary elections from federal judicial review, repealed state laws regulating primaries, thereby allowing political parties to make their own rules, including rules excluding blacks from voting or party membership. Such exclusionary schemes were eventually held unconstitutional.

First, in *Nixon v. Condon*,[24] after holding that racial discrimination in voting was not delegable, the Supreme Court struck down a Texas statute authorizing the state Democratic party to fix qualifications for voting in primaries. Then, in *Smith v. Allwright*, the Court held a rule of the Democratic party of Texas limiting membership to whites, passed without the aid or authorization of the legislature, unconstitutional for the reason that the equal right to vote "is not to be nullified by a state through casting its electoral process in a form which permits a private organization to practice racial discrimination in the election."[25]

The rule in *Smith v. Allwright* was later applied to prevent exclusion of blacks from voting in elections held by an ostensibly private club that duplicated the functions of primaries held by political parties. "It violated the Fifteenth Amendment," the Supreme Court said, "for a state, by such circumvention, to permit within its borders the use of any device that produces an equivalent of the prohibited elections."[26]

Other forms of discrimination by political parties, such as rules requiring members to take an oath supporting the "social and educational separation of races," have also been held unconstitutional.[27]

Can proof of payment of a poll tax be required for voting in federal or state elections?

No. The poll or head tax was never regarded as a legitimate revenue measure, but, like the literacy test, was enacted as a "clog" upon the franchise to keep blacks from voting.[28] Nonetheless, the Supreme Court initially ruled in 1937 that proof of payment of the tax was an appropriate condition for suffrage within the power of states to impose.[29] Numerous attempts were subsequently made to abolish the poll tax through federal legislation. It was not until 1964, however, with ratification of the Twenty-fourth Amendment, that the tax was banned in federal elections. Two years later, the Supreme Court, reversing its earlier decision, declared use of the poll tax in state elections to be in violation of the equal protection clause of the Fourteenth Amendment because "the affluence of the voter or payment of any fee" was not a proper "electoral standard."[30]

Are literacy or education tests for registering and voting Constitutional?

Not if they are used to exclude racial minorities from voting. The Supreme Court, as well as numerous lower courts, have now ruled that "interpretation tests" which require registrants to read and explain the state or federal Constitution are unconstitutional where they grant unlimited discretion to local voter registrars and are used to exclude blacks from registration. Under the circumstances, the test is "not a test but a trap, sufficient to stop even the most brilliant man on his way to the voting booth," and is invalid under both the Fourteenth and Fifteenth Amendments.[31]

Literacy and similar tests for voting are also banned by the Voting Rights Act of 1965.

Is discrimination or intimidation by private individuals against racial minorities in registering and voting unlawful?

Yes. Although the Supreme Court has held that neither the Fourteenth nor Fifteenth Amendment prohibits private acts of discrimination,[32] it has held that article I, section 4, of the Constitution granting authority to Congress to regulate federal elections justifies congressional prohibition of private discrimination in registering and voting for federal officials.[33] Physical assaults and threats against minority registrants have been enjoined, as have different forms of economic coercion.[34]

In one case from Tennessee, blacks who registered, and whites who assisted them, were blacklisted and denied credit and the right to buy necessities by local businessmen. Tenant farmers and sharecroppers who were blacklisted were also evicted by their white landowners. In a lawsuit filed to stop the intimidation, a court held that injunctions should be issued against the businessmen and the landowners to end their interference with the rights of blacks to register and vote.[35]

What other kinds of intentional discrimination have been struck down under the Constitution and federal voting laws?

Just about every kind imaginable. Racial discrimination in voting has taken many forms, and has included such crude measures as segregated polling places,[36] segregated voter registration procedures and the discriminatory administration of the literacy test,[37] purges of blacks from registration lists,[38] the requirement that the race of every candidate for elective office appear on the ballot,[39] the arrest and prosecution of blacks conducting voter registration drives,[40] and the disfranchisement of persons convicted of crimes selected on the basis that the crimes were believed to be more frequently committed by blacks.[41] More subtle practices have been "slowdowns" in processing minority registration applications,[42] and resignation from office by state officials leaving plaintiffs in voting rights lawsuits with no one to sue.[43] All of these practices have been held to be unlawful.

A classic example of racial discrimination in voting, at once crude and ingenious, involved the city of Tuskegee, Alabama, which redrew its city limits from a square into a "strangely irregular twenty-eight-sided figure."[44] The result of the alteration was to remove from the electorate all but four or five of the city's black voters, while not removing a single white voter or resident. The Supreme Court had little trouble in finding that the reapportionment was discriminatory in violation of the Fifteenth Amendment.

The Voting Rights Act, as we shall see, is a further deterrent to such racial gerrymanders since covered jurisdictions seeking to change voting lines now have the burden under section 5 of the act to prove the absence of a discriminatory purpose or effect.

Are so-called ballot integrity or security programs that are conducted by political parties or groups to purge persons from the voter roles who are suspected of being improperly registered or no longer residents permissible?

Not if the purpose of the programs is to remove minorities

from the voter roles or discourage or intimidate them from voting. In a Louisiana case, the Republican party orchestrated a mailing of approximately three hundred thousand letters targeted to minority voters. The envelopes were marked "Do Not Forward," and those that were returned were sent to local county registrars with a demand that the voters—over 95 percent of whom were black and lived in predominantly black or exclusively black precincts—be purged on the grounds that they were not residents or were illegally registered. The court concluded that the party had not adequately investigated whether the voters were legally registered and that the ballot security program was "an insidious scheme by the Republican Party to remove blacks from the voting roles."[45] The court enjoined the attempted purging of minority voters as being in violation of the Fifteenth Amendment.

What is minority vote dilution?

Minority vote dilution, as distinguished from vote denial, is the impairment of the equal opportunity of minority voters to participate in the political process and to elect candidates of their choice. Even where the right to register and vote is freely available, a minority's voting strength may be impaired, or diluted, in a variety of ways, including through use of such procedures as at-large elections; by racially gerrymandered reapportionment plans that unnecessarily fragment (crack), submerge (stack), or concentrate (pack) the minority population; through use of numbered posts, staggered terms of office and majority vote requirements; by laws prohibiting single shot voting; by discriminatory annexations and the abolition of elected or appointed offices.

How do at-large elections dilute minority voting strength?

When voting is at-large, all the voters in a jurisdiction elect all the officials. The majority, if it votes as a bloc, can choose all the officeholders, thereby depriving a discrete minority of an effective opportunity to elect any representatives of its choice. At-large elections are a "winner take all" system that favors the numerical majority.

In what way can the requirement that a candidate receive a majority of the votes dilute minority voting strength?

A majority vote requirement, as opposed to election by a

plurality, gives a clear advantage to majority candidates. If one black and several whites were to run for a single elective office in a majority white district, and if voting were along racial lines, it is conceivable that the white votes would be so evenly distributed among the white candidates that the black candidate would receive the most, or a plurality, of the votes cast. However, if the black candidate fell short of a majority—which would be likely since blacks would be a minority of voters—he or she would be forced into a runoff election with the white candidate who had received the next highest number of votes. In the runoff, the white voters could regroup behind the sole white candidate and easily elect that person to office. In the words of the Supreme Court, a majority vote requirement "enhance[s] the opportunity for racial discrimination."[46]

Aside from its direct effect, a majority vote requirement discourages minority candidates from seeking office in majority white jurisdictions where voting is along racial lines. Minority candidates could not generally expect to get enough white crossover votes to win in such jurisdictions and consequently frequently do not run for office.

How do numbered posts and staggered terms of office dilute minority voting strength?

Staggering the terms of office restricts the number of offices filled at any one election by having terms expire in different years. Numbered post requirements force candidates to run for individual seats, or posts, rather than for a given number of vacancies. Both procedures isolate candidates in head to head contests and—where voting is racially polarized—limit the chances of minorities for election. Both procedures also limit the opportunities for single shot, or bullet, voting and deprive minorities of the ability to concentrate their votes on a single candidate in a multicandidate field.

How do anti-single-shot laws dilute minority voting strength?

A minority candidate would have a chance to be elected by a plurality of the vote if the majority split its votes among several majority candidates and the minority engaged in single shot voting (i.e., concentrated its votes behind one or a limited number of candidates). Laws that prohibit single shot voting in essence force minority voters to vote for opposition candidates and thus undermine the chances of election of the candidates favored by the minority.

What is cracking, stacking, and packing?

Cracking, stacking, and packing are techniques of racial gerrymandering used in reapportionment to minimize minority political influence. *Cracking* is the fragmenting of an area of heavy minority concentration and dispersing it among several districts so that no district has a majority of minority population. *Stacking* is combining concentrations of minority population with larger concentrations of majority population, again to ensure that no district has a majority of minority population. *Packing* is concentrating the minority population into one or more districts to minimize the number of districts in which the minority is the majority.

Is the dilution of minority voting strength unconstitutional?

Yes. The prohibition on minority vote dilution has its roots in the one person, one vote decisions of the Supreme Court decided on the basis of the equal protection clause of the Fourteenth Amendment, and which held that voting power must be apportioned equally among the electorate based upon population.[47] In subsequent cases the Court held that voting strength could be unconstitutionally diluted on the basis of race as well as population inequality. Section 2 of the Voting Rights Act, discussed in more detail below, also prohibits minority vote dilution.

Are at-large elections, numbered posts, staggered terms, majority vote requirements and other voting procedures that can dilute minority voting strength automatically unconstitutional?

No. These procedures are not unconstitutional per se, but their use is unlawful where they were adopted purposefully to discriminate or where, in the context of the facts of a given jurisdiction, they interact with social and historical conditions to cause an inequality in the opportunities enjoyed by black and white voters to elect their preferred candidates.[48]

Is the prohibition against minority vote dilution contrary to the democratic idea of majority rule?

No. A fundamental principle embodied in the Bill of Rights is that there are limitations on majority control and power. Minorities do have rights, including the right of equal political participation, which may be antithetical to the majority but which are deserving of protection and may not be abridged. The notion of simple majority rule is in fact ignored throughout the Constitution, e.g., in the provisions requiring super-majorities for impeachment and ratification of treaties.[49]

How is a violation of constitutionally protected voting rights proved?

In its first decision invalidating an at-large election system because it diluted minority voting strength, *White v. Regester* (decided in 1973),[50] the Supreme Court applied a "totality of circumstances" analysis. The Court considered, aside from the fact that few minorities had been elected to office, a broad range of factors affecting minority political participation: (1) a history of discrimination; (2) the existence of racially exclusive slating groups; (3) cultural and language barriers; (4) depressed minority voter registration; (5) lack of responsiveness by elected officials to the needs of the minority community; and (6) the use of election devices, such as numbered posts and majority vote requirements. Based upon the "totality of the circumstances" the Court concluded that minorities "had less opportunity than did other residents in the district to participate in the political processes and to elect legislators of their choice."[51] The *White v. Regester* analysis, which examined the effect of a challenged practice to determine its constitutionality, was routinely applied in subsequent voting cases.

In 1980, in *City of Mobile v. Bolden*,[52] the Court established a subjective intent standard for vote dilution claims and essentially repudiated *White v. Regester*. The plurality held that a plaintiff had to prove that a challenged practice was racially motivated and that proof of the factors identified in cases such as *White v. Regester* was insufficient to prove an unconstitutionally discriminatory purpose.

Did Congress take any action in response to the *Bolden* decision?

Yes. Unhappy with the subjective intent standard of *Bolden*,

Congress amended the Voting Rights Act in 1982 to provide that a violation of section 2 of the act, as opposed to the Constitution, could be established by showing either the discriminatory purpose or result of a challenged practice. Congress rejected exclusive reliance upon the intent standard for three basic reasons: it was "unnecessarily divisive" because it required plaintiffs to prove that local officials were racists, the burden of proof was "inordinately difficult," and it "ask[ed] the wrong question."[53] The "right question" was whether minorities had an equal opportunity to participate in the political process and elect candidates of their choice. Amended section 2 is discussed in more detail in the section of this chapter dealing with the Voting Rights Act.

Did the Supreme Court ever reconsider *Bolden*?

Yes. Two days after Congress amended section 2, the Supreme Court decided *Rogers v. Lodge*,[54] a vote dilution case from Burke County, Georgia, and all but reversed its earlier decision in *Bolden*. While the Court continued to require proof of racial purpose, it said that such purpose could be inferred from circumstantial evidence: "discriminatory intent need not be proved by direct evidence. 'Necessarily, an invidious discriminatory purpose may often be inferred from the totality of the relevant facts.'"[55] The effect of *Lodge* was to restore the constitutional test for vote dilution contained in *White v. Regester.*

Is the appropriate standard for determining a constitutional violation of voting rights of major importance today?

No, except in those cases where courts use constitutional analysis in resolving issues of intent under section 2. Since Congress amended section 2 in 1982 to include a results test, and given the requirement that courts decide cases on statutory grounds if possible, most voting rights cases are now decided under the statute rather than the Fourteenth or Fifteenth Amendments. An understanding of the development of constitutional standards in this area of the law is necessary, however, to understand the intent of Congress in passing the 1982 amendments and to determine questions of racial purpose.

How are the Fourteenth and Fifteenth Amendments enforced?

The traditional methods of enforcing the Fourteenth and

Fifteenth Amendments have been prosecutions by the federal government for violations of criminal statutes protecting voting rights,[56] lawsuits by victims of discrimination under the various statutes enacted by Congress to enforce the Fourteenth and Fifteenth Amendments,[57] and suits by the attorney general under the same statutes to remedy individual violations as well as patterns and practices of voting discrimination. The Department of Justice and jurisdictions covered by section 5 of the Voting Rights Act of 1965 have been given administrative responsibilities in connection with the implementation of changes in voting procedures. These procedures, designed to protect Fourteenth and Fifteenth Amendment rights, are discussed below in this chapter. There are no administrative requirements that must be complied with prior to filing a lawsuit in court.[58]

What remedies are available for constitutional violations?

As in any case involving a constitutional violation, a court is obligated to exercise its equitable powers so that it fully and completely remedies the dilution of minority voting strength. The scope of the remedy will thus depend upon the nature and extent of the violation. Remedies for violations in voting cases include court orders ending the discrimination, retroactive relief such as the setting aside of elections,[59] the establishment of new election procedures, and awards of attorneys' fees[60] and damages.[61]

Can a person be made to disclose his or her race as a condition for registering to vote?

Yes, if state law requires it. Many states require persons to list their race on voter registration forms. If the forms are not fully completed, registration may be denied. None of these compulsory disclosure laws have been held unconstitutional in themselves by the Supreme Court,[62] but their discriminatory misuse, for example to deny registration only to noncomplying racial minorities,[63] or the misuse of the information itself—for example to segregate or purge blacks on voter lists—would be patently unlawful.[64] Although racial classification was used in the past to exclude minorities from the elective process, the modern justification for requiring disclosure of race, aside from the incidental value it may have in identifying registrants and

minimizing voter fraud, is to aid the government in formulating
and evaluating legislative programs to assist minorities and the
courts in fashioning remedies for past discrimination.

In a related context, the Voting Rights Act amendments of
1975 authorize the director of the census to conduct surveys
and compile registration and voting statistics on the extent to
which racial minorities are registered to vote and have voted
in elections.[65] The main purpose of the surveys is to assist the
Congress in evaluating the effectiveness of federal voting rights
legislation and the need for additional remedial measures.
Some persons object to supplying the government with racial
information not only because of their fear of its misuse but
because of their beliefs that governmental concepts of race
and ethnic origin are loose and unscientific and constitute an
invasion of privacy. To meet these concerns, the act provides
that no person may be compelled to disclose race, color, or
national origin in response to any census survey taken under
the act and that no penalty may be imposed for failure to make
such disclosures.[66]

To further ensure privacy, the amendments also provide that
the confidentiality and criminal penalties provisions that are
normally applicable to processes used to collect census data are
applicable to surveys under the act.

Given the importance of racial information, if government
is to legislate intelligently and courts are to fashion effective
remedies for past discrimination, the balance between individual rights and the public need for accurate data seems best
struck by requiring disclosure of racial information, but guaranteeing protection against its discriminatory misuse and ensuring privacy by separating racial or ethnic information from
personal identifying information such as name and address.

THE VOTING RIGHTS ACT OF 1965

**What are the basic provisions of the Voting Rights Act of
1965?**

The Voting Rights Act of 1965, amended in 1970, 1975, 1982,
and 1992,[67] abolished tests or devices for voting which had been
used in the past to disfranchise racial minorities.[68] The term
tests or devices includes literacy tests, educational require-

ments, good character tests, and exclusively English language registration procedures or elections conducted solely in English where a single linguistic minority comprises more than 5 percent of the voting age population of the jurisdiction. A second provision of the act, section 5, requires "covered" jurisdictions to gain approval or preclearance from federal authorities before implementing changes in voting laws or procedures to make certain that they do not have the purpose or effect of abridging the right to vote on account of race, color, or membership in a language minority.[69] The act also provides for federal voter registrars and observers, absentee balloting in presidential elections, and bilingual ballots for language minorities.[70] Section 2 of the act, which was amended in 1982, provides that voting practices are unlawful if they result in discrimination, whether or not they were enacted or are being maintained with a discriminatory purpose.[71]

The basic provisions and amendments of the Voting Rights Act of 1965 have been held to be constitutional by the Supreme Court.[72]

Is the Voting Rights Act ban on literacy and education tests for voting nationwide?

Yes. Literacy or other tests as a condition for voting were suspended by the Voting Rights Act of 1965 initially only in those states in which Congress found there had been pervasive discrimination against blacks in registration and in which literacy tests had been specifically designed to disfranchise racial minorities. Later, the ban on literacy and other tests was made nationwide and permanent by amendments to the act in 1970 and 1975. The Supreme Court held the nationwide ban constitutional after concluding that literacy tests had reduced voter participation in a discriminatory manner throughout the country and not merely in those states originally covered by the act.[73]

Do the preclearance procedures of section 5 also apply nationwide?

No. Section 5 covers only those states in which less than half of eligible persons are actually registered or voted in either the 1964, 1968, or 1972 presidential elections *and* if a test or device was used for registering or voting. When this formula is not met in a state as a whole, coverage may apply in any "political subdivision" within the state that satisfies the formula. The attorney general and the director of the census are responsible for determining whether the conditions for coverage are met in particular jurisdictions.

What is a "political subdivision" for the purposes of the act?
"Political subdivision" is defined in the act as any county or parish or subdivision of a state that conducts registration for voting.[74] A list of jurisdictions now covered by section 5 is as follows:[75]

Alabama: whole state
Alaska: whole state
Arizona: whole state
California, 4 counties: Kings, Merced, Monterrey, and Yuba
Florida, 5 counties: Collier, Hardee, Hendry, Hillborough, and Monroe
Georgia: whole state
Louisiana: whole state
Michigan, 2 towns: Buena Vista and Clyde
Mississippi: whole state
New Hampshire, 10 towns: Antrim, Benton, Boscawen, Millsfield, Newington, Pinkhams Grant, Rindge, Stewartstown, Stratford, and Unity
New York, 3 counties: Bronx, Kings, and New York
North Carolina, 40 counties: Anson, Beaufort, Bertie, Bladen, Camden, Caswell, Chowen, Cleveland, Craven, Cumberland, Edgecomb, Franklin, Gaston, Gates, Granville, Greene, Guilford, Halifax, Harnett, Hertford, Hoke, Jackson, Lee, Lenoir, Martin, Nash, Northampton, Onslow, Pasqutank, Perquamans, Person, Pitt, Robeson, Rockingham, Scotland, Union, Vance, Washington, Wayne, and Wilson
South Carolina: whole state
South Dakota, 2 counties: Shannon and Todd
Texas: whole state
Virginia: whole state

Are all political units within designated jurisdictions covered by section 5?

Yes. Section 5 covers all entities or political units within designated jurisdictions that exercise power over any aspect of the electoral process, without regard to whether such units actually register voters or conduct elections.

Thus, cities that do not register voters,[76] political parties,[77] and entities such as school boards that neither register voters nor conduct elections,[78] located within designated jurisdictions, are subject to section 5 where they exercise control over some aspect of the elective process.

Is coverage under section 5 permanent?

No. Congress enacted section 5 in 1965 as a temporary, five year measure to combat the extraordinary defiance of equal voting rights in certain sections of the country and because of the failure of litigation to end discrimination and the repeated attempts by local jurisdictions to evade the law by enacting new and different discriminatory practices. Congress extended section 5 in 1970, 1975, and 1982 after concluding that the special provision was still needed to protect minority voting rights. The statute is now scheduled to expire in the year 2007.

Can a jurisdiction remove itself from coverage prior to the expiration of section 5?

Yes. While the decision of the attorney general and the director of the census that a given jurisdiction is covered is not reviewable,[79] covered jurisdictions, down to the county level, may seek to "bail out" from section 5 coverage pursuant to section 4(a) of the act by filing a declaratory judgment action in the federal court in the District of Columbia.[80] Section 4(a), which was substantially revised in 1982, requires a jurisdiction as a condition for bail out to show that during the preceding ten years it has: (1) complied with the law as specified in the statute, e.g., has not used a discriminatory literacy test for voting, has not violated the voting rights laws, has fully complied with section 5, has not received a section 5 objection, has not engaged in any discriminatory conduct; and (2) undertaken constructive efforts to ensure equal political participation by minorities, e.g., has expanded opportunities for minority voter registration, has eliminated voting procedures that inhibit or dilute equal political access, has attempted to eliminate voter intimidation. The bail out formula was designed not only to ensure that discrimination-prone jurisdictions remained covered by section 5, but to provide local jurisdictions with an incentive to change their voting practices by eliminating structural and other barriers to minority political participation. Very few jurisdictions have sought bail out since the 1982 amendments were enacted.

May a court as part of its remedial order require a noncovered jurisdiction to comply with section 5?

Yes. A court can require a jurisdiction to preclear some or all of its voting changes by applying the so-called pocket trigger of section 3.[81]

Congress designed section 3 to reach pockets of discrimination in parts of the country not otherwise covered by section 5. Any federal court that has found a violation of voting rights protected by the Fourteenth or Fifteenth Amendments may require as part of its remedial order that the jurisdiction comply with section 5 preclearance.[82]

Is coverage under section 5 of real significance?

Yes. Coverage under section 5 is enormously significant, for it means that no change in voting procedures in a covered jurisdiction may be implemented unless the change has first been cleared to ensure that it does not have the purpose or effect of denying or abridging the right to vote on account of race, color, or membership in a language minority. Section 5 thus provides an effective safeguard against enactment of new forms of discrimination, and it places the burden of litigation or administrative proceedings and delay upon the perpetrators and not the victims of possibly discriminatory practices.[83]

What kinds of changes in voting are covered by section 5?

Any change in voting sought to be implemented after 1 November 1964 (or 1968 or 1972, depending on when the jurisdiction came under preclearance) in a covered jurisdiction is subject to section 5, with the exception of changes formulated and ordered by federal courts. Even federal court orders are subject to section 5 to the extent that they implement voting changes "reflecting the policy choices of the elected representatives of the people."[84] It is immaterial whether the change is major or minor, or is brought about by legislation, constitutional amendment, political party rule, custom and practice, or is ordered by a state court.[85] The Supreme Court has generally given section 5 the broadest possible construction to include such seemingly inconsequential changes in voting as the relocation of a polling place.[86] Other changes held to be within the scope of section 5 because of their potential impact on voting include annexations (even of vacant land), staggering of terms of office, majority vote requirements, changes to single-member or multimember districts, abolition of elective or appointive offices, changing of precinct lines, redistricting, changes in filing fees or other candidacy requirements, a change in the date of an election, the transfer of the power to appoint members of a county racing commission from locally elected officials to the governor, and a requirement that the probate judge pay the salaries of persons in her office who had previously been paid by the county commission.[87] Even a rule adopted by a county school board that its employees must take unpaid leaves of absence while campaigning for elective political office was held to be a change in voting for which preclearance was required.[88]

In a recent section 5 case, however, a divided Supreme Court held that changes that affect only the distribution of power among elected officials are not required to be precleared.[89]

Does section 5 apply to voting changes affecting the election of nonlegislative officials such as judges?

Yes. Although the courts have held that the one person, one vote rule of the Fourteenth Amendment is not applicable to the election of judges, section 5 has been held to apply to all voting without limitation as to who, or what, is the object of the vote. Applying this standard, the courts have specifically required preclearance of statutes affecting the election of state court judges.[90]

Is a change in voting enacted prior to 1 November 1964, but not implemented until after 1 November 1964 subject to section 5?

Yes, so long as the change in voting alters the practice in effect on 1 November 1964 (or 1968 or 1972, depending on the date of coverage of the jurisdiction), it is subject to the preclearance procedures of section 5 regardless of when the change was actually enacted. For example, in 1962 the state of Mississippi enacted a law requiring the city of Canton to change from ward to at-large elections for aldermen. The city ignored the law in its 1965 elections and, as in previous years, elected aldermen by wards. In 1969 the city for the first time implemented the change in the law and switched to at-large elections. It refused to comply with section 5 on the ground that it had no choice but to conform to the 1962 state statute. The Supreme Court nonetheless enjoined use of at-large elections until the city complied with section 5 since the procedure actually in force and effect on 1 November 1964 was voting by wards.[91]

How is preclearance obtained?

Preclearance of changes in voting may be obtained in two ways. The change may be submitted administratively to the attorney general who has sixty days from the date the submission is deemed completed within which to note any objection (or 120 days if the Department of Justice requests, or a jurisdiction voluntarily submits, additional information). If the attorney general does not object, the proposed change may be implemented. If the attorney general notes an objection, the change is rendered null and void and preexisting legally enforceable law remains in effect.

The second method by which a covered jurisdiction may obtain preclearance, whether or not submission has been made to the attorney general, is to bring a lawsuit before a special three-judge federal district court in the District of Columbia. If the court rules that the change has neither the purpose nor the effect of denying or abridging the right to vote on account of race, color, or membership in a language minority, it may be implemented. If the court makes no such ruling, the change may not take effect.

Because of the time and expense of legal proceedings, administrative submission to the attorney general has been the usual method of seeking clearance of proposed changes in voting.

Do persons affected by proposed changes in voting have the right to make their views known, either to the attorney general or the federal court, before clearance is granted or denied?

Yes. The attorney general has issued guidelines involving

administrative submissions,[92] which allow interested persons or organizations to request and receive notice of submissions, and more importantly, to submit evidence and arguments in favor of or against proposed changes. Persons potentially affected by changes in voting laws are also permitted to intervene in court proceedings in the District of Columbia to assert any interests they might have. In this manner, persons affected by changes in voting laws play an important role in enforcing the preclearance procedures of section 5 of the Voting Rights Act. Persons wishing to receive notice of submissions, or who have questions about voting laws in their jurisdictions, should contact the Chief, Voting Section, Civil Rights Division, Department of Justice, Washington, D.C. 20530.

Can the decision of the attorney general in objecting or failing to object to a change in voting be appealed?

No. The Supreme Court has ruled that the decision of the attorney general to object or approve a change in voting is final and not appealable.[93] However, if the attorney general makes an objection, a covered jurisdiction has the option of bringing a lawsuit seeking a favorable ruling from the federal court in the District of Columbia.[94] If the attorney general approves a change, persons affected also may seek to enjoin its enforcement, but only in traditional lawsuits attacking the change on constitutional or statutory grounds filed in the federal courts in the jurisdiction where the voting change was proposed.[95]

Can decisions of the federal court in the District of Columbia approving or disapproving changes in voting be appealed?

Yes. Decisions of the federal court in the District of Columbia approving or disapproving changes in voting are reviewed directly by the Supreme Court pursuant to its appellate jurisdiction.[96]

Once a submission is made, how does the attorney general or the federal court determine whether to grant clearance?

The standard for preclearance is whether the proposed change has the purpose or effect of denying or abridging the right to vote on account of race, color, or membership in a language minority. Discriminatory purpose under section 5 has been defined as the sort of invidious purpose that would support a challenge to official action under the equal protection clause of the Fourteenth Amendment.[97] Discriminatory effect under section 5 has generally been defined as retrogression, i.e., whether a change will make members of the minority group worse off than they were before the change. In determining retrogression, the attorney general and the courts normally compare the submitted change to the practice lawfully in effect at the time of the submission.

Some changes in voting, for example those that expand access to registration or increase the hours during which polling places remain open, would obviously be unobjectionable. Other changes, such as those that make registration and voting more difficult, would be denied preclearance. If the attorney general or the court cannot determine whether a change might have a prohibited effect, preclearance must still be denied; for under section 5 there is a presumption that a submission is discriminatory, and if the submitting authority cannot rebut the presumption, implementation of the proposed change must be denied.[98]

The allocation of the burden of proof to the submitting jurisdiction was a critical and innovative feature of section 5 and has proved to be a substantial curb to the introduction of new, discriminatory voting procedures. Not surprisingly, many section 5 submissions turn on the failure of the jurisdiction to carry its burden of proof rather than on a positive finding of discrimination by the courts or the attorney general.

Does a change that increases minority participation in the elective process—but does so only partially—"deny or abridge" the right to vote?

Generally no. In *Beer v. United States*,[99] the Supreme Court was asked to review a decision of the federal court in the District of Columbia denying preclearance to a reapportionment plan for the city of New Orleans. The lower court had ruled that although the new plan created two single-member districts with a majority of black voters where before there had been none, the plan was objectionable because it failed to eliminate pre-Voting Rights Act at-large seats for the city council which restricted the opportunities of minorities for election. The Supreme Court reversed the ruling, concluding that an "ameliorative new legislative apportionment cannot violate Section 5 unless the new apportionment itself so discriminates on the basis of race or color as to violate the Constitution."[100] In other words, a change in election procedures that removes some but not all barriers to voting ordinarily will not violate section 5.

Even an ameliorative, nonretrogressive change violates section 5 if its purpose is to limit minority political participation. During congressional reapportionment in Georgia in 1982, the general assembly increased the black percentage in the fifth congressional district from 50 percent to 57 percent. Although the state argued the change could not be objectionable under the *Beer* standard of retrogression, the court nonetheless denied preclearance. It concluded that the legislature had rejected an alternative plan creating a 69 percent black fifth district because, in the words of the chairman of the house reapportionment committee, it didn't want to create a "nigger district."[101] Although the plan was not technically retrogressive, it was the product of intentional discrimination and was denied preclearance.

Have the courts created any exceptions to the retrogression standard?

Yes. In recognition of its limitations and potential harshness, the courts have created a number of exceptions to the strict application of the retrogression rule. For example, a new legislative plan cannot be approved, even if it is not retrogressive compared with the preexisting legislative plan, if it diminishes minority voting strength when compared with an intervening court-ordered plan.[102] Preexisting districts that have not themselves been precleared may also not be used in determining if a submission is retrogressive.[103]

In *Wilkes County, Georgia v. United States*,[104] the court created another important exception to the retrogression standard where a preexisting plan is malapportioned. Under such circumstances, any new plan must be measured for retrogression based not upon the preexisting plan but upon "options for properly apportioned . . . plans."[105]

Has Congress taken any action to modify the *Beer* retrogression standard?

Yes. Congress indicated its disagreement with the strict retrogression standard of *Beer* when it amended section 2 of the Voting Rights Act in 1982. According to the senate report that accompanied the amendment, "it is intended that a section 5 objection also follow if a new voting procedure itself so discriminates as to violate section 2."[106] Thus, preclearance should be denied a voting practice, even if not intentionally discriminatory or retrogressive, if it would have a discriminatory result. This interpretation of the interplay between section 2 and section 5 is included in the regulations for section 5 enforcement issued by the attorney general in 1987 in which he concludes that a section 5 objection should be entered "to prevent a clear violation of amended section 2."[107]

Do annexations of territory that increase majority voting strength "deny or abridge" the rights of minorities under section 5?

No, provided the purpose of the annexation is not to dilute minority voting strength and minorities are ensured fair representation in government in proportion to their percent of the postannexation population. In one section 5 case, the Supreme Court approved annexations by the city of Richmond, Virginia, which reduced the black population from 55 to 45 percent of the electorate because there had been no discriminatory purpose and blacks were ensured fair representation in government of the enlarged city.[108] Nevertheless, the decision does sanction a change which had the net effect of watering down the political strength of minority voters. One of the justices implied that the decision was a limited one and created a special "municipal hardship" exemption from section 5 coverage in favor of annexations.

Is there anything to keep a covered jurisdiction from ignoring section 5 and implementing changes in voting without having received preclearance?

Yes. The attorney general or any person affected by a change in voting may seek an injunction against enforcement by filing an action before a three-judge court in the covered jurisdiction.[109] In such a proceeding, the sole issues are whether the jurisdiction is covered, whether the change affects voting, and whether there has been preclearance. If both the jurisdiction and the changes are covered and there has been no preclearance, the three-judge court *must* prohibit implementation of the change. The court has no jurisdiction to resolve whether the change has the purpose or effect of abridging the right to vote on account of race, color, or membership in a language minority since these issues may be resolved only by the attorney general or the federal court in the District of Columbia.[110] To expedite judicial review, appeals from the decisions of three-judge courts are reviewed directly by the Supreme Court pursuant to its appellate jurisdiction.[111]

The Voting Rights Act also makes it a crime to fail to comply with preclearance requirements[112] although there have been no known prosecutions for the offense.

If an uncleared change has been implemented, can the courts grant retroactive relief?

Yes. In the event an uncleared change has actually been implemented, the court must not only enjoin its future use, but fashion a remedy to undo the violation of the Voting Rights Act, such as shortening of terms of office or ordering new elections under the preexisting election laws.[113] The Supreme Court has indicated, however, that in certain circumstances it is appropriate to enjoin further use of an uncleared change but allow local officials an opportunity to seek federal approval. The court may then order new elections if approval is denied.[114]

What is the standard for proving vote dilution under the results test of amended section 2?

The legislative history of the 1982 amendments sets out certain readily verifiable factors derived from *White v. Regester* and other voting cases courts should ordinarily consider in dilution cases. The factors include racial bloc voting; a history of discrimination; depressed levels of minority employment, income, and education; few minorities elected to office; the presence of formal or informal organizations that endorse or "slate" candidates for public office; the existence of racial campaign appeals; and the use of devices that enhance discrimination, such as numbered posts and a majority vote requirement. Other factors having possible probative value, but which should generally be avoided because of their subjective nature, are a lack of responsiveness by elected officials to the legitimate needs and interests of the minority community and a tenuous policy underlying the use of the challenged practice.

Has the Supreme Court approved the use of the results test in section 2 cases?

Yes. In *Thornburg v. Gingles*[115] the Court applied section 2 to invalidate multimember districts in North Carolina's 1982 legislative reapportionment. A majority of the Court established a three-part test for determining when at-large voting violated the results standard of the statue. First, the minority must be able to show that it is sufficiently large and geographically compact to constitute a majority in one or more single-member districts. Second, it must show that it is politically cohesive or tends to vote as a bloc. Third, it must show that the majority votes sufficiently as a bloc usually to defeat the minority's preferred candidates. The Court adopted, in its words, a "functional" view of the political process and isolated the most important factors identified in the legislative history of section 2 bearing on challenges to at-large voting. The other factors, such as the history of discrimination, racial campaign appeals, and so forth were deemed supportive of, but not essential to, a vote dilution claim.

What is bloc voting and how is it proved?

The Supreme Court adopted a simple, common sense definition of bloc voting in *Gingles*. According to the Court, bloc voting exists "where there is 'a consistent relationship between [the] race of the voter and the way in which the voter votes,' . . . or to put it differently, where 'black voters and white voters vote differently.'"[116] Bloc voting that is legally significant, i.e., that will sustain a section 2 violation, exists in general where "a white bloc vote . . . normally will defeat the combined strength of minority support plus white 'crossover' votes."[117]

Bloc voting can be proved through statistical analysis showing a correlation between the race of voters and the race of candidates. Two standard methods of analysis are bivariate ecological regression and homogeneous precinct analysis, both of which were approved by the Court in *Gingles*. Bloc voting may also be shown by the testimony of experienced politicians who are familiar with voting patterns in the jurisdiction and by such factors as few minority candidates or elected officials and a history of discrimination.[118]

Is it necessary to show that voters are motivated by race?
No. It is enough to show simply that voters of different races are voting differently. According to *Gingles*, "[a]ll that matters under . . . [section] 2 and under a functional theory of vote dilution is voter behavior, not its explanations."[119]

What kind of voting practices are subject to challenge under section 2?
Section 2 applies to any "standard, practice, or procedure" affecting voting. While most section 2 challenges have been to electoral structures such as at-large elections and districting plans, the legislative history of the 1982 amendments, as well as the plain language of the statute, make it clear that section 2 applies to all voting rights practices, including those that are episodic and do not involve permanent structural barriers. The courts have given section 2 a broad construction and have held that such practices as the failure to appoint blacks as poll officials, the requirement of separate or dual registration for city and county elections, and the form or structure of a referendum question were subject to challenge under section 2.[120]

Can a single-member districting plan be challenged under section 2 on the ground that it fails to create minority controlled districts where it is possible to draw them?
Yes. A three-judge court, after concluding that voting was racially polarized and that blacks were unable to elect black candidates of their choice in majority white districts, invalidated portions of Arkansas's legislative districting because it failed to create reasonably contiguous and compact minority-controlled districts in parts of the state where it was possible to draw them.[121]

Does section 2 also apply to voting practices affecting the election of nonlegislative officials, such as judges and administrators?
Yes. The courts have held that the "plain language" of the statute provides that it applies to the election of any candidate for public office, regardless of the duties or functions involved, including judges (trial and appellate) and administrators.[122] A state's justification for its particular system of electing judges, however, is a proper factor for the courts to consider among

the "totality of circumstances" in determining a section 2 violation and an appropriate remedy.

Are single-member offices, such as mayors and governors, immune from vote dilution challenges?

No. The method of electing a single-member office (e.g., where there is only one such office in the voting area, or where all the duties of an office are exercised by a single official[123]) is subject to challenge under section 2. Thus, for example, the configuration of a municipality that produced a racially discriminatory distribution of voting power, or a particular practice, such as closing the polls at noon, that resulted in dilution of minority voting strength could be challenged under section 2 regardless of whether the election was for a single-member officeholder or not.[124]

Can the form of government, as opposed simply to the method of elections, be challenged under section 2?

Yes. The court held in *Carrollton Branch of NAACP v. Stallings*[125] that the sole commissioner (one person) form of government in Carroll County, Georgia was subject to a dilution challenge, both because there was evidence that the sole commissioner system was adopted in 1951 with a discriminatory purpose and because it resulted in discrimination within the meaning of amended section 2. The case was eventually settled on the basis of the adoption by the county of a five-member board of commissioners elected from districts. In a similar case, the court of appeals held that the at-large elected sole commissioner form of government in Bleckley County, Georgia violated the result standard of section 2 and that on remand the district court should consider adopting as a remedy the five-seat single-member district plan used by the board of education.[126]

What kind of remedies are required for section 2 violations?

In amending section 2 Congress declined to specify any particular remedies for violations of the statute. Instead, the legislative history provides that a "court should exercise its traditional equitable powers to fashion the relief so that it completely remedies the prior dilution of minority voting strength and fully provides equal opportunity for minority citizens to participate and to elect candidates of their choice."[127]

In cases involving challenges to at-large elections, the courts have generally ordered single-member districts as a remedy, a proportionate number of which contain a majority of minority group members. The Supreme Court, noting the impact of at-large voting upon minorities, has expressed a preference for single-member districts, and has concluded that they are required in court-formulated reapportionment plans unless a special combination of circumstances justifies a different result.[128] Greater leeway is allowed for experimentation in legislatively formulated plans, however.[129]

In addition to new, racially fair election procedures, successful plaintiffs in section 2 cases are entitled to special elections, orders ending the discrimination, and awards of damages and attorneys fees.

Are "mixed" plans that contain some combination of single-member districts, multimember districts, and at-large seats acceptable as remedies in vote dilution cases?

That depends on whether the plans meet the complete and full remedy standard of section 2. If retaining any at-large or multimember seats would merely perpetuate rather than ameliorate the voting rights violation, they cannot be used.[130]

Can a jurisdiction retain the use of a chairperson or executive officer elected at-large in a remedial plan?

Not if it would carry forward the voting rights violation or dilute the voting strength and influence of the other members of the governing body.[131] Thus, in a case from Dallas County, Alabama, the court rejected a remedial plan in which four commissioners were to be elected from single-member districts with the probate judge, elected at-large, serving as chairperson ex officio. The court of appeals held that the "election plan does not fully cure the infirmities which caused the district court in the first instance to declare the county's at-large electoral system violative of section 2."[132] An at-large elected chairperson would be permitted, however, if there was a clearly delineated job description along with other safeguards that would guarantee no infringement by the chairperson on the work of the other members of the governing body.[133]

Are there alternatives to electing a chairperson at-large?
Yes. They include choosing the chairperson on a rotating basis from the membership of the governing body, having the governing body elect the chairperson, or hiring a chief administrative officer.

Are single-member districts always the best alternative to at-large elections?
No. While single-member districts are the most commonly used alternative to at-large elections, they do not always provide an adequate remedy, as where the minority population is geographically dispersed and it is impossible to construct a proportionate number of districts in which the minority is a majority of the population. Under the circumstances, other nonmajoritarian election procedures, such as limited or cumulative voting, may provide a more complete and full remedy for the vote dilution.

What are limited and cumulative voting?
In a limited voting system, each voter has fewer votes than the number of seats to be filled. In a cumulative system, each voter has as many votes as seats to be filled, but may express a preference by giving all her votes to one candidate or dividing her votes among several candidates. If the minority votes cohesively, both systems enhance the opportunity for the minority to elect candidates of its choice and prevent the majority from sweeping the field.[134]

Are practices such as limited and cumulative voting exotic and contrary to American electoral traditions?
No. Limited and cumulative voting have often been used in the United States and have consistently withstood constitutional challenges. While one court has held that they were not required as a remedy for a section 2 violation,[135] they have been voluntarily adopted by the defendants in an increasing number of section 2 cases, and have been approved by the courts and precleared by the attorney general under section 5 of the Voting Rights Act.[136]

Has the amendment of section 2 had any appreciable impact on voting rights litigation?

Yes. The amendment of section 2, and the decisions in *Lodge* and *Gingles,* represented a strong congressional and judicial commitment to equality in voting and support of vote dilution claims. They also accelerated the pace of voting rights litigation and have brought about the decline of at-large elections and the increased use of district voting, which in turn has facilitated minority political participation and officeholding.

Has the amendment of section 2 and the increased use of district voting caused political resegregation and polarization where none existed before?

No. Congress considered such arguments when it amended section 2 and rejected them as unfounded. According to Congress, the testimony and other evidence presented to it belied the predictions and speculations that the amendment of section 2 would be a divisive factor that would cause the polarization of communities on the basis of race. Numerous courts had applied the results standard to set aside at-large elections and none of the dire consequences predicted by the critics of section 2 had occurred. Congress concluded that racial polarization was unfortunately an existing fact of political life and that criticism of the results standard and district voting was "like saying that it is the doctor's thermometer which causes high fever." [137] Because Congress rejected these arguments and speculations when it enacted the amendments to the act in 1982, they are no longer factors to consider in vote dilution cases under section 2.

Social science studies also indicate that the increased minority officeholding brought about by district voting has been associated with a substantial shift in responsiveness to minority interests and the inclusion of minorities in decision making. The presence of minority elected officials has tended to break down polarization and racial stereotyping, and has increased minority access to government. [138]

Can voting lines be drawn to *increase* minority participation in elective government?

Yes. It is permissible, both under the Constitution and the Voting Rights Act, for a state or its political subdivisions to take race into account in drawing district voting lines to ensure minority participation in politics or to remedy the continuing effects of past discrimination in voting. Thus, in a case from New York, the Supreme Court approved a reapportionment plan creating several majority black districts in Kings County over the objections of whites who had been included in those districts for the reasons that the plan overall neither stigmatized nor fenced out any racial group but promoted a fair allocation of political power.[139]

Are racial minorities entitled to elect minority candidates to office in proportion to their presence in the population?
No. The 1982 amendments of the Voting Rights Act provide that nothing in the act established "a right to have members of a protected class elected in numbers equal to their proportion in the population."[140] According to the legislative history, the purpose of the disclaimer was to make clear that at-large elections were not unlawful per se, that minorities could not establish a violation of section 2 merely by showing that they had not been elected to office in proportion to their numbers in the population, and that minorities were not entitled to racial quotas for officeholding.[141] Although not entitled to proportional representation, minorities are entitled to a proportional, or equal, opportunity to elect candidates of their choice.

How are federal examiners and observers appointed under the Voting Rights Act? What do they do?
The attorney general is authorized by the Voting Rights Act to direct that federal examiners and/or observers be sent to covered jurisdictions from which twenty or more meritorious, written complaints alleging voter discrimination have been received or if the attorney general determines that appointment is necessary to protect the equal right to vote.[142]

Examiners may register or list qualified voters.[143] Those listed are issued registration certificates and may vote in all federal, state, and local elections. The list of persons registered is sent monthly to local officials who must enter their names on election rolls. Federal observers act as poll watchers and determine whether all the eligible persons are allowed to vote and that ballots are properly counted.

Persons wishing to have either examiners or observers appointed in their jurisdictions should make a request directly to the Attorney General, Department of Justice, Washington, D.C. 20530.

Have examiners and observers been used extensively?

No. Federal examiners have been used sparingly, and primarily during the first years of the Voting Rights Act. The mere threat of appointment of examiners has generally been sufficient to ensure registration of minority voters.

Federal observers have been more widely used than examiners. During the first ten years of the Voting Rights Act, more than 6,500 observers were sent to monitor elections in covered jurisdictions.[144] The use of federal observers in more recent times has significantly declined.

Are language minorities entitled to special protection in voting?

Yes. The 1975, 1982, and 1992 amendments of the Voting Rights Act require jurisdictions containing significant numbers of language minorities to conduct bilingual elections and registration campaigns.[145] Jurisdictions subject to the requirements are those covered by section 5 and in which a single language minority is more than 5 percent of eligible voters, as well as noncovered jurisdictions in which (1) more than 5 percent or 10,000 of the voting age citizens are members of a single language minority who do not "speak or understand English adequately enough to participate in the electoral process" and (2) if the rate of citizens in the language minority group who have not completed the fifth grade is higher than the national rate of persons who have not completed the fifth grade. If an Indian reservation meets these criteria a political subdivision that contains all or any part of that reservation is also subject to the bilingual election requirements. Affected jurisdictions are required to provide registration or voting notices, forms, instructions, assistance, or other materials or information relating to the electoral process, including ballots, in the language of the applicable language minority group if such items and services are provided in English.

Many states also make statutory provision for assistance to illiterate voters or those who do not read or understand English, while several court decisions have held that the right to receive assistance in voting is protected by the Constitution.[146]

Which language minorities are entitled to the special bilingual election and registration provisions of the Voting Rights Act? Which jurisdictions are covered?

The Voting Rights Act defines language minorities as American Indians, Asian-Americans, Alaskan Natives, and those of Spanish heritage.[147] Jurisdictions required to provide bilingual election procedures for one or more language minorities include the entire states of Alaska, Arizona, and Texas and more than 280 counties and townships, too numerous to list here, in California, Colorado, Connecticut, Florida, Hawaii, Idaho, Illinois, Massachusetts, Michigan, Mississippi, Montana, Nevada, New Jersey, New Mexico, New York, North Carolina, North Dakota, Oklahoma, Oregon, Pennsylvania, Rhode Island, South Dakota, Utah, and Wisconsin.[148]

Does the act make any special provision for minorities with no written languages?

Yes. The act provides that where the language of the applicable minority group is oral or unwritten or, in the case of Alaskan natives, if the dominant language is historically unwritten, the affected jurisdiction is required to furnish oral instructions, assistance, or other information relating to registration and voting.[149]

How are the bilingual provisions of the act enforced?

Enforcement of the bilingual provisions of the act is the responsibility of the covered jurisdictions themselves, the attorney general, and private citizens. Affected jurisdictions have the initial duty of determining what actions by them are necessary for compliance with the act. Then, the attorney general, through section 5 preclearance procedures and by his authority to bring litigation, has the duty to prevent or remedy discrimination based on the failure to use the applicable minority language in the electoral process.[150] The attorney general also has the responsibility of defending suits brought for termination of Voting Rights Act coverage. Finally, private individuals may file complaints with the attorney general or institute litigation to force compliance with the act.

Are the bilingual registration and election provisions of the act permanent?

No. The bilingual registration and election provisions of the Voting Rights Act are scheduled to expire on 6 August 2007.

What has been the overall impact of the Voting Rights Act on minority political participation?

It has been substantial. Prior to 1965 there were fewer than one hundred black elected officials in the seven southern states originally targeted by the act and fewer than two hundred nationwide.[151] As of January 1990 the number had grown to 3,394 in the targeted states and 7,370 nationwide.[152] Nonblack minorities have posted similar gains.

At the time of passage of the act there were only about 994,000 black registered voters in the targeted states.[153] By 1990 the number had increased to approximately 3,758,000.[154] Similar increases in black, Hispanic, and Native American registration have been recorded in other parts of the country.

Despite the undeniable progress, minorities clearly have not yet achieved equality of political participation measured by officeholding and voter registration and turnout. Nationally, blacks comprise 11 percent of eligible voters but hold fewer than 1.5 percent of elected offices.[155] Hispanics are 7 percent of the population but less than 1 percent of officeholders, while the population-percent ratio of Indians to Indian officeholders is similarly low.[156] Registration and turnout statistics, which are depressed for all voters, also show racial disparities. According to a survey conducted by the bureau of the census after the 1988 presidential election, 68 percent of whites but only 65 percent of blacks and 36 percent of Hispanics of voting age were registered to vote, while 60 percent of whites but only 52 percent of blacks and 29 percent of Hispanics of voting age actually voted.[157]

NOTES

1. Universal suffrage was not granted to women until ratification of the Nineteenth Amendment in 1920.
2. *E.g.*, 42 U.S.C. §§ 1983 and 1985; 18 U.S.C. §§ 241 and 242 *et seq.*
3. The various acts are codified in 42 U.S.C. §§ 1971 and 1973 *et seq.*

4. *Lane v. Wilson*, 307 U.S. 268, 275 (1939).
5. *Smith v. Allwright*, 321 U.S. 649 (1944); *Terry v. Adams*, 345 U.S. 461 (1953).
6. 16 Stat. 140–46 (1870).
7. 16 Stat. 433 (1871).
8. *United States v. Reese*, 92 U.S. 214 (1876); *James v. Bowman*, 190 U.S. 127 (1903).
9. 28 Stat. 36.
10. *South Carolina v. Katzenbach*, 383 U.S. 301, 310 n.9 (1966); and *Journal of the Constitutional Convention of the State of South Carolina*, 464, 469, 471 (1895).
11. *Political Participation, A Report of the United States Commission on Civil Rights, Washington, D.C., May, 1968*, 8 and n. 46.
12. 42 U.S.C. § 1971(a)(1).
13. 42 U.S.C. §§ 1983 and 1985.
14. 18 U.S.C. §§ 241 and 242.
15. *See, e.g., United States v. Stone*, 188 F. 836 (D. Md. 1911); *see also* Christopher, *The Constitutionality of the Voting Rights Act of 1965*, 18 Stan. L. Rev. 1 (1965).
16. *See, e.g., Smith v. Allwright*, 321 U.S. 649 (1944), brought under 42 U.S.C. § 1983, a provision of the Civil Rights Act of 1871.
17. *Guinn v. United States*, 238 U.S. 347 (1915), noted in *Nevett v. Sides*, 571 F.2d 209, 220 n.14 (5th Cir. 1978).
18. *Id.*, 238 U.S. at 359.
19. 71 Stat. 637.
20. 74 Stat. 90.
21. 78 Stat. 241.
22. 79 Stat. 445.
23. *Nixon v. Herndon*, 273 U.S. 536 (1927).
24. 286 U.S. 73 (1932).
25. 321 U.S. 649, 664 (1944).
26. *Terry v. Adams*, 345 U.S. 461, 469 (1953).
27. *Brown v. Baskin*, 78 F. Supp. 933, 937 (E.D.S.C. 1948); *Brown v. Baskin*, 80 F. Supp. 1017 (E.D.S.C. 1948), *aff'd* 174 F.2d 391 (4th Cir. 1949).
28. *Ratliff v. Beale*, 74 Miss. 247, 20 So. 865, 869 (1896).
29. *Breedlove v. Suttles*, 302 U.S. 277 (1937).
30. *Harper v. Virginia State Board of Elections*, 383 U.S. 663, 666 (1966).
31. *Louisiana v. United States*, 380 U.S. 145, 153 (1965). *See also Schnell v. Davis*, 336 U.S. 933 (1949); *United States v. Raines*, 189 F. Supp. 121 (M.D. Ga. 1960).
32. *James v. Bowman*, 190 U.S. 127 (1903); *United States v. Reese*, 92 U.S. 214 (1876). *Cf. Terry v. Adams*, 345 U.S. 461, 484 (1953).

33. *Ex parte Yarbrough*, 110 U.S. 651 (1884), affirming convictions under the predecessor of 18 U.S.C. § 241 for a private conspiracy to deprive a black of the right to vote; *United States v. Classic*, 313 U.S. 299 (1941).

34. *United States v. Original Knights of the Ku Klux Klan*, 250 F. Supp. 330 (E.D. La. 1965) (three-judge court), invoking the Civil Rights Act of 1957, 42 U.S.C. § 1971(c).

35. *United States v. Beaty*, 288 F.2d 653 (6th Cir. 1961). *See also United States v. Deal*, 6 R. Rel. Law Rep. 474 (W.D. La. 1961).

36. *Bell v. Southwell*, 376 F.2d 659 (5th Cir. 1967).

37. *United States v. Raines*, 189 F. Supp. 1212 (M.D. Ga. 1960).

38. *Reddix v. Lucky*, 252 F.2d 930 (5th Cir. 1958).

39. *Anderson v. Martin*, 375 U.S. 399 (1964).

40. *United States v. McLeod*, 385 F.2d 34 (5th Cir. 1967).

41. *Hunter v. Underwood*, 471 U.S. 222 (1985).

42. *Alabama v. United States*, 371 U.S. 37 (1962).

43. *United States v. Mississippi*, 380 U.S. 128 (1965).

44. *Gomillion v. Lightfoot*, 364 U.S. 339, 341 (1960).

45. *Long v. Gremillion*, Civ. No. 142,389 (Ninth Jud. Dist., Rapides Parish, La., Oct. 14, 1986).

46. *White v. Regester*, 412 U.S. 755, 766 (1973).

47. *Gray v. Sanders*, 372 U.S. 368 (1963); *Reynolds v. Sims*, 377 U.S. 533 (1964).

48. *Thornburg v. Gingles*, 478 U.S. 30, 47 (1986).

49. *Gordon v. Lance*, 403 U.S. 1, 6 (1971).

50. 412 U.S. 755 (1973).

51. *Id.*, at 766, 769.

52. 446 U.S. 55 (1980).

53. *Thornburg v. Gingles*, 478 U.S. 30, 44 (1986)

54. 458 U.S. 613 (1982).

55. *Rogers v. Lodge*, 458 U.S. 613, 618 (1982).

56. 18 U.S.C. §§ 241 and 242.

57. 42 U.S.C. §§ 1971 and 1973 *et seq*.

58. *Reddix v. Lucky*, 252 F.2d 930, 938 (5th Cir. 1958). *See also* 42 U.S.C. § 1973j(f).

59. *See, e.g.*, *Bell v. Southwell*, 376 F.2d 659 (5th Cir. 1967).

60. 42 U.S.C. §§ 1973l(e) and 1988.

61. *Lane v. Wilson*, 307 U.S. 268 (1939).

62. *Cf.*, *United States v. Rickenbacker*, 309 F.2d 462 (2d Cir. 1962), *cert. denied*, 83 S. Ct. 542 (1963); *United States v. Steele*, 461 F.2d 1148 (9th Cir. 1972).

63. *Cf.*, *Yick Wo v. Hopkins*, 118 U.S. 356 (1886).

64. *Reddix v. Lucky*, 252 F.2d 930 (5th Cir. 1958); *Bell v. Southwell*, 376 F.2d 659 (5th Cir. 1967).
65. 42 U.S.C. § 1973aa-5(a).
66. 42 U.S.C. § 1973aa-5(b).
67. 79 Stat. 437; 84 Stat. 315; 89 Stat. 402; 96 Stat. 134; 106 Stat. 921; codified as 42 U.S.C. § 1973 *et seq.*
68. 42 U.S.C. § 1973aa.
69. 42 U.S.C. § 1973c.
70. 42 U.S.C. §§ 1973d, f, cc and aa-1a.
71. 42 U.S.C. § 1973.
72. *South Carolina v. Katzenbach*, 383 U.S. 301 (1966); *Katzenbach v. Morgan*, 384 U.S. 641 (1966); *Oregon v. Mitchell*, 400 U.S. 112 (1970); *City of Rome v. United States*, 446 U.S. 156 (1980); *Thornburg v. Gingles*, 478 U.S. 30 (1986).
73. *Oregon v. Mitchell*, 400 U.S. 112 (1970).
74. 42 U.S.C. § 1973l(c)(2).
75. 28 C.F.R. pt. 51, app. (1990).
76. *United States v. Board of Commissioners*, 435 U.S. 110 (1978).
77. *MacGuire v. Amos*, 343 F. Supp. 119 (M.D. Ala. 1972).
78. *Dougherty County v. White*, 439 U.S. 32 (1978).
79. *Briscoe v. Bell*, 432 U.S. 404 (1977).
80. 42 U.S.C. § 1973b(a).
81. 42 U.S.C. §§ 1973a(c).
82. *Jeffers v. Clinton*, 740 F. Supp. 585 (E.D. Ark. 1990).
83. *South Carolina v. Katzenbach*, 383 U.S. 301, 335 (1966).
84. *McDaniel v. Sanchez*, 453 U.S. 130, 153 (1981).
85. *Hathorn v. Lovorn*, 457 U.S. 255 (1982); *Gresham v. Harris*, 695 F. Supp. 1179 (N.D. Ga. 1988), *aff'd sub nom.*, *Poole v. Gresham*, 110 S. Ct. 2556 (1990).
86. *Perkins v. Matthews*, 400 U.S. 379 (1971).
87. *City of Pleasant Grove v. United States*, 479 U.S. 462 (1987); *NAACP v. Hampton County Election Commission*, 470 U.S. 166 (1985); *Hardy v. Wallace*, 603 F. Supp. 174 (N.D. Ala. 1985); *Huffman v. Bullock County*, 528 F. Supp. 703 (M.D. Ala. 1981).
88. *Dougherty County v. White*, 439 U.S. 32 (1978)
89. *Presley v. Etowah County Commission*, 112 S. Ct. 820 (1992).
90. *Clark v. Roemer*, 111 S. Ct. 2096 (1991).
91. *Perkins v. Matthews*, 400 U.S. 379 (1971).
92. 28 C.F.R. §§ 51.1 *et seq.*
93. *Morris v. Gressette*, 432 U.S. 491 (1977).
94. *Beer v. United States*, 425 U.S. 130 (1976).
95. *Allen v. State Board of Elections*, 393 U.S. 544 (1969).

96. 42 U.S.C. § 1973c; *Beer v. United States*, 425 U.S. 130 (1976).

97. *Mississippi v. United States*, 490 F. Supp. 569, 583 (D.D.C. 1979).

98. *McCain v. Lybrand*, 465 U.S. 236 (1984).

99. 425 U.S. 130 (1976).

100. *Id.*, at 141.

101. *Busbee v. Smith*, 549 F. Supp. 494, 501 (D.D.C. 1982).

102. *Mississippi v. Smith*, 541 F. Supp. 1329, 1333 (D.D.C. 1982).

103. *Id.*; 28 C.F.R. § 51.54(b)(3).

104. 450 F. Supp. 1171 (D.D.C. 1978).

105. *Id.*, at 1178.

106. S. Rep. No. 417, 97th Cong., 2d Sess. 12 n.31 (1982).

107. 28 C.F.R. § 51.55(b)(2).

108. *Richmond v. United States*, 422 U.S. 358 (1975).

109. *Allen v. State Board of Elections*, 393 U.S. 544 (1969).

110. *Perkins v. Matthews*, 400 U.S. 279 (1971); *Clark v. Roemer*, 111 S. Ct. 2096 (1991).

111. 42 U.S.C. § 1973c; *Presley v. Etowah County Commission*, 112 S. Ct. 820 (1992).

112. 42 U.S.C. §§ 1973j.

113. *Perkins v. Matthews*, 400 U.S. 379 (1971).

114. *NAACP v. Hampton County Election Commission*, 470 U.S. 166 (1985).

115. 478 U.S. 30 (1986).

116. *Id.*, at 53 n. 21.

117. *Id.*, at 56.

118. *United States v. Marengo County Commission*, 731 F.2d 1546 (11th Cir. 1984).

119. 478 U.S. at 73.

120. *Harris v. Graddick*, 615 F. Supp. 239 (M.D. Ala. 1985); *PUSH v. Allain*, 674 F. Supp. 1245 (N.D. Miss. 1987); *Lucas v. Townsend*, 908 F.2d 851 (11th Cir. 1990), *vacated and remanded on other grounds, sub nom., Board of Education & Orphanage for Bibb County v. Lucas*, 111 S. Ct. 2845 (1991).

121. *Jeffers v. Clinton*, 730 F. Supp. 196, 198 (E.D. Ark. 1989).

122. *Chisom v. Roemer*, 111 S. Ct. 2354 (1991); *Houston Lawyers' Association v. Attorney General of Texas*, 111 S. Ct. 2376 (1991); *Dillard v. Crenshaw County, Alabama*, 831 F.2d 246, 1251 (11th Cir. 1987).

123. *See SCLC v. Siegelman*, 714 F. Supp. 511, 518 (M.D. Ala. 1989), discussing definitions of single-member offices.

124. *Houston Lawyers' Association v. Attorney General of Texas*, 111 S. Ct. 2376, 2381 (1991). The decision in *Houston Lawyers' Association* thus supersedes *Butts v. City of New York*, 779 F.2d 141, 148–49 (2d Cir. 1985), which held that vote dilution principles did not apply

to a challenge to a 40 percent plurality vote requirement in elections for mayor, city council president, and comptroller of New York City because it was impossible for minorities to win a "share" of such single-member offices.

125. 829 F.2d 1547 (11th Cir. 1987).
126. *Hall v. Holder*, 955 F.2d 1563 (11th Cir. 1992).
127. S. Rep. No. 417, 97th Cong., 2d Sess. 31 (1982).
128. *Connor v. Finch*, 431 U.S. 407 (1977).
129. *Wise v. Lipscomb*, 437 U.S. 535 (1978).
130. *United States v. Dallas County Commission*, 850 F.2d 1433, 1440 (11th Cir. 1988).
131. *Dillard v. Crenshaw County, Alabama*, 831 F.2d 246 (11th Cir. 1987).
132. *United States v. Dallas County Commission*, 850 F.2d 1430, 1432 (11th Cir. 1988).
133. *Dillard v. Crenshaw County, Alabama*, 831 F.2d 246, 253 (11th Cir. 1987).
134. P. Karlan, *Maps and Misreading: The Role of Geographic Compactness in Vote Dilution Litigation*, 24 Harv. C.R.-C.L.L. Rev. 173, 223–36 (1989).
135. *McGhee v. Granville County*, 860 F.2d 110 (4th Cir. 1988).
136. *E.g., Dillard v. Town of Cuba*, 708 F. Supp. 1244, 1246 n.3 (M.D. Ala. 1988).
137. S. Rep. No. 417, 97th Cong., 2d Sess. 34 (1982).
138. L. McDonald, *The Quiet Revolution in Minority Voting Rights*, 42 Vand. L. Rev. 1249, 1277–79 (1989).
139. *United Jewish Organizations v. Carey*, 430 U.S. 144 (1977).
140. 42 U.S.C. § 1973(b).
141. S. Rep. No. 417, 97th Cong., 2d Sess. 23–24, 27, 31 (1982).
142. 42 U.S.C. §§ 1973d and f.
143. 42 U.S.C. § 1973e.
144. *The Voting Rights Act: Ten Years After, A Report of the United States Commission on Civil Rights*, Washington, D.C., January, 1975, 35.
145. 42 U.S.C. §§ 1973h(f)(4) and aa-1a.
146. *E.g., Puerto Rican Organization for Political Action v. Kusper*, 490 F.2d 575 (7th Cir. 1973).
147. 42 U.S.C. § 1973aa-1a(e).
148. 28 C.F.R. pt. 55, app. (1990); 57 Fed. Reg. 43213 (Sept. 18, 1992).
149. 42 U.S.C. § 1973aa-1a(c).
150. 42 U.S.C. § 1973aa-2.
151. *Political Participation, A Report of the United States Commission on Civil Rights, Washington, D.C., May, 1968*, 15.

152.   *Black Elected Officials: A National Roster, 1990, Joint Center for Political and Economic Studies,* 10–11 (1991).
153.   *Political Participation, A Report of the United States Commission on Civil Rights, Washington, D.C., May, 1968,* 12–13.
154.   *Black Elected Officials: A National Roster, 1990, Joint Center for Political and Economic Studies,* 27, 129, 195, 249, 329, 383, 433 (1991).
155.   *Id.,* at ix.
156.   NALEO Education Fund, *1988 National Roster of Hispanic Elected Officials.*
157.   U.S. Bureau of the Census, Current Population Reports, Series P-20, No. 440, Voting and Registration in the Election of November, 1988, 2–4, U.S. Government Printing Office, Washington, D.C., 1989.

III

EMPLOYMENT

Discrimination in employment on the basis of race is prohibited by various modern civil rights laws, most importantly by Title VII of the Civil Rights Act of 1964, by the Thirteenth and Fourteenth Amendments, and by several of the Reconstruction era civil rights acts. Although there are many prohibitions against employment discrimination, they do not apply uniformly to all employers, nor do they make all discriminatory practices unlawful.

What are the major federal prohibitions against employment discrimination?

There are two general categories of federal prohibitions against employment discrimination. The first includes the modern civil rights acts and executive orders. The primary prohibition in this category is Title VII of the Civil Rights Act of 1964,[1] which specifically prohibits employment discrimination by large private employers; by most state, county, and municipal governments; by most labor unions; and by agencies of the federal government. In addition, in 1965 President Johnson issued Executive Order (E.O.) No. 11246 (later amended by E.O. No. 11375),[2] which requires all federal contracts to include an "equal opportunity clause." By signing a contract containing such a clause, the private contractor agrees not to discriminate in hiring and to take affirmative action to eliminate discrimination. Firms with at least fifty employees that contract with the government for fifty thousand dollars or more must also file affirmative action plans setting forth steps for achieving equal employment. The executive orders are enforced by the Office of Federal Contract Compliance Programs (OFCCP) in the Department of Labor.

The second category includes prohibitions that are more than a hundred years old: the Fourteenth Amendment and part of the Civil Rights Act of 1871 (42 U.S.C. § 1983), which prohibit discrimination in state and local government employment; and the Thirteenth Amendment and part of the Civil Rights Act of 1866 (42 U.S.C. § 1981), which prohibit discrimination in making and enforcing contracts for public and private employment. Section 1981 has been held to apply to discrimination against Jews[3] and Arabs,[4] as well as African Americans.

Are there important differences between Title VII of the Civil Rights Acts of 1964 and the older Reconstruction era prohibitions against employment discrimination?

Yes. There are three important differences. First, although Title VII and the older federal prohibitions sometimes cover the same employers, very often they do not. These differences give more options to minorities seeking to challenge discrimination.

Second, Title VII is administered by a federal agency, the Equal Employment Opportunity Commission (EEOC), which means that there are federal agency regulations in which the EEOC has described the types of prohibited discrimination.[5] The EEOC is also an enforcement agency. This means that an administrative charge of discrimination must be filed with the EEOC by a person who has been discriminated against before the person can go to court and also that the charge of discrimination might be resolved administratively without going to court. Under the older federal prohibitions, there is no administrative agency. Accordingly, there are no agency regulations, there are no administrative remedies, and there is little hope of stopping discrimination without going to court.

Third, Title VII prohibits a larger variety of discriminatory practices than do the older federal prohibitions. For example, Title VII generally prohibits not only intentionally discriminatory practices but also forbids practices that have a discriminatory effect;[6] the older prohibitions, on the other hand, prohibit only intentionally discriminatory practices.[7] The third difference is very important, because it is difficult in this modern age to prove intentional discrimination, especially since no employer will admit that it engages in intentional discrimination. For this reason, minority persons who believe they have been discriminated against should always try to obtain their rights to nondiscrimination under Title VII.

Are most employers covered by Title VII of the Civil Rights Act of 1964, as amended?

Yes. Title VII covers, and hence prohibits discrimination by, all private, state, county, and municipal employers with fifteen or more employees and that are engaged in interstate commerce (the transfer of goods and services between two or more states).[8] As far as the federal government is concerned, when Title VII was first enacted it applied only to federal agencies employing civil service schedule employees.[9] As a result of passage of the Civil Rights Act of 1991, Congress, the agencies of the legislative branch of government, and presidential appointments are subject to Title VII.[10] Title VII also covers and thus prohibits employment discrimination by employment referral agencies, labor unions with fifteen or more members, and labor apprenticeship programs.[11]

Given Title VII's broad coverage, it again needs to be stressed that minority persons who believe that they have been discriminated against should always try to obtain their rights to nondiscrimination under Title VII. In order to obtain such rights, however, it is necessary to comply with several administrative requirements under Title VII. These administrative requirements are discussed below in this chapter.

Does the application of 42 U.S.C. § 1981 also depend on the size of the employer and whether the employer is engaged in interstate commerce?
No. Section 1981 was designed to enforce the Constitution and applies to claims of discrimination based on race without regard to the size or number of employees of the employer and without regard to whether the employer is engaged in interstate commerce.

Do the states have laws prohibiting discrimination in employment?
Yes. All the states except Alabama, Arkansas, Georgia, and Mississippi have laws prohibiting discrimination in employment. In many instances, the EEOC must defer to or cooperate with the agency created to enforce the state civil rights laws.[12] Many counties and cities also have enacted laws making certain forms of employment discrimination unlawful.

May a discriminated-against person bring claims under both federal and state laws?
Yes. In some circumstances a victim of discrimination may

be able to assert claims under Title VII, section 1981, and state law. In other circumstances, however, a person may have no remedy at all, for example when he or she waited too long before asserting a section 1981 claim, works for an employer who employs fewer than fifteen employees, and lives in a state that does not have a law prohibiting racial discrimination in employment.

PROHIBITED DISCRIMINATORY PRACTICES

What are the basic prohibitions against employment discrimination under Title VII?

Title VII of the Civil Rights Act of 1964 makes it unlawful for an employer, on grounds of race, sex, religion, color, or national origin to discriminate with respect to "compensation, terms, conditions, or privileges of employment," and to classify employees or applicants "in any way which would deprive or tend to deprive any individual of employment opportunities."[13] The statute prohibits discrimination in hiring, firing, promotion, transfer, job training, and apprenticeship decisions.[14]

Employment agencies are prohibited from engaging in racial discrimination in referrals for employment,[15] and labor organizations may not exclude from membership, limit, or segregate any individual because of race, sex, religion, color, or national origin or refuse to make referrals "or otherwise adversely affect his status as an employee or as an applicant for employment."[16]

What if an employer fires or retaliates against an employee for filing an EEOC complaint or speaking out against discriminatory employment practices?

Title VII provides that it is illegal for an employer or other entity covered by the statute to retaliate in any way against a person who files a charge of discrimination or cooperates with the EEOC.[17] Title VII has also been interpreted to prohibit the discharge of an employee for lawful civil rights activities whether or not they involve the EEOC.[18]

Not all forms of protest against discrimination are protected by Title VII. The courts have tended to balance the goal of fair employment laws "to protect persons engaging reasonably in activities opposing . . . discrimination" with the right of employers to fairly select and supervise personnel.[19] An employee who had filed a charge of discrimination with EEOC, for example, was not protected from discharge where the employer showed that the employee had a long history of absenteeism and that other employees with similar records had also been discharged.[20]

In determining if an employer's actions are prohibited by Title VII, some courts have asked whether the employee's protest was "calculated to inflict needless economic hardship on the employer."[21] For example, one court held that an employer could fire an employee whose complaint went beyond legitimate accusations of discrimination and disclosed confidential information to newspaper reporters and circulated rumors that the company was in financial trouble.[22] An employee was protected from retaliation, however, for writing and circulating a petition protesting racial discrimination and urging other employees to assert their legal rights.[23] The courts have also protected complaining employees who had a reasonable belief that a practice was discriminatory, even if the charge was later found to be without merit.[24]

What is the standard for determining whether a practice is unlawful under Title VII?

Unfortunately, the law concerning Title VII is very unsettled at the present time. During the 1980s the Supreme Court decided a number of cases that substantially modified earlier rulings that had been favorable to minority claimants. Congress enacted the Civil Rights Act of 1991 to reverse these rulings, but the courts have only begun to interpret and apply the new law. As a consequence, Title VII law is in a state of flux.

In general, however, an employment practice is unlawful under Title VII if it (1) constitutes "disparate treatment" of a protected individual or (2) has a "disparate impact" upon a protected group. Where the disparate treatment has become the employer's standard operating procedure, the discrimination is said to constitute an unlawful "pattern and practice." In pattern-and-practice cases, the discriminated-against person alleges that the employer engaged in systematic disparate treatment of a protected class.[25]

How is a violation of the disparate treatment standard of Title VII shown?

In *McDonnell-Douglas Corp. v. Green*,[26] the Supreme Court explained the nature of proof necessary to make out a case of disparate treatment of a job applicant on the basis of race. The minority applicant must show that:

1. She belongs to a racial minority;
2. She applied and was qualified for a job for which the employer was seeking applicants;
3. Despite her qualifications, she was rejected; and
4. After her rejection, the position remained open and the employer continued to seek applicants from persons with similar qualifications.

Of course, a person making a complaint should adapt the facts to reflect the particular adverse employment action (discipline, layoff, promotion, transfer, retaliation, or wages).[27] Upon proving these elements, a person is said to have established a prima facie case of discrimination.

The employer must then "articulate some legitimate, nondiscriminatory reason for the employee's rejection."[28] Legitimate reasons are any reasons that are not discriminatory. Employers are given broad authority in their employment decisions, and as long as those decisions are not based on prohibited reasons, they will stand. Thus, an employer can claim it made the decision based on business conditions or because it simply liked a different applicant or employee better. The employer need not prove the absence of a discriminatory motive.[29]

Once the employer articulates a legitimate reason for its decision, the minority applicant then must "be afforded a fair opportunity to show that [the employer's] stated reason for [the] rejection was in fact pretext."[30] For example, in a lawsuit against the Jackson, Mississippi police department, black officers dismissed for allegedly accepting bribes argued that they had been discriminated against. They satisfied their initial burden of proof; the employer then argued that accepting bribes was a legitimate nondiscriminatory reason for dismissal. The federal court of appeals held that the reason appeared pretextual because white officers accused at the same time of accepting bribes were never even investigated, much less dismissed.[31]

When an employment practice affects a large number of employees, statistics may help prove a violation. For example, an inference of discrimination can be raised by showing a significant statistical disparity between the number of protected group members in the employer's work force as compared to the number of qualified members in the workforce within the geographical area from which the employer recruits employees.[32]

Even where the employer has produced enough evidence to raise a genuine issue of fact as to whether it was motivated by a legitimate, nondiscriminatory reason, the plaintiff can still prevail. To prove pretext, the claimant should look for evidence that the employer departed from its usual practices, applied different criteria to minorities, has a history of discriminating, or created a hostile work environment.

How is a violation of the disparate impact standard of Title VII shown?

Disparate impact cases, unlike disparate treatment cases, do not require proof of a discriminatory intent.[33] That is so because Title VII is also aimed at "the *consequences* of employment practices, not simply the motivation" of an employer.[34] Because disparate impact cases focus on the effects of employment practices, statistics are extremely important and normally provide the evidence of the discrimination.

There are three general steps in proving disparate impact under Title VII. First, the person discriminated against must be able to show that the practice, even if neutral on its face, has a disproportionate impact against racial minorities. Second, once the practice is shown to be discriminatory, the employer then must have evidence that the practice is "related to job performance"[35] or is "essential to effective job performance."[36] Third, a challenged practice, even if it is job-related, will still be found unlawful if the discriminated-against person can "show that other tests or selection devices, without a similarly undesirable racial effect, would also serve the employer's legitimate interest in 'efficient and trustworthy workmanship.'"[37]

Unlike disparate treatment cases, disparate impact cases require the employer to persuade the court that its practice is job related or justified by business necessity.[38]

What types of employment practices have been found to have a discriminatory impact, not job related and therefore unlawful under Title VII?

Following the steps just discussed, the Supreme Court has found a number of practices unlawful. In a 1971 case, for example, *Griggs v. Duke Power Co.*,[39] the company had a policy requiring employees seeking better jobs in the company to have either a high school diploma or make a certain score on an aptitude test. Because of the heritage of unequal educational opportunities, fewer blacks than whites finished high school and fewer blacks than whites made high scores on the aptitude tests. The power company's requirements thus denied better employment to a disproportionate number of minorities. The Supreme Court held the diploma and test requirements violated Title VII because they had a discriminatory impact against racial minorities, and the company had not shown them to be job related. Job relatedness might be shown, for example, if high scorers on the test performed better on the job than low scorers. The Supreme Court said that Title VII "proscribes not only overt discrimination but also practices that are fair in form, but discriminatory in operation. The touchstone is business necessity. If an employment practice which operates to exclude [racial minorities] cannot be shown to be related to job performance, the practice is prohibited."[40]

In 1975 in *Albemarle Paper Co. v. Moody*,[41] the Supreme Court reviewed another written test that had a discriminatory impact on minority applicants. The Court held that the employer's evidence of job relatedness was insufficient and that use of the test was unlawful under Title VII. In 1977 the Court reviewed a minimum height requirement that had a discriminatory impact; since the employer had no evidence of job relatedness, the Court held the minimum height requirement unlawful under Title VII.[42]

Lower federal courts have found a number of other practices unlawful under Title VII. A few examples will indicate the breadth of the general rule against practices with a discriminatory effect. (1) An employer's practice of discharging employees whose wages have been garnished (for nonpayment of debts) has been found unlawful under Title VII.[43] (2) An employer's rejection of applicants with arrest records,[44] or even with conviction records,[45] has been found unlawful under Title VII. (3) An employer's use of word of mouth recruitment[46] or prior work experience requirements,[47] where the employer employs few minorities, has been found unlawful under Title VII.

What is the current status of the law as it relates to proof of disparate impact under Title VII?

The decision of the Supreme Court in *Wards Cove Packing Co. v. Atonio* in 1989[48] made it much more difficult for plaintiffs to succeed in disparate impact cases. First, the Court held that the plaintiff must identify each specific discriminatory employment practice and present statistical evidence that shows the practice caused the statistical disparity. This is difficult to do since it is often a combination of practices, not a single practice, that has caused a disparity in the work force.

Second, the Court said that once the employer produces evidence of a business justification (less than a business necessity), the employee must persuade the court that the challenged practice either does not serve a legitimate business goal or can be accomplished (at the same cost and burden to the employer) by a less discriminatory practice.

Third, the Court held that the relevant statistics could not be based on comparisons of the internal work force. Thus, even where the structure of the industry renders any other statistical comparison meaningless, such comparison may not be used. Under the Court's decision, the statistics must compare the job holders with the number of qualified members of the work force (in the *Wards Cove* case the general population).

One of the main purposes of the Civil Rights Act of 1991 was to restore the law to what it was prior to the decision in *Wards Cove*. The act returns the burden of proof to employers, requiring them to justify practices adversely affecting minorities. It provides that employers must show that their employment practices are "job related for the position in question and consistent with business necessity."[49] It also adopted the meaning and definition of the terms "job related" and "business necessity" as they were used in *Griggs v. Duke Power Co.*, discussed above. Although the act did not reverse the holding in *Wards Cove* that required a claimant to identify a particular employment practice that caused the disparate impact, it permits a claimant to show the disparate impact caused by an employer's decision-making process as a whole when she can show that the various elements of the process are not capable of separation for analysis.

Can an employer administer ability or other tests in determining whether to hire someone?

Yes. Title VII explicitly says that an employer may use "ability tests" in the hiring process.[50] However, any such test must operate fairly with respect to one race as to another.[51] Thus, a test that does not provide the same opportunity for selection to minorities who perform equally well on the job as members of the majority, or that predicts job performance differently because of race, would not be a fair test and would not be job related for the position in question and consistent with business necessity.

Are there any employment practices that have a discriminatory effect and are not job related that are lawful under Title VII?

Yes. There is one major exception to the general rule against practices with a discriminatory effect. In 1977 the Supreme Court held that seniority systems, regardless of their discriminatory impact against minorities and regardless of whether they are job related, are lawful under Title VII—unless they were formulated with an intent to discriminate.[52] This decision was based upon the legislative history of a specific section of the Title VII statute, which states that a "bona fide seniority . . . system" is not to be considered unlawful.[53] In addition, the Court has held that a discriminatory intent cannot be inferred but must be proved by facts showing actual motive.[54] Thus, it is very difficult to prove that a seniority system violates Title VII.

Can an employer ever base an employment decision on race?

No. An employer may make employment decisions on the basis of sex, religion, or national origin in very limited circumstances where the characteristics are a bona fide occupational qualification reasonably necessary to the normal operation of the employer's business (called the BFOQ exception).[55] However, there is no BFOQ exception that allows employment decisions to be based on race.

Can an employer who makes employment decisions based simply on subjective criteria be deemed to violate Title VII?

Yes. Many employers base their employment decisions wholly or in part on nonobjective criteria, such as personal preference, judgment, or a persons "ability to get along with people." An employer who makes employment decisions based on such factors is still subject to the restrictions of Title VII, in both disparate treatment and disparate impact cases.[56]

Can there be a violation of Title VII where discrimination was only one of several factors in an employer's decision?

Yes. In a 1989 case, *Price Waterhouse v. Hopkins*,[57] the Supreme Court said that if a plaintiff establishes discrimination as a motive for the employer's decision the burden of proof shifted to the employer to prove that there were other legitimate reasons for the decision. If the employer could show that it would have made the same decision even in the absence of the discriminatory reason, there would be no violation of Title VII. While *Price Waterhouse* allowed plaintiffs to prevail in so-called mixed motive cases where an employer failed to carry its burden of rebuttal, it also tolerated discrimination where an employer could show a legitimate, nondiscriminatory reason for its decision.

The Civil Rights Act of 1991 addressed the anomaly of *Price Waterhouse* and provided that intentional discrimination in employment is always unlawful and that a discriminated against person is entitled to appropriate injunctive relief and attorneys' fees.[58] The plaintiff cannot recover any monetary damages, however, if the employer shows that it would have made the same decision anyway.

Does Title VII prohibit discrimination in working conditions?

Yes. An employer may not engage in such practices as discriminatory promotions or job assignments. In addition, an employer may not engage in *or permit* such discriminatory practices as on-the-job harassment, the use of racial epithets, the closer supervision of minority workers, or the uneven application of disciplinary rules. The EEOC has held that an employer must take reasonable steps to maintain an atmosphere free of intimidation and insults directed against protected group members.[59]

To support a hostile work atmosphere claim, the plaintiff must prove that management was aware, or should have been aware, of the offensive or discriminatory conduct but failed to correct it.[60] Thus, a person who is being discriminated against should complain to the employer (in writing, preferably) to allow an opportunity to remedy the discriminatory working conditions and to help establish that the employer was aware of the conditions but failed to remedy them.[61]

Does Title VII apply to Americans working for United States companies abroad?

Yes. Although the Supreme Court had held to the contrary,[62] Congress amended Title VII in 1991 to provide that the statute applies to United States citizens working for American companies abroad.[63] The actions of a company otherwise prohibited by Title VII are exempt from coverage to the extent that they would violate the law of the foreign country in which the company's workplace is located. Thus, for example, an American company abroad would not violate Title VII by complying with a foreign country's restrictions on the employment opportunities of women or a racial group.

Are employers and other organizations that are not covered by Title VII covered by other federal prohibitions against employment discrimination?

Yes. Many employers and other organizations (including those covered by Title VII) are covered by the Reconstruction era constitutional amendments and civil rights acts. For example, all private employers, and unions too, whatever their size, are prohibited from engaging in intentional discrimination by the Thirteenth Amendment and by the Civil Rights Act of 1866 (42 U.S.C. § 1981).[64] Similarly, all state, county, and municipal employers are prohibited from engaging in intentional discrimination by the Thirteenth and Fourteenth Amendments and by the Civil Rights Acts of 1866 and 1871 (42 U.S.C. § 1983). Note that small employers and unions thus are covered only by the Reconstruction era prohibitions, while large employers and unions also are covered by Title VII.

Are practices that have a discriminatory effect and are not job related also unlawful under the older Reconstruction era federal prohibitions against discrimination?

No. Practices that are neutral on their face are not unlawful under the Reconstruction era prohibitions unless such practices are intentionally discriminatory. In 1976, in *Washington v. Davis*,[65] the Supreme Court held that an employer's use of a written aptitude test, which had a disproportionately discriminatory impact against racial minorities, was not unlawful under the older laws. The Court held that proof of racially discriminatory intent or purpose is required to show a violation of the Fourteenth Amendment. The Court found that the employer had a good record of hiring minority members in recent years and had established a special minority recruitment program. The Court thus concluded that there was insufficient proof of discriminatory intent. In the absence of these findings, the Court might have ruled the use of the test to be intentionally discriminatory. Yet most practices that are unlawful under Title VII merely because they have a discriminatory impact would be held lawful under the older prohibitions.

Does section 1981 prohibit racial harassment and other on-the-job discrimination?

Yes. The Supreme Court ruled in a controversial case in 1989, *Patterson v. McLean Credit Union*,[66] that section 1981 prohibited discrimination *only* in making and enforcing employment contracts and did not prohibit racial harassment during the course of employment. Congress reversed the decision when it enacted the Civil Rights Act of 1991, by providing that the equal right under section 1981 to make and enforce contracts includes "making, performance, modification, and termination of contracts and the enjoyment of all benefits, terms, and conditions of the contractual relationship."[67]

How can one know if a discriminatory employment practice is intentionally discriminatory?

Discriminated-against persons usually believe, and correctly so, that discriminatory action is intentional. The problem is proving it because few if any employers will admit to intentional discrimination. In 1977 the Supreme Court recognized this problem and said that it was not necessary to prove that the challenged practice "rested solely on racially discriminatory purposes" but only that "a discriminatory purpose has been a motivating factor."[68] The Court next stated that determining whether a "discriminatory purpose was a motivating factor demands a sensitive inquiry into such circumstantial and direct evidence of intent as may be available."[69] A "starting point" is the racial "impact" of the action or practice.[70] The "historical background of the decision" is another source of evidence.[71] "Departures from the normal procedural sequence also might afford evidence that improper purposes are playing a role."[72]

Overall, a lengthy investigation of all of the facts is necessary to develop proof that indicates intentional discrimination. Obtaining the necessary proof sometimes can be very difficult. For this reason, nearly all persons who have been discriminated against assert their rights under Title VII, where proof of discriminatory impact is sufficient proof of discrimination.

REMEDIES FOR EMPLOYMENT DISCRIMINATION

What types of remedies are available to persons who have been discriminated against in employment in violation of Title VII?

The Supreme Court has held that one of the purposes of Title VII is "to make persons whole for injuries suffered on account of unlawful employment discrimination."[73] Applying this standard, the courts have ordered as remedies for Title VII violations: (1) termination of the discrimination; (2) hiring, reinstatement, or promotion; (3) awards of backpay and retroactive seniority; and sometimes (4) affirmative hiring steps such as goals and timetables. In addition to these remedies, court-awarded attorneys' fees, including the cost of hiring expert witnesses,[74] are available for the "prevailing party" in a Title VII lawsuit.[75]

How much backpay is available to a person who has been discriminated against in violation of Title VII?

Pursuant to the make-whole objective of Title VII, an award of backpay is determined by the amount of pay that normally would have been earned if there had been no discrimination. Backpay awards may also include interest, overtime, shift differentials, vacation and sick pay, and pension plan contributions.[76] There are, however, two important limitations.

First, backpay is calculated no further back than two years prior to the date upon which the administrative charge of discrimination was filed with the EEOC.[77] Thus, for example, even if you have been continuously and discriminatorily denied a promotion for ten years by a private employer, you are eligible under Title VII to receive backpay only starting two years before filing your charge of discrimination with the EEOC.

Second, the amount of backpay for which you are theoretically eligible is reduced by "interim earnings or amounts earnable with reasonable diligence by the person or persons discriminated against."[78] For example, if you earned $300 a week until 3 January 1990, when you were discriminatorily fired, and if you refused to look for any other work until 3 July 1990, when you immediately found work at $250 a week, you probably would be able to recover no more than $50 a week backpay for your six months of unemployment as well as thereafter.

Are monetary damages, other than backpay, an available remedy under Title VII for unlawful employment discrimination?

Yes, but only to those, e.g., women, who cannot recover damages under section 1981. Prior to passage of the Civil Rights Act of 1991, the courts held that backpay was the only monetary remedy available under Title VII.[79] That was because backpay was the only monetary remedy mentioned in the Title VII statute[80] and because pain and suffering and punitive damages were said not to be necessarily consonant with the make-whole objective of the statute. In 1991, however, Congress enacted legislation creating a new cause of action, or claim,[81] for intentional discrimination in employment against persons protected by Title VII and the Americans with Disabilities Act, such as women and the disabled, who could not recover damages under section 1981, which is restricted to claims of discrimination based upon race. The cause of action provides for the recovery of compensatory and punitive damages and for a jury trial. Congress placed a ceiling or cap on the amount of damages that can be recovered under the new statute based on the number of covered employees in the employer's workforce—15 to 100 employees: $50,000; 101 to 200: $100,000; 201 to 500: $200,000;

over 500: $300,000. The monetary relief that was previously recoverable under Title VII, such as backpay, is excluded from the cap. The cap does, however, apply to each complaining party rather than an entire group of employees affected by a discriminatory policy or practice.

Are remedies similar to those available under Title VII also available in lawsuits filed under the older Reconstruction amendments and civil rights acts?

Yes. But remember that proof of discriminatory intent is necessary under the Reconstruction amendments and civil rights acts. Once a person has proved intentional discrimination in court under these older laws, similar remedies are available. The backpay remedy operates the same way as under Title VII, except that the two administrative limitations on backpay in the Title VII statute are not directly applicable to lawsuits filed under the older prohibitions.[82]

Are monetary damages, other than backpay, available under the older civil rights prohibitions?

Yes. Once a court determines that an employer has engaged in intentional discrimination, persons discriminated against may receive not only backpay but also other out-of-pocket damages and possible pain and suffering damages.[83] Additionally, if the discrimination is found to have been malicious, persons discriminated against may receive punitive damages. These remedies are very difficult to obtain because it is hard to prove intentional discrimination, much less malicious discrimination.

Under Title VII, is retroactive seniority an available remedy for unlawful employment discrimination?

Yes. Although the Supreme Court held in 1977 that seniority systems that have a discriminatory effect are not unlawful per se,[84] the Court did not overrule its earlier decision in 1975 holding that persons discriminated against were entitled to the seniority they would have earned had they not been discriminated against.[85] This means that even though a seniority system may itself be lawful, a person who has been unlawfully discriminated against is entitled to full retroactive seniority.

Who is eligible for retroactive seniority under Title VII? How is it awarded?

Any person who has been unlawfully discriminated against is eligible for retroactive seniority. This includes a person denied a transfer to a more lucrative job for which she was qualified. It also includes a person who was unlawfully denied employment in the first place or who was deterred from applying for employment.[86] The retroactive seniority is available from the date the initial discrimination occurred. Thus, as soon as the complainant is placed in the sought after job, whether by a court order or otherwise, retroactive seniority is accumulated—thereby protecting the complainant against future layoffs.

Are other remedies, such as affirmative hiring of minorities and goals and timetables for accomplishing the hiring, available under Title VII or the Constitution to make up for extensive past discrimination?

Yes. The federal courts have broad powers to impose remedies that operate both retrospectively to redress past discrimination and prospectively to ensure that the discrimination does not recur. In most employment cases a court need only require an employer to stop practicing the discrimination and award make-whole relief to the individual victims of the discriminatory practices. In some instances, however, where the discrimination has been persistent or egregious, or where necessary to dissipate the lingering effects of pervasive discrimination, it may be necessary to require the employer to take affirmative steps to end discrimination effectively to enforce Title VII. Under the circumstances, a court might require a recalcitrant employer—public or private—to hire qualified minorities roughly in proportion to the number of qualified minorities in the work force.[87]

In one case, for example, after finding that a city had discriminated in employment in its police and fire departments, the court required the defendants to make 50 percent of its entry level and/or officer appointments from a pool of qualified minority applicants, with such hiring goals remaining in effect until the city's work force reflected the minority composition of the labor force.[88]

How does a court determine whether affirmative action remedies are necessary in a particular case?

In addition to examining how extensive the past discrimination has been, the courts look at a variety of other factors in determining whether to require affirmative hiring and goals and timetables as remedies, including the availability and efficacy of alternative remedies; the flexibility, duration, and waivability of the relief; the impact of the relief on the rights of third parties; and the relationship of the numerical goals to the relevant labor market.

Applying these standards, the Supreme Court in *United States v. Paradise*[89] approved a remedy requiring Alabama, which had systematically excluded blacks from employment in its Department of Public Safety, to promote one black trooper for each white trooper elevated in rank, as long as qualified black candidates were available, until the state implemented an acceptable promotion plan. The Court found the affirmative action remedy permissible because it was "flexible, waivable, and temporary in application" and did not impose an unacceptable burden on innocent third parties.[90]

Can a court award seniority retroactively to a class as part of a general affirmative action remedy?

No. The Supreme Court, relying on the legislative history and the provision in Title VII permitting the routine application of a seniority system absent proof of an intention to discriminate, has held that a court can award competitive seniority only where the beneficiary of the award has actually been a victim of illegal discrimination.[91]

Are voluntary affirmative action plans by private employers designed to integrate the work force and forestall possible employment discrimination litigation permissible under Title VII?

Yes, depending on the facts and circumstances involved. In *United Steelworkers of America v. Weber*,[92] the leading case, the union and the company (Kaiser Aluminum & Chemical Company) entered into a voluntary affirmative action agreement to eliminate conspicuous racial imbalance in the company's almost exclusively white craft work force. Pursuant to the agreement, the company set a goal of 39 percent minority representation (the minority representation in the surrounding labor force), adopted a hiring ratio of one minority for every white (so that 50 percent of the new skilled craft employees would be minority workers), and estimated that its goal would be reached under a thirty-year timetable (meaning that the program would be in effect past the year 2000). A white employee brought suit claiming that this numerically based program was reverse racial discrimination prohibited by Title VII, but the Supreme Court rejected the challenge.

The Court acknowledged that Title VII protected whites as well as blacks from racial discrimination in employment but concluded that the statute did not forbid all voluntary race conscious affirmative action. In the Court's view, the spirit and intent of Title VII was to break down old patterns of racial segregation and hierarchy, and to open job opportunities for minority workers. The Court then found that the specific plan adopted by the company was permissible in that it did not require the discharge of white workers nor was it an absolute bar to their advancement, and it was a temporary measure, not intended to maintain racial balance but simply to eliminate a manifest racial imbalance.

Are voluntary affirmative action plans adopted by state and local governments also permitted under Title VII?

Yes, provided they meet the same standards as are applicable to affirmative actions plans adopted by private employers.[93]

Are voluntary affirmative action plans that give preferential protection against layoffs to minority employees lawful under Title VII?

No. In *Wygant v. Jackson Board of Education*,[94] the Court invalidated on Fourteenth Amendment grounds an affirmative action agreement under which a school board gave preferential protection against layoffs to minority employees. The agreement provided that in the event it became necessary to reduce the number of teachers through layoffs, teachers with the most seniority would be retained, except that at no time would there be a greater percentage of minority teachers laid off than the percentage of minority teachers employed at the time of the layoffs. When layoffs later became necessary, adherence to the agreement resulted in the layoff of nonminority teachers, while

minority teachers with less seniority were retained. The nonminority teachers brought suit and the Supreme Court invalidated
the preferential protection agreement. According to the Court,
while hiring goals impose a diffuse burden, layoffs impose the
entire burden of achieving racial equality on particular individuals, and as a result were too intrusive. The school board's
affirmative action plan was invalid because it was not "sufficiently narrowly tailored" to accomplish purposes that otherwise might be legitimate.[95]

**Are federal laws that set aside a certain percentage of fed-
eral funds to be used in contracts with minority firms to increase minority employment opportunities lawful under the
Constitution?**

Yes. In *Fullilove v. Klutznick*,[96] the Supreme Court dismissed a Fourteenth Amendment challenge by nonminority
contractors to a federal statute[97] requiring for one year at least
10 percent of federal public works funds to be used, or "set
aside," in contracts with minority owned business enterprises.
The Court approved the provision in part because of the deference due an act of Congress. In addition, the Court found that
it was within the power of Congress to act on the assumption
that in the past some nonminority businesses may have reaped
benefits over the years from the exclusion of minority firms
from contracting and employment opportunities and because
the "actual 'burden' shouldered by nonminority firms is relatively light."[98] The Court also emphasized that the set aside was
flexible in that it could be waived where minority businesses
were not available or attempted to exploit the remedial aspects
of the program by charging an unreasonable price (a price not
attributable to the effects of past discrimination).

**Are minority set-aside programs adopted by cities and states
treated the same as those adopted by Congress?**

No. The Supreme Court has not deferred to state and local
set aside programs as it has to those of Congress, but has
required the jurisdiction "to demonstrate a compelling interest
in apportioning public contracting on the basis of race."[99] Failing to meet this strict test was a set-aside adopted by the city
of Richmond requiring prime contractors to whom the city
awarded contacts to subcontract at least 30 percent of the dollar

amount of the contract to one or more minority business enterprises. The Court found the city had failed to produce any evidence or findings that nonminority contractors had systematically excluded minority businesses from subcontracting opportunities or that there was a significant statistical disparity between the number of qualified minority contractors willing and able to perform a particular service and the number of such contractors actually engaged by the locality or the locality's prime contractors. Because the city had failed to identify the need for remedial action, its set-aside program violated the Fourteenth Amendment. The Court indicated, however, that such a plan would be constitutional if an adequate factual predicate were offered to support it. Indeed, since the Richmond decision, a number of local set-asides have been approved by the lower federal courts.[100]

Does affirmative action violate the make-whole rationale of Title VII by benefiting those who are not themselves victims of discrimination?

No. The Supreme Court has held that the purpose of affirmative action remedies is not to make identified victims whole but to dismantle prior patterns of employment discrimination and to prevent discrimination in the future. Relief is provided to the class as a whole rather than to individual members.[101]

Does affirmative action treat people unfairly who are themselves innocent of discrimination by denying them employment and other opportunities?

That depends, as noted above, on how heavy and intrusive the burdens of affirmative action are. The courts are solicitous of the plight of third parties when affirmative action plans are adopted. However, because of the nation's dedication to eradicating racial discrimination even innocent third parties may be called upon to bear some of the burdens of affirmative action, provided those burdens are diffuse and not overly intrusive. Affirmative action is admittedly a controversial subject and presents complex legal issues involving judicial standards of review and burdens of proof. For these reasons, affirmative action is discussed in more detail in chapter 10 of this book under the general topic of race conscious remedies.

Is it necessary to file a lawsuit under Title VII to obtain its remedies for employment discrimination?

No, but it is highly advisable to prepare as if a lawsuit were going to be filed. Some charges of discrimination are resolved informally between the individual and the employer. Other charges are resolved administratively. However, since many employers do not want to volunteer the appearance of wrongdoing, they will not settle a charge unless the individual has strong proof of discrimination and appears able and willing to file a lawsuit. Thus, to be in the best position, a person discriminated against should always file a timely administrative charge under Title VII and should comply with the other prerequisites to filing a Title VII lawsuit.

Can those who were not parties to a litigated or consent judgment ever challenge the judgment on the grounds that it discriminates against or affects them?

Yes, under some circumstances. In a 1989 case the Supreme Court held that white fire fighters, who had failed to intervene in earlier employment discrimination proceedings brought by blacks in which consent decrees were entered that included goals for hiring blacks as fire fighters and for promoting them, could challenge employment decisions taken pursuant to those decrees. That is, they could bring a subsequent lawsuit claiming that they were being denied promotions because of their race in favor of less qualified blacks.[102] When it enacted the Civil Rights Act of 1991, Congress significantly limited the circumstances under which a person could collaterally attack a judgment in an employment discrimination case. The act provides that once it is determined that a person had notice of the proceedings and a reasonable opportunity to intervene but had failed to act, a subsequent attack on the judgment is precluded. The act also precludes persons from raising a challenge after the court had already rejected a similar claim which (1) involved the same legal grounds as the later challenge; (2) involved a factual situation similar to that of the later challenge; and (3) was adequately litigated by the prior challenger.[103] The purpose of the 1991 law is to provide a framework to achieve finality and fairness in employment discrimination cases that include hiring or promotion orders that might affect the rights of nonminorities.

Do the provisions of the Civil Rights Act of 1991 apply retroactively or only to conduct occurring after the date of passage (21 November 1991)?

The answer is not entirely clear in every case. The act states generally that it takes effect on the date of enactment. The courts will have to determine, based upon the legislative history, which is somewhat contradictory, and the general rules governing statutory construction, whether this language means that the act applies to pending cases and conduct that can still be challenged or is limited to conduct occurring after 21 November 1991. Two provisions of the act, however, specify that they will not apply retroactively: section 109, the provision extending Title VII extraterritorially to protect American citizens working for American companies abroad and section 402, exempting the Wards Cove Packing Company from the changes made by the act.

PROCEDURES UNDER TITLE VII OF THE CIVIL RIGHTS ACT OF 1964

In order to be protected by Title VII in nonfederal employment, are there any procedural steps which must be taken?

Yes. The procedural steps are important and must be strictly adhered to. If the state or locality does not have a fair employment agency that can enforce a state or local law prohibiting discrimination in employment, the claim must be filed with the EEOC within 180 days of the discriminatory act.[104] If there is a state or local fair employment agency, the charge must be brought to that agency within the time limits specified by the local law.

The generally accepted view is that a complainant's Title VII action is not barred by failing to file a charge within a state limitations period if the state period is shorter than the 180 day period under the federal statute.[105] The EEOC will not, however, investigate a Title VII charge until the state or local agency has had 60 days to review the charge, or if an investigation has begun within 60 days.

Filing a charge with a state or local agency does not mean that a complainant does not also have to file a charge with EEOC. A charge must always be filed with the EEOC within

180 days of the discriminatory act or a person may lose the right to sue under Title VII.[106] The Supreme Court has held that no extensions of time will be granted merely because a person pursued her discrimination charge through contract grievance machinery,[107] arbitration procedures,[108] or a federal court action under section 1981.[109]

Are there exceptions to the 180-day time limit for filing a charge of discrimination?

Yes, there are two important, but limited, exceptions. First, a person can become a plaintiff in a class action lawsuit under Title VII if the representative of the class has met all of the time requirements. The Supreme Court has held that only one Title VII plaintiff need comply with the time requirements.[110] The class may not, however, include persons whose Title VII claims would have been time barred when the class representative's charges were filed.[111]

Second, a person can file a charge of discrimination after the 180-day time period has elapsed if the discriminatory practice is one that is deemed to be "continuing."[112] For example, if an employer has a lower salary scale for blacks than other employees, each pay period constitutes another act of discrimination, and the 180 period begins to run anew with the receipt of each paycheck.

Many acts of discrimination, however, have been held not to be continuing.[113] In *Lorance v. AT&T Technologies*,[114] for example, the Supreme Court held that for purposes of challenging an intentionally discriminatory seniority system, the 180-day time period starts to run when the plan first goes into effect, and not when it actually affects a particular employee. In essence, the Court required the employees to anticipate the discriminatory effects of the seniority system and initiate suit to prevent future applications no matter how speculative or unlikely they might be.

Has Congress taken any action to ameliorate the harshness of the *Lorance* decision?

Yes. Congress attempted to ameliorate the harshness of *Lorance* when it enacted the Civil Rights Act of 1991. It provided that a cause of action arises under Title VII, i.e., the 180-day time period begins to run when a discriminatory seniority system is adopted, when a person becomes subject to it, *or* when an individual is actually injured by its application.[115]

Where and how do you file a charge of discrimination under Title VII?

A person may file an administrative charge of discrimination with any district or regional office of the EEOC, or with the main office of the EEOC in Washington, D.C. The EEOC has an official form for filing administrative charges.

The charge must be signed and sworn to,[116] it must detail or at least summarize the nature of the discrimination,[117] and it must give the name of every employer and union involved in the discrimination.[118]

What does the EEOC do after it receives a charge of discrimination?

Within 10 days after receiving a charge, the EEOC must notify the employer of the allegation of discrimination.[119] The EEOC is then supposed to investigate the charge to determine if there is "reasonable cause" to believe a violation of Title VII has occurred or refer the charge to the appropriate state or local human-rights agency, if one exists, for 60 days.[120] The investigation by the EEOC is supposed to last no longer than 120 days after the filing of the charge or after the 60-day local or state agency deferral period.[121]

If the EEOC finds "reasonable cause," it will try to conciliate the complaint, i.e., try to convince both sides to settle the matter informally. If it fails, the EEOC can file a lawsuit on behalf of the complaining party in federal district court against the employer for injunctive and other relief.[122]

Is there much chance that the EEOC will resolve and successfully conciliate the charge of discrimination?

No. Since the EEOC has a large backlog of charges of discrimination and since it has been unable to resolve many charges, it is unlikely that your charge will be administratively resolved by the EEOC.

If the EEOC does not resolve a charge of discrimination, can a complainant go to court under Title VII to seek to remedy the discrimination?

Yes. A complainant may sue in court after 180 days have elapsed since the filing of the charge and after receiving a "right-to-sue letter" from the EEOC (to sue private employers) or from the Justice Department (to sue state, county, and municipal employers).[123] Alternatively, if the EEOC certifies that it will not investigate the charge within 180 days, an individual may ask for a right-to-sue letter and bring suit immediately. However, the individual *must* sue, if at all, within 90 days after receiving the right-to-sue letter.[124]

It is very important that a person contemplating litigation seek an attorney *before* requesting a right-to-sue letter. Although 90 days may sound like a long time, it may take longer than that to find an attorney willing to take the case, and for her to review the facts and prepare the necessary court papers. Title VII allows a court to appoint an attorney to represent a complainant, but many courts are reluctant to force an attorney to represent a client if the attorney is otherwise unwilling to do so.[125]

There is another hitch. The person suing, the plaintiff, can name as defendants in the lawsuit only the employers, unions, and individuals named in the administrative charge filed with the EEOC; and the person suing can raise as claims only those matters reasonably growing out of the administrative charge.[126] Thus, the administrative charge to the EEOC always should be as broad as possible.

Can a person who can't afford a lawyer still file a lawsuit under Title VII?

Yes. Under Title VII a poor person can file a lawsuit *in forma pauperis*, which means that a poor person can sue without paying court costs.[127] And one can always file a lawsuit pro se, which means that a person can represent oneself. But since the law is very complicated and since, as the saying goes, a person who represents oneself has a fool for a client, it is best to try to find a lawyer. Anyone who has a problem finding a lawyer should contact the organizations listed in appendix B at the end of this book. If this fails, the EEOC might be of assistance, or a court might be able to appoint a lawyer.

If a discriminated-against minority person cannot file a lawsuit under Title VII, are there other possible means of obtaining relief from a court?

Yes, there are several other possible means of obtaining relief. First, the EEOC can sue private employers and unions, and the Justice Department can sue state, county, and municipal employers.[128] Although they file very few lawsuits, it is sometimes worth contacting them to see if they will sue. Second, a person can always sue private employers under the Thirteenth Amendment and the Civil Rights Act of 1866, and state, county, and municipal employers under the Thirteenth and Fourteenth Amendments and under the Civil Rights Acts of 1866 and 1871. An individual can file such a lawsuit without complying with any of Title VII's procedural requirements, but the lawsuit must be filed within the period allowed by the applicable state statute of limitations.[129] In order to win, however, an individual must be able to prove that the discrimination was intentionally discriminatory, and that is often difficult to do.[130]

In addition to the foregoing lawsuits, Title VI of the Civil Rights Act of 1964[131] and the Justice System Improvement Act of 1984[132] prohibit discrimination in employment in federally funded programs or activities. The substantive provisions and methods of enforcing these laws are discussed in chapter 7 dealing with federally assisted discrimination.

How does a person file a charge of discrimination against an employer that has contracts with the federal government?

Employees who work for companies that have contracts with the federal government and that are prohibited from discriminating by Executive Order (E.O.) No. 11246 (as amended by E.O. No. 11375) may file charges of discrimination with the Office of Federal Contract Compliance Programs (OFCCP) of the Department of Labor within 180 days of the violation.[133] The OFCCP has full responsibility for the administration and enforcement of the executive order. In cases of racial discrimination, however, the OFCCP has restricted its role to reviewing the employment records of companies that have contracts with the federal government. Individual complaints filed with OFCCP are transferred to the EEOC for investigation and processing under Title VII. If E.O. No. 11246 applies, a person should file a complaint with the OFCCP even if she plans to file a Title VII charge with the EEOC since the employer will be subject to losing its federal contracts if it is found to have violated the law.

How about discrimination in federal agencies? Are the Title VII procedures the same?

No. Persons seeking the protection of Title VII against federal agencies—other than Congress, the agencies of the legislative branch, and presidential appointments—are governed by a separate set of complicated procedures that are even more difficult to follow than those applicable to discrimination by nonfederal employers. Furthermore, the initial steps must be undertaken not with the EEOC but instead with the federal agency itself.

1. Within 90 days of the discriminatory act, the individual must bring the matter to the attention of the federal agency's Equal Employment Opportunity Counselor.
2. After informal proceedings with the Counselor, and within only 15 days of the final interview with the Counselor, the individual must file a formal written, signed complaint with the agency. Thereupon, the agency will investigate the complaint and attempt an informal "adjustment" of the matter.
3. If an informal adjustment is not reached, and if the individual desires an agency hearing on the complaint, the individual within 15 days of the agency's proposed disposition must request a hearing. With or without the hearing, the agency will reach a "final" agency decision, which the individual may appeal to the EEOC.
4. If the individual wishes to sue the agency, the lawsuit must be filed within 30 days of notice of the final agency decision or of the EEOC decision.

Obviously, these time periods are very short, but they must be complied with if one is to be protected at all by Title VII in federal employment.[134]

Is there a good chance that the responsible federal agency will resolve the charge of discrimination?

No. Most federal agencies have reputations for being unable to resolve their own discrimination.

If the responsible agency or the EEOC does not satisfactorily resolve or "adjust" a complaint of discrimination, can an individual go to court under Title VII to seek to remedy the discrimination?

Yes, the individual can file a lawsuit against the federal agency. But there are two different time periods that apply. First, if there is a final decision by the responsible agency (and the individual elects not to appeal to the EEOC) or by the EEOC (after an appeal), the individual must file the lawsuit, if at all, within 30 days of that final decision. Second, if 180 days have elapsed since the filing of the administrative complaint and there has not yet been a final decision, the individual then may file a lawsuit even before there is a final administrative decision. Additionally, the administrative steps and time periods mentioned before also must be complied with. If they are not, the court will dismiss the lawsuit.[135]

If an individual gets to court under Title VII against a federal agency, may the court receive additional evidence about the discrimination, other than what was introduced in the administrative process?

Yes. Although federal agencies for many years argued that the court could do no more than review the administrative record, the Supreme Court in 1976 rejected that argument and held that the courts should admit all evidence relevant to the formal administrative complaint.[136] In other words, once in court, individuals can prove discrimination against federal employers just the same as against nonfederal employers.

Can a person sue a federal agency under Title VII if he or she cannot afford an attorney?

Yes. The answer is the same with regard to a federal agency as it is with a nonfederal employer. Under Title VII, a person may file free of cost in court and may represent him or herself.[137] However, finding a lawyer is recommended.

How are employment discrimination complaints against Congress and the agencies of the legislative branch and in presidential appointments processed under Title VII?

In the Senate, complaints of discrimination in employment are investigated, not by the EEOC of the executive branch, but by the Office of Senate Fair Employment Practices pursuant to a special set of rules enacted by Congress. Upon completion of the administrative process an appeal may be taken to the United States Court of Appeals for the District of Columbia. In the

House of Representatives employment discrimination claims are investigated by a review board pursuant to rules promulgated by the House. The chief official of each agency of the legislative branch is required to establish remedies and procedures to be used in processing complaints of employment discrimination. Complaints by presidential appointees against the President or other appointing authority in the executive branch are processed by the EEOC; an appeal may be taken to the United States Court of Appeals for the District of Columbia.

If a person cannot file a lawsuit against a federal agency or entity under Title VII because of noncompliance with the administrative steps and time requirements, are there other possible means of obtaining relief from a court?

As a practical matter, no. Neither the EEOC nor the Justice Department is authorized to sue federal agencies for employment discrimination. Although the Fifth Amendment and the Civil Rights Act of 1866 prohibit employment discrimination in the federal government, federal officials have been held entitled to various immunities to civil suit.[138] Moreover, the Supreme Court in 1976 held that Title VII is the exclusive remedy for suing federal employers covered by Title VII.[139] Other prohibitions on employment discrimination are therefore irrelevant.

NOTES

1. 42 U.S.C. §§ 2000e *et seq.*
2. Exec. Order No. 11246, 30 Fed. Reg. 12319, 3 C.F.R. 1964–1965, Comp. p. 339, as amended by Exec. Order No. 11375, 32 Fed. Reg. 14303, 3 C.F.R. 1966–1970, Comp. p. 684.
3. *Shaare Tefila Congregation v. Cobb*, 481 U.S. 615 (1987).
4. *Saint Francis College v. Al-Khazraji*, 481 U.S. 604 (1987).
5. 29 C.F.R. § 1606 and § 1607.
6. *Griggs v. Duke Power Co.*, 401 U.S. 424 (1971).
7. *Washington v. Davis*, 426 U.S. 229 (1976).
8. 42 U.S.C. § 2000e(b) and § 2000e-2(a).
9. 42 U.S.C. § 2000e-16.
10. Sections 117, 302, and 320 of the Civil Rights Act of 1991.
11. 42 U.S.C. §§ 2000e(c)-(e) and §§ 2000e-2(b)-(d).

12. 42 U.S.C. § 2000e-5(e).
13. 42 U.S.C. § 2000e-2(a).
14. 42 U.S.C. § 2000e-2(d).
15. 42 U.S.C. § 2000e-2(b).
16. 42 U.S.C. § 2000e-2(c).
17. 42 U.S.C. § 2000e-3(a). *See Rutherford v. American Bank of Commerce*, 565 F.2d 1162 (10th Cir. 1977); *Drew v. Liberty Mutual Insurance Co.*, 480 F.2d 69 (5th Cir. 1973), *cert. denied*, 417 U.S. 935 (1974).
18. *McDonnell-Douglas Corp. v. Green*, 411 U.S. 792 (1973).
19. *Hochstadt v. Worcester Foundation for Experimental Biology*, 545 F.2d 222 (1st Cir. 1976).
20. *Brown v. Ralston Purina Co.*, 557 F.2d 570 (6th Cir. 1977).
21. *EEOC v. Kallir, Philips, Ross, Inc.*, 401 F. Supp. 66, 71 (S.D.N.Y. 1975), *aff'd*, 559 F.2d 1203 (2d Cir. 1977).
22. *Hochstadt v. Worcester*, 545 F.2d 222 (1st Cir. 1976).
23. EEOC Dec. No. 70-119, 10 FEP 811 (1969).
24. *Berg v. La Crosse Cooler Co.*, 613 F.2d 1041 (7th Cir. 1980); *Sias v. City Demonstration Agency*, 588 F.2d 692 (9th Cir. 1978).
25. *Hazelwood School District v. United States*, 433 U.S. 299 (1977).
26. 411 U.S. 792 (1973).
27. *Loeb v. Textron*, 600 F.2d 1003, 1014 n.12 (1st Cir. 1979).
28. *McDonnell-Douglas Corp. v. Green*, 411 U.S. 792, 802 (1973).
29. *Board of Trustees of Keene State College v. Sweeney*, 439 U.S. 24, 25 n.2 (1978).
30. *McDonnell-Douglas Corp. v. Green*, 411 U.S. 792, 804 (1973).
31. *Corley v. Jackson Police Department*, 566 F.2d 994 (5th Cir. 1978). *See also Turner v. Texas Instruments, Inc.*, 555 F.2d 1251 (5th Cir. 1977); *cf. McDonald v. Santa Fe Trail Transportation Co.*, 427 U.S. 273, 283 (1976).
32. *Wards Cove Packing Co. v. Atonio*, 490 U.S. 642 (1989). *See, International Brotherhood of Teamsters v. United States*, 431 U.S. 324 (1977).
33. *International Brotherhood of Teamsters v. United States*, 431 U.S. 324, 349 (1977).
34. *Griggs v. Duke Power Co.*, 401 U.S. 424, 432 (1971)(emphasis in original).
35. *Id.*, at 431.
36. *Dothard v. Rawlinson*, 433 U.S. 321, 331 (1977).
37. *Albemarle Power Co. v Moody*, 422 U.S. 405, 425 (1975).
38. *Griggs v. Duke Power Co.*, 401 U.S. 424, 431 (1971).
39. 401 U.S. 424 (1971).
40. *Id.*, at 431.
41. 422 U.S. 405 (1975).

42. *Dothard v. Rawlinson*, 433 U.S. 321 (1977).

43. *Wallace v. Debron Corp.*, 494 F.2d 674 (8th Cir. 1974).

44. *Gregory v. Litton Systems*, 472 F.2d 631 (9th Cir. 1972); *Carter v. Gallagher*, 452 F.2d 315 (8th Cir. 1971), *modified on other grounds, en banc*, 452 F.2d 327 (8th Cir.), *cert. denied*, 406 U.S. 950 (1972).

45. *Green v. Missouri Pacific Railroad Co.*, 523 F.2d 1290 (8th Cir. 1975).

46. *E.g.*, *Reed v. Arlington Hotel Co.*, 476 F.2d 721 (8th Cir.), *cert. denied*, 414 U. S. 854 (1973); *United States v. Georgia Power Co.*, 474 F.2d 906 (5th Cir. 1973).

47. *Sabol v. Snyder*, 524 F.2d 1009 (5th Cir. 1975); *Rowe v. General Motors Corp.*, 457 F.2d 348 (5th Cir. 1972).

48. 490 U.S. 642 (1989).

49. Section 105 of the Civil Rights Act of 1991.

50. 42 U.S.C. § 2000e-2(h).

51. *Albemarle Paper Co. v. Moody*, 422 U.S. 405 (1975).

52. *International Brotherhood of Teamsters v. United States*, 431 U.S. 324 (1977). *See also Acha v. Beame*, 570 F.2d 57, 64–65 (2d Cir. 1978).

53. 42 U.S.C. § 2000e-2(h).

54. *Pullman Standard v. Swint*, 456 U.S. 273 (1982).

55. 42 U.S.C. § 2000e-(2)(e)(1).

56. *Furnco Construction Corp. v. Waters*, 438 U.S. 567 (1978); *U.S. Postal Service Board of Governors v. Aikens*, 460 U.S. 711 (1983); *Watson v. Fort Worth Bank and Trust*, 487 U.S. 977 (1988).

57. 490 U.S. 228 (1989).

58. Section 107 of the Civil Rights Act of 1991.

59. *Rogers v. EEOC*, 454 F.2d 234 (5th Cir. 1972).

60. 2 Larson, *Employment Discrimination*, § 84.10 n.12 (1990).

61. *Watkins v. Scott Paper*, 530 F.2d 1159 (5th Cir. 1976).

62. *Equal Employment Opportunity Commission v. Aramco*, 111 S. Ct. 1227 (1991).

63. Section 109 of the Civil Rights Act of 1991.

64. *Patterson v. McLean Credit Union*, 491 U.S. 164 (1989).

65. 426 U.S. 229 (1976). The reasoning of the Supreme Court in *Washington v. Davis*, requiring proof of intent to discriminate under the Fourteenth Amendment and the Civil Rights Act of 1871, may also require proof of intent to discriminate under the Thirteenth Amendment and the Civil Rights Act of 1866. This latter issue was presented to but not decided by the Supreme Court in 1979 in *County of Los Angeles v. Davis*, 440 U.S. 625 (1979).

66. 491 U.S. 164 (1989).

67. Section 101 of the Civil Rights Act of 1991.

68. *Village of Arlington Heights v. Metropolitan Housing Development Corp.*, 429 U.S. 252, 265–66 (1977).

69. *Id.*, at 266.
70. *Id.*
71. *Id.*, at 267.
72. *Id.*
73. *Albemarle Paper Co. v. Moody*, 422 U.S. 405, 418 (1975).
74. *See,* Section 113 of the Civil Rights Act of 1991, modifying in Title VII cases the ruling in *West Virginia University Hospitals v. Casey*, 111 S. Ct. 1138 (1991), that successful civil rights plaintiffs could not recover the costs of hiring expert witnesses.
75. 42 U.S.C. § 2000e-5(k). A prevailing plaintiff will ordinarily receive attorneys' fees, whereas a prevailing defendant can be awarded attorneys' fees only if the plaintiff's lawsuit was plainly frivolous. *See Christiansburg Garment Co. v. EEOC*, 434 U.S. 412 (1978).
76. *Royal v. Bethlehem Steel Corp.*, 636 F. Supp. 833 (E.D. Tex. 1986); *Boosma v. Greyhound Food Management, Inc.*, 639 F. Supp. 1448 (W.D. Mich. 1986).
77. 42 U.S.C. § 2000e-5(g).
78. *Id. Albemarle Paper Co. v. Moody*, 422 U.S. 405 (1975); *Pettway v. American Cast Iron Pipe Co.*, 494 F.2d 211 (5th Cir. 1974).
79. *Richerson v. Jones*, 551 F.2d 918, 926–28 (3d Cir. 1977); *Pearson v Western Electric Co.*, 542 F.2d 1150 (10th Cir. 1976); *EEOC v. Detroit Edison Co.*, 515 F.2d 301, 308–10 (6th Cir. 1975), *vacated and remanded on other grounds*, 431 U.S. 951 (1977).
80. 42 U.S.C. § 2000e-5(g).
81. To be codified as 42 U.S.C. § 1981A.
82. *Brown v. Gaston County Dyeing Machine Co.*, 457 F.2d 1377 (4th Cir.), *cert. denied*, 409 U.S. 982 (1972).
83. *Cf. Sullivan v. Little Hunting Park*, 396 U.S. 229 (1969).
84. *International Brotherhood of Teamsters v. United States*, 431 U.S. 324 (1977).
85. *Franks v. Bowman Transportation Co.*, 424 U.S. 747 (1975).
86. *International Brotherhood of Teamsters v. United States*, 431 U.S. 324 (1977).
87. *Local 28 of Sheet Metal Workers v. EEOC*, 478 U.S. 421, 449 (1980), and cases cited.
88. *United States v. City of Buffalo*, 721 F. Supp. 463 (W.D.N.Y. 1989). *Also see, Firefighters Institute for Racial Equality v. St. Louis*, 588 F.2d 235 (8th Cir. 1978); *Morrow v. Dillard*, 580 F.2d 1284 (5th Cir. 1978); *EEOC v. Contour Chair Lounge Co.*, 596 F.2d 809 (8th Cir. 1979), *aff'g* 457 F. Supp. 393 (E.D. Mo. 1978).
89. 480 U.S. 149 (1987).
90. *Id.*, at 178.
91. *Firefighters Local Union No. 1784 v. Stotts*, 467 U.S. 561 (1984).

92. 443 U.S. 193 (1979).

93. *Johnson v. Transportation Agency, Santa Clara County, California,* 480 U.S. 616, 627 (1987).

94. 476 U.S. 267 (1986).

95. *Id.,* at 283.

96. 448 U.S. 448 (1980).

97. Section 103(f)(2) of the Public Works Employment Act of 1977, 42 U.S.C. § 6701 *et seq.*

98. *Fullilove v. Klutznick,* 448 U.S. 448, 484 (1980).

99. *City of Richmond v. J. A. Croson Co.,* 488 U.S. 469, 505 (1989).

100. *E.g., Coral Construction Co. v. King County,* 729 F. Supp. 734 (W.D. Wash. 1989); *Cone v. Hillsborough County,* 908 F.2d 908 (11th Cir. 1990).

101. *Local 28 of Sheet Metal Workers v. EEOC,* 478 U.S. 421, 474 (1986).

102. *Martin v. Wilks,* 490 U.S. 755 (1989).

103. Section 108 of the Civil Rights Act of 1991.

104. 42 U.S.C. § 2000-5(e).

105. *Bonham v. Dresser Industries Inc.,* 569 F.2d 187 (3d Cir. 1977); *Davis v. Valley Distributing Co.,* 522 F.2d 827 (9th Cir. 1975).

106. 42 U.S.C. § 2000-5(e).

107. *International Union of Electrical, Radio and Machine Workers v. Robbins & Meyers, Inc.,* 429 U.S. 229, 236 (1976).

108. *Alexander v. Gardner-Denver Co.,* 415 U.S. 36 (1974).

109. *Johnson v. Railway Express Agency, Inc.* 421 U.S. 454 (1975).

110. *Albemarle Paper Co. v. Moody,* 422 U.S. 405 (1975).

111. *East Texas Motor Freight Systems Inc., v. Rodriguez,* 431 U.S. 395 (1977).

112. *Bethel v. Jendoco Const. Corp.,* 570 F.2d 1168, 1173–75 (3d Cir. 1978); *Clark v. Olinkraft, Inc.,* 556 F.2d 1219 (5th Cir. 1977); *Williams v. Norfolk and Western Railway Co.,* 530 F.2d 539 (4th Cir. 1975).

113. *Smith v. American President Lines,* 571 F.2d 102 (2d Cir. 1978); *Smith v. Arkansas State OEO,* 538 F.2d 226 (8th Cir. 1976).

114. 490 U.S. 900 (1989).

115. Section 112 of the Civil Rights Act of 1991.

116. 42 U.S.C. § 2000e-5(b). Failure to swear to the charge deprives the EEOC of administrative jurisdiction and may result in the dismissal of your subsequent lawsuit. *EEOC v. Appalachian Power Co.,* 568 F.2d 226 (8th Cir. 1976).

117. Any subsequent lawsuit is limited only to those issues which are "reasonably related" to the allegations in the administrative charge. *Jenkins v. Blue Cross Mutual Hospital Insurance, Inc.,* 538 F.2d 164, 165 (7th Cir. 1976); *Smith v. Delta Air Lines,* 486 F.2d 512 (5th Cir. 1973).

118. Persons or parties not named in the administrative charge will be

dismissed from any subsequent lawsuit. *E.g., Williams v. General Foods Corp.*, 492 F.2d 399, 404–5 (7th Cir. 1974).

119. 42 U.S.C. §§ 2000e-5(b), (e); 29 C.F.R. § 1601.14

120. *See* 42 U.S.C. §§ 2000e-5(c) and (e), and *Love v. Pullman Co.*, 404 U.S. 522 (1972).

121. 42 U.S.C. § 2000e-5(b).

122. 42 U.S.C. §§ 2000e-5(b),(f)(1).

123. *Mohasco Corp. v. Silver*, 447 U.S. 807 (1980).

124. 42 U.S.C. § 2000e-5(f). *Bradshaw v. Zoological Society of San Diego*, 569 F.2d 1066 (9th Cir. 1978); *Page v. U. S. Industries, Inc.*, 556 F.2d 346 (5th Cir. 1977), *cert. denied*, 434 U.S. 1045 (1978). *But see Zambuto v. American Telephone & Telegraph Co.*, 544 F.2d 1333 (5th Cir. 1977), *and DeMatteis v. Eastman Kodak Co.*, 520 F.2d 409 (2d Cir. 1975), both holding that the ninety-day period to file suit begins to run not upon receipt of the right-to-sue notice but upon receipt of a notice that the EEOC charge has been dismissed.

125. 42 U.S.C. § 2000e-5(f). The appointment of an attorney is discretionary, and the court will require the claimant to show that he or she has tried to find an attorney or is financially unable to afford one. *Spanos v. Penn Central Transportation Co.*, 470 F.2d 806 (3d Cir. 1972).

126. *Williams v. General Foods Corp.*, 492 F.2d 399 (7th Cir. 1974); *Jenkins v. Blue Cross Mutual Hospital Insurance, Inc.*, 538 F.2d 164 (7th Cir. 1976).

127. 42 U.S.C. § 2000e-5(f)(1).

128. 42 U.S.C. § 2000e-5(f).

129. *See Johnson v. Railway Express Agency*, 421 U.S. 454 (1975) and the cases cited therein at 459 n.6.

130. *E.g., Washington v. Davis*, 426 U.S. 229 (1976).

131. 42 U.S.C. § 2000d *et seq.*

132. 42 U.S.C. § 3789d(c).

133. 41 C.F.R. § 60-1.21.

134. 42 U.S.C. § 2000e-16, and 5 C.F.R. §§ 713 *et seq.*, modified by Presidential Reorganization Plan No. 1, 43 Fed. Reg. 19807 (May 9, 1978), and implemented by Exec. Order No. 12106, 44 Fed. Reg. 1053 (Jan. 3, 1979).

135. *Richardson v. Wiley*, 569 F.2d 140 (D.C. Cir. 1977).

136. *Chandler v. Roudebush*, 425 U.S. 840 (1976).

137. 42 U.S.C. § 2000e-16(d) incorporates 42 U.S.C. §§ 2000e-5(f)-(k).

138. *Penn v. Schlesinger*, 497 F.2d 970 (5th Cir. 1974) (*en banc*); *Davis v. Passman*, 422 U.S. 228 (1979).

139. *Brown v. General Services Administration*, 425 U.S. 820 (1976).

IV
Education

The modern civil rights era in many respects was initiated by the Supreme Court's historic, unanimous decision in *Brown v. Board of Education*.[1] "Separate educational facilities," the Supreme Court declared, "are inherently unequal."[2]

Within several years, the *Brown* decision was widely applied by the Supreme Court to end segregation in numerous government facilities and services.[3] Segregation in public education, however, did not end with the Supreme Court's 1954 decision. Indeed, the Supreme Court did not even devise a remedy for unconstitutional segregation until the following year. In 1955, in *Brown II*,[4] the Supreme Court declined to impose a nationwide remedy but instead merely directed the school boards in the five consolidated cases that comprised *Brown* to replace their dual school systems with unitary systems with "all deliberate speed."[5]

For nearly twenty years after *Brown I* and *Brown II*, most school districts focused on "deliberate" and not "speed" and pursued numerous strategies to resist desegregation. The Supreme Court consistently rejected these tactics but accepted delays.

In the Little Rock case in 1958 the Court discounted white hostility to desegregation, declaring that the "constitutional rights of [black children] are not to be sacrificed or yielded" because of white opposition to those rights.[6] In 1963, in another case, the Court rejected voluntary transfer plans that allowed white students to transfer out of desegregated schools.[7] That same year, the Court eliminated another resistance tactic—the requirement that plaintiffs in a desegregation lawsuit exhaust state administrative remedies before seeking federal court relief—a tactic that had been urged successfully on several lower courts.[8] A year later, in 1964, the Court required the reopening of a school system that chose to close its schools rather than to desegregate, noting that "[t]he time for mere 'deliberate speed' had run out."[9] The following year the Court banned as too slow the use of a new delaying strategy: one grade per year desegregation plans.[10] In 1968 the Court invalidated freedom of choice desegregation plans and ordered the elimination of all segregation "root and branch."[11] In 1969 the Court rejected resistance tactics attempted by the federal government and repeated the duty of all school districts to desegregate their schools and classrooms "at once."[12] Finally, in 1971, in the case of *Swann v. Charlotte-Mecklenburg Board of Education,*[13] the Court approved the reassignment of students and realignment of school transportation routes (busing) in order to desegregate school systems effectively.

Despite the resistance to desegregation, the right of racial minorities to be free of legally enforced segregated education was established as a fundamental principle of civil rights law. In varying degrees, this tenet has been expanded in recent years to include the right to be free of legally segregated interdistrict education (including remedies that use transfers among school districts in a metropolitan area), the right to a bilingual education for non-English-speaking minority students, and the right to nondiscriminatory admissions procedures in private schools. These rights, however, are enforceable in most instances only through lawsuits filed by aggrieved minorities against offending school boards.

PUBLIC SCHOOL SEGREGATION

Is a school that is almost all of one race unconstitutional?

It depends. On the federal level, racial imbalance is not unconstitutional unless it results from intentional acts of discrimination. As interpreted by state courts, the question is as yet unanswered. Although school districts have the power to require that "each school have a prescribed ratio of [minority] to white students reflecting the proportion for the district as a whole," there is *no* general requirement of racial balance in schools, and courts will not order districts to balance.[14] On the other hand, the use of "mathematical ratios" to assign students to schools on the basis of race is an appropriate "starting point in the process of shaping a remedy" to overcome past practices of unconstitutional segregation.[15] In other words, racial balance and student reassignment on the basis of race are legally required only where school districts have engaged in legal segregation in violation of the equal protection clause of the Fourteenth Amendment.

This question is being addressed at the state level. Plaintiffs in *Sheff v. O'Neill*, a Connecticut case, argue that racial imbalance, even when not caused intentionally, may be unconstitutional under state constitutions despite absence of intentional acts.

What forms of school segregation violate the Fourteenth Amendment's guarantee of equal protection of the laws?

The most basic form of unconstitutional segregation was the intentional state-imposed dual school system formerly used throughout the South, which in *Brown I* was held to violate the Fourteenth Amendment.[16] Under a state-enforced dual school system, black students were required by state law to attend separate, all black schools.

What is the remedy for an unconstitutional state-imposed dual school system?

Segregated school systems are required "to effectuate a transition to . . . racially nondiscriminatory school system[s][17] and affirmatively to eliminate all aspects of the dual systems "until it is clear that state-imposed segregation has been completely removed."[18]

Since many school districts still have not complied with this mandate, they have to be forced to desegregate through lawsuits. In such lawsuits,

> Where plaintiffs prove that a current condition of segregated schooling exists within a school district where a dual school system was compelled or authorized by statute at the time of *Brown I* in 1954, the school district and the state are under a continuing affirmative duty "to effectuate a transition to a racially nondiscriminatory school system," that is to eliminate from the public schools within their school system "all vestiges of state-imposed segregation."[19]

If a school district or a state fails to carry out this affirmative duty, a federal court may order appropriate remedies.[20]

Remedies for achieving this goal were spelled out in detail in *Swann v. Charlotte-Mecklenburg Board of Education*.[21] They include the reassignment of teachers and students according to mathematical ratios based upon race, the alteration of attendance zones and feeder patterns, and the realignment of bus transportation routes.[22] In another case, the Supreme Court held that such services as special reading programs for students and in-service human relations training for teachers were proper remedies for the continuing effects of past discrimination.[23]

Does school segregation in the North and West, which was not imposed by state law, also violate the Fourteenth Amendment?

Generally, yes. Most of the segregation in the North and West was caused by the *intentional* policies and practices of school authorities. This violates the Fourteenth Amendment as much as segregation imposed by state statutes in the South. The key criteria under the Constitution are that the desegregation be imposed by the government and be intentional. It does not have to be written into the law.

In *Keyes v. School District No. 1*, a 1973 decision involving the Denver, Colorado schools, the Supreme Court outlined some of the policies and practices that create a segregated school system and accordingly violate the Fourteenth Amendment:

> First, it is obvious that a practice of concentrating Negroes in certain schools by structuring attendance zones or designating "feeder" schools on the basis of race has the reciprocal effect of keeping other nearby schools predominantly white. Similarly, the practice of building a school . . . to a certain size and in a certain location, "with conscious knowledge that it would be a segregated school," has a substantial reciprocal effect on the racial composition of other nearby schools. So also, the use of mobile classrooms, the drafting of student transfer policies, the transportation of students, and the assignment of faculty and staff, on racially identifiable bases, have the clear effect of earmarking schools according to their racial composition, and . . . causing further racial concentration within the schools.[24]

If a school district claims that it has not engaged in intentional discrimination but has only followed a neighborhood assignment policy, is that school district thereby absolved of responsibility for segregation of its schools?

No. School districts frequently argue that the existence of any school segregation is merely the result of residential segregation. Such bald claims are closely examined by the courts, as was done by the Supreme Court in *Keyes:* "the mere assertion of such a policy is not dispositive where, as in this case, the school authorities, have been found to have practiced de jure segregation in a meaningful portion of the school system by techniques that indicate that the 'neighborhood school' concept has not been maintained free of manipulation."[25]

A close review of a purported neighborhood assignment policy often reveals that students are not in fact assigned to the nearest school but are racially assigned and that school assignment patterns and feeder patterns have been changed to parallel racial residential changes.[26]

If only a portion of a school system is intentionally segregated, is the entire system required to desegregate and correct racial imbalance?

Yes, if the discrimination has been significant and has had a systemwide impact.[27] There is no requirement that segregation be practiced in every school before an entire system is made to desegregate. The Supreme Court has held that the existence of "intentionally segregative school board actions in a meaningful portion of a school system . . . creates a presumption that other segregated schooling within the system" similarly is intentionally segregative.[28] When there is a systemwide impact, meaning that the entire school system is segregated, the entire system is required to desegregate.

There is an exception to the systemwide imposition of these appropriate remedies—when only a very small portion of a school system is unconstitutionally segregated and the segregation has no significant impact on the system as a whole. In this situation, a federal court can impose remedies only in the unconstitutionally segregated portion of the school system in order to correct the "incremental segregative effect" of the unconstitutional segregation.[29]

Are the remedies for segregation caused by school authorities carrying out intentionally discriminatory policies and practices the same as those for segregation caused by state statutes?

Yes. When an entire school system is segregated, the appropriate remedies in the North and the West are identical to those in the South. When an entire school system is unconstitutionally segregated, the school system, the state, and if necessary, a federal court must provide affirmative remedies for desegregating the school district. These remedies, as noted, include reassignment of students and teachers, alteration of attendance zones and feeder patterns, and the realignment of bus routes (sometimes increasing the amount of transportation).[30] The remedies also include compensatory and remedial education programs (which include testing and counseling) and additional teacher training.[31]

When a school district is unconstitutionally segregated and a court-ordered desegregation plan is imposed, will the plan stay in effect for many years? Can it be altered to correct increasing racial imbalance in the school district?

Once a desegregation plan is imposed, it usually will stay in effect for at least several years so as to insure that all vestiges of segregation are removed from the school district. Several federal courts have indicated that districts must remain in compliance with the desegregation decree for at least three successive years.[32]

However, courts have used different standards in determining whether a school system has successfully converted its unconstitutional dual system of education to a unitary school system. The Supreme Court recently addressed this issue in *Oklahoma v. Dowell*, where it stated that the courts generally use "dual" to "denote a school system which has engaged in intentional segregation of students by race," and "unitary" to describe "a school system which has been brought into compliance with the command of the Constitution,"[33] i.e., the Fourteenth Amendment. Unitary status is "one in which all of the students have equal access to the opportunity for education, with the publicly provided educational resources distributed equitably and with the expectation that all students can acquire a community defined level of knowledge and skills consistent with their individual efforts and abilities."[34] The Court stated that further defining these terms may not be useful.

The Court further held in *Dowell* that federal supervision of local school systems was intended to be temporary.[35] The Court set out the standard that lower courts are to use to determine if a desegregation decree can be dissolved. First, the school district must comply in "good faith" with the court order, since it was mandated; and second, the school district must eliminate "to the extent practicable"[36] all vestiges of segregation. These vestiges include the "existing policy and practice with regard to faculty, staff, transportation, extracurricular activities, and facilities." [37]

However, a desegregation decree does "not mean that every school in every community must always reflect the racial composition of the school system as a whole."[38] *Swann* stated earlier that the use of mathematical ratios is only a starting point for shaping the remedy, not a set requirement.[39]

Thereafter, as the Supreme Court in *Swann* observed, neither school districts nor the courts "are constitutionally required to make year-by-year adjustments of the racial composition of student bodies once the affirmative duty to desegregate has been accomplished and racial discrimination through official action is eliminated from the system."[40] Thus, "in the absence of a showing that either the school authorities or some other agency of the State has deliberately attempted to fix or alter demographic patterns to affect the racial composition of the schools, further intervention by a district court should not be necessary."[41] That is, if the district has never segregated or has completed desegregation, it is under no duty to make adjustments to racial imbalances within its boundaries.

In *Freeman v. Pitts*,[42] a recent Supreme Court case, the Court issued a confusing set of opinions. One area in *Pitts,* on which the Court was clear, is that a school district under a desegregation order can achieve unitary status incrementally. For example, one year the district can become unitary in student assignments, and the following year in teacher placement. *Pitts* reflects the Court's impatience and ambivalence about what to do with school districts under court order to desegregate. Many of these cases are twenty and thirty years old. Some members of the Court do not want merely to abandon the effort to desegregate, and yet they are wary about continuing court supervision.

In view of the flight of whites from desegregated schools, aren't desegregation remedies useless when applied to inner-city schools?
No. First, even in predominantly minority school districts, many whites do remain after desegregation. And there is no difference, in principle, between desegregating a school district with 70 percent minority and 30 percent white students, and desegregating one with the reverse proportions. The objective in both situations is to eliminate the effects of intentional racial segregation caused by school authorities.

Second, white flight is not a recent phenomenon due solely to school desegregation but rather is an ongoing process that began with suburbanization after World War II. In fact, much of the white suburbanization and the concomitant concentration of minorities in the central cities was caused by government action.[43] In addition, there are districts that have not experienced white flight. Nonetheless, this situation in many metropolitan areas may have been caused in violation of the Fourteenth Amendment, and thus may be remediable in court through desegregation plans that include city as well as suburban school districts.

When a central city school district is predominantly minority and suburban districts are predominantly white, does this interdistrict segregation violate the Fourteenth Amendment?
Interdistrict segregation is a violation of the Fourteenth Amendment only if the suburban districts as well as the central-city district are shown to have engaged in interdistrict constitutional violations (for example, when white students are transferred by city districts to suburban districts) or if government officials have otherwise contributed unconstitutionally to segregated residential patterns.

In 1974 the Supreme Court reviewed an interdistrict case involving metropolitan Detroit, in which unconstitutional segregation was proved only against the Detroit school district. Thereafter, many suburban districts were brought into the lawsuit by the federal district court for purposes of determining the scope of the interdistrict remedy.[44] On review, the Supreme

Court, in a 5 to 4 decision, held that an interdistrict remedy was improper. The Court said that "an interdistrict remedy might be in order" if it is shown "that there has been a constitutional violation within one district that produces a significant segregative effect in another district."[45] The Court also stated that "an interdistrict remedy" might be "proper, or even necessary" if it were shown "that state officials had contributed to the separation of the races by drawing or redrawing school district lines, or by purposeful, racially discriminatory use of state housing or zoning laws."[46] Much of this evidence is available in some metropolitan areas, but it was not sufficiently proven in the Detroit case.

Within the last ten years state courts have begun to address interdistrict segregation under state equal protection clauses. In California, a court decided that interdistrict remedies in school desegregation cases can be applied only if there is a showing of de jure, intentional segregation, but all other desegregation techniques can be utilized to alleviate de facto segregation.[47] In *Sheff v. O'Neill*, a Connecticut case, plaintiff parents and schoolchildren contend that the conditions of racial and economic segregation in educational opportunity between the Hartford and suburban schools and the failure of the state to provide the children of Hartford with an adequate education violate the Connecticut Constitution's education, equal protection, and equality of rights provisions. Although the case has not gone to trial, the Hartford Superior Court denied the defendants' motion to dismiss, holding that the plaintiffs have stated valid claims.

Have any interdistrict school desegregation lawsuits been successful after the Supreme Court's decision in the Detroit case?

Yes. As a result of two successful lawsuits, interdistrict desegregation is now in effect in metropolitan Louisville, Kentucky, and in metropolitan Wilmington, Delaware. Both lawsuits obtained an interdistrict remedy for the violation of the equal protection clause under the federal Constitution. The Supreme Court did not review either case.

In Louisville, the interdistrict remedy was based primarily upon the existence of interdistrict school segregation whereby the city and suburbs had assigned minority students to all black schools in the city and had never fully desegregated their separate school systems.[48]

In Wilmington, the interdistrict school remedy was premised primarily on unconstitutional government contributions to segregated residential patterns.[49] For example, nearly all low-cost public housing in the metropolitan area had been placed in Wilmington; deeds containing racially restrictive covenants had been accepted by government officials; and the *State Real Estate Commission Handbook* had encouraged racially homogeneous neighborhoods, as had the *Federal Mortgage Underwriting Manual*.

If minority students believe that they are unconstitutionally segregated, how can they enforce their rights?

Virtually the only way to eliminate discrimination in public education is through a lawsuit filed by students and their parents or guardians under the Fourteenth Amendment, under part of the Civil Rights Act of 1871, or under the education article or protection clause of a state constitution.[50]

The main remedies available are those already discussed. Monetary damages have rarely if ever been recovered. Attorneys' fees, however, are awarded to plaintiffs whose lawsuits against school districts "bring about compliance" with the law.[51] In *Missouri v. Jenkins*, the Court awarded enhancement of attorneys' fees to compensate for payment delay and also compensated paralegal and law clerk work using market rates.[52]

Aside from federal lawsuits brought by individuals, are there any other ways to remedy discrimination in public schools?

Yes. First, the Department of Justice is authorized by two civil rights statutes to file discrimination lawsuits against school districts. Under one section of Title IV of the Civil Rights Act of 1964, the Department of Justice may file a lawsuit if it receives a written charge from parents alleging discrimination and if the department certifies that the complainants are unable to bring a lawsuit on their own behalf.[53] Similarly, under several sections of the Equal Education Opportunities Act of 1974, the Department of Justice may file a lawsuit on behalf of any "individual denied an equal educational opportunity."[54] Although the Department of Justice files very few such lawsuits, it is worth sending an administrative charge of discrimination to the Department of Justice, Washington, D.C. 20530.

A second possibility involves desegregation enforcement by the Department of Education (DOE). Under Title VI of the Civil Rights Act of 1964, the DOE is required to terminate its federal funding to discriminatory school districts.[55] This potentially powerful remedy for unconstitutional discrimination is initiated by the filing of an administrative charge of discrimination with any regional office of the DOE or with its main office (DOE, Office for Civil Rights, 330 Independence Avenue, SW, Washington, D.C. 20201). Because of the importance of this latter remedy, it is discussed in detail in chapter 7.

Finally, an individual can bring a claim against the school district under a state constitution or statutes. As many as twenty states have had suits that directly challenge violations of the state's education or equal protection clause.

SCHOOL FINANCING AND BILINGUAL EDUCATION

Do racial minorities enjoy other educational rights?

No and yes. Although enforcement of the right to a desegregated education has exposed many education inequities besides segregation, these have not been uniformly addressed. Three important areas of educational inequities other than segregation are disparities in school financing, the absence of bilingual education, and the absence of a minimally adequate education. As to school financing, the Supreme Court has held that there is no enforceable right under the Fourteenth Amendment to equitable school financing, but a growing number of state courts have held that such a right exists. The federal courts, on the other hand, have held that there is a right to a bilingual education for non- and limited-English-speaking minorities. Finally, minimally adequate education is now being addressed in state courts under state constitutions.

What are the inequities in school financing?

Public school districts in nearly every state are supported primarily by a combination of (1) state funds awarded fairly equally to each district based upon the number of students attending schools in the district and (2) local property taxes.

Local property taxes not only provide the greatest monetary support for school districts but also are very inequitable. For example, a poor, predominantly minority urban school district may tax its residents heavily but raise relatively little revenue for its schools, whereas a rich, predominantly white suburban school district may tax its residents only slightly but still raise much greater revenues for its schools. These inequities in school financing are particularly harsh to low income minorities because of the high taxation imposed and the low revenues raised for schools.

If school financing inequities are so patent, why are they not unconstitutional under the Fourteenth Amendment?

In 1972, in *San Antonio School District v. Rodriguez*,[56] the Supreme Court, in a 5 to 4 decision, held that school financing inequities do not violate the Fourteenth Amendment's guarantee of equal protection of the laws because education is not a fundamental right under the federal constitution. However, several state courts have interpreted their state constitutions differently.

The inequities in San Antonio were typical. The poorest school district, which was 96 percent minority, had an average property value for taxation per student of $6,000; at a property tax rate of $1.05 per $100 of property, the school district raised only $26 for the education of each student. The wealthiest school district, which was 19 percent minority, had an average property value for taxation per student of $49,000; at a property tax rate of only $0.85 per $100 of property, this school district raised $333 per student. With the addition of state and federal funds (more federal funds usually go to poor districts than to wealthy districts), the poor district could spend only $356 per student as compared to $594 per student in the wealthy district. Based upon these financing disparities, poor and minority parents alleged that the use of local property taxes was discriminatory and unconstitutional under the Fourteenth Amendment.

Not so, replied the Supreme Court. Although it conceded that "substantial disparities exist,"[57] it held that the strict standard of review usually applied to distinctions that disadvantage minorities, was inapplicable because there was no intentional racial discrimination. Applying the more lenient rational basis standard of review, the Supreme Court held that the disparities were rational primarily in view of this country's long tradition of local control of schools, and that "some inequality" was not a sufficient basis for striking down the financing system.[58] The Court did note that if children attending school in the poorly financed area were denied an education altogether, a Fourteenth Amendment claim might exist.[59]

Can school financing inequities be challenged other than through a lawsuit filed under the Fourteenth Amendment?
Yes. A number of school financing challenges have been brought in state courts alleging discrimination in violation of the equal protection clauses of state constitutions. Since interpretations of state constitutions are not reviewable by the Supreme Court, state courts can differ from the Supreme Court's interpretation of the Fourteenth Amendment in *Rodriguez*.

In early cases, California,[60] Connecticut,[61] and New Jersey,[62] interpreted their state constitutions to prohibit property tax school financing inequalities. More recently, four state courts have found that school district disparities violated their state's equal protection clause—Arkansas, California, Connecticut, and Wyoming. Another six states have found these disparities in violation of the state's education clause—Kentucky, Montana, New Jersey, Texas, Washington, and West Virginia.

What is bilingual education?
Bilingual education generally means the effective education of students who do not speak English or who have limited-English-speaking ability who come from environments where the dominant language is other than English. In order to provide an effective bilingual education, schools teach the students English but they teach all other subjects in the students' dominant language, usually Spanish, until the students are able to learn other subjects in English.

Bilingual education recently has been heralded as an educational priority. Congress, in enacting the Bilingual Education Act, recognized "the special educational needs of the large numbers of children of limited English speaking ability in the United States" and declared "it to be the policy of the United States to provide financial assistance to local educational agencies to develop and carry out" bilingual educational programs.[63]

Do non- or limited-English-speaking students have a right to a bilingual education?

Yes, said the Supreme Court in *Lau v. Nichols*,[64] at least when there are a substantial number of non- or limited-English-speaking students who speak the same dominant language.

Lau was a lawsuit filed on behalf of 1,800 Chinese-speaking students who were being taught only in English by the San Francisco school district. They argued that they were being discriminated against in violation of the Fourteenth Amendment and of Title VI of the Civil Rights Act of 1964[65] which bans discrimination "based on the ground of race, color, or national origin" in "any program or activity receiving Federal financial assistance."[66] The Supreme Court agreed that they had been discriminated against in violation of Title VI: "There is no equality of treatment merely by providing students with the same facilities, textbooks, teachers, and curriculum; for students who do not understand English are effectively foreclosed from any meaningful education."[67]

The decision in *Lau*, brought on behalf of Chinese-speaking students, has its greatest impact in requiring bilingual education for Spanish-speaking students, members of the largest language minority in the country.

How do non- or limited-English-speaking students enforce their right to a bilingual education?

The primary way, which was used in *Lau*, is to file suit against the school district alleging a violation of Title VI.[68] Before such a lawsuit can be filed, an administrative charge of discrimination must be filed with the federal agency that administers Title VI with regard to schools, the Department of Education (DOE). The charge may be resolved administratively by the DOE without having to file a lawsuit. Complaints should be sent to any DOE regional office or the main office (DOE, Office for Civil Rights, 330 Independence Avenue, SW, Washington D.C. 20201).

Because of the importance of this administrative remedy under Title VI, it is discussed in detail in chapter 7.

How do courts interpret "minimally adequate education"?

A minimally adequate education is dependent on the statutory provisions that set up programs and/or requirements intended to improve the educational performance of students, whether or not a student is considered "at risk."[69] While education finance cases address funding inequities between the richest and poorest school systems, minimum standard cases address the state's failure to provide an adequate education. Thus, in minimum standard cases, when states set standards the student must reach, the state is effectively indicating what is required for a minimum education. Although the federal courts have held that education is not a fundamental right under the Fourteenth Amendment, many state courts hold that it is a fundamental right under state law. The two prongs, setting the standard and establishing a right, provide the basis for a claim for a minimally adequate education.

DISCRIMINATION IN PRIVATE SCHOOLS

Are there any prohibitions against discrimination in private, as opposed to public, schools?

Yes. As we have seen, the constitutional prohibition against discrimination in public education is the Fourteenth Amendment's guarantee of equal protection of the laws. The Fourteenth Amendment, however, applies only to state and local governments and their offices and not to entities that are primarily private.

But this does not mean that discrimination is permitted in private schools: there are federal statutes that prohibit private school discrimination. The two laws that have been used to date are one part of the Civil Rights Act of 1866,[70] which protects minority contract rights; and Title VI of the Civil Rights Act of 1964, which prohibits discrimination in programs or activities receiving federal financial assistance.

If a private school intentionally denies admission to a minority student, is that an unlawful denial of the right to contract in violation of the Civil Rights Act of 1866?

Yes. As noted, part of the Civil Rights Act of 1866 guarantees all persons the same right "to make and enforce contracts . . . as is enjoyed by white citizens." This law, the Supreme Court has held, prohibits private schools from intentionally denying admission to minority students, and makes the private schools liable for court-awarded damages.[71]

Enforcement of the Civil Rights Act of 1866 is accomplished only through litigation, and the lawsuits must be timely filed within the applicable state statute of limitations.[72]

What types of discrimination in private schools are prohibited by Title VI? How is the law enforced?

Title VI, as noted, generally prohibits all forms of discrimination based "on the grounds of race, color, or national origin" in "any program or activity receiving federal financial assistance."[73] So long as a private school receives federal financial assistance, it generally is prohibited from engaging in discrimination.

Title VI is enforced through administrative procedures and sometimes through lawsuits—both of which are discussed in chapter 7.

AFFIRMATIVE ACTION IN ADMISSIONS

What is affirmative action in educational admissions?

Affirmative action in admissions embodies two closely related concepts. First, affirmative action requires special recruitment of minority students. This requires colleges and universities that are predominantly white, that may have used or may still use admissions criteria that discriminate against minority applicants, and that may have discriminatory reputations in minority communities, to expand their pool of applicants to include minority applicants. Second, affirmative action requires that the minority race of an applicant be considered as a positive factor in admissions. This allows colleges and universities to overcome past and current admissions practices that discriminate against minorities and to increase the admission of minorities to their schools.

Why is affirmative action used in higher education? And is it widely used?

Prior to the late 1960s, there was no affirmative action in education. At that time, although racial minorities constituted approximately 19 percent of the population of the United

States, they were vastly underrepresented in higher education and, as a result, in professional life. For example, less than 2 percent of all doctors, lawyers, medical students, and law students were minority persons. As of 1970, two black medical schools, Howard and Meharry, had trained more than 75 percent of all minority doctors in the country.

During the late 1960s and early 1970s, colleges, universities, and graduate schools (especially medical and law schools) began to expand student enrollments substantially. Some, but not most, began to adopt and implement affirmative action admissions programs, for three reasons.

First, some institutions of higher education sought to overcome past and current practices that discriminated against minorities. They decided that such discrimination was wrong and that they (especially the public institutions) had an obligation to serve all segments of the community, not just the white portions of the community. And because they were expanding their enrollments, they resolved to give some of their expanded admissions to minority applicants.

Second, some institutions also realized that the grade point averages and written aptitude tests used as admissions criteria not only discriminated against minority applicants (because of the segregated and inferior public education given to minorities for so long) but also were not very useful in making admissions decisions. Additionally, some institutions evaluated applicants by criteria that were clearly unrelated to the student's ability to perform, such as their parents' wealth and whether their parents were alumni. Since these criteria have a discriminatory impact upon minority applicants, some of the institutions resolved to overcome this pattern by also giving extra weight to the minority status of the qualified applicants.

Finally, some of the institutions simply believed that the admission of more than a token number of minority students was necessary to provide a genuinely diverse student body in which all students would learn from each other and would benefit from a robust exchange of ideas and viewpoints.

Accordingly, many, but not most, institutions of higher education implemented affirmative action programs during the late 1960s and early 1970s. Some of those programs set aside a minimum number of admissions for minority applicants, but most simply added race as another of the many positive factors that were used to make admissions decisions.

Is it lawful to use an affirmative action admissions program which sets aside a minimum number of admissions for disadvantaged minority applicants and which considers disadvantaged minority applicants separately from all other applicants?

Probably not. In *Regents of the University of California v. Bakke*,[74] the Supreme Court reviewed a medical school's affirmative action admissions program, which set aside sixteen out of one hundred places for disadvantaged minority students, using criteria for the disadvantaged minority applicants that were different from the criteria used for other applicants, thus considering the disadvantaged minority applicants separately from all other applicants. In a close and confusing vote, the Supreme Court invalidated this program.

Four of the nine members of the Supreme Court, led by Justice Stevens, voted to strike down this dual admissions program and implicitly other race conscious programs under Title VI of the Civil Rights Act of 1964. Four other members of the Supreme Court led by Justice Brennan voted to uphold the program, and thus virtually any other race conscious program, as lawful under Title VI and as constitutional under the Fourteenth Amendment. The ninth member of the Court, Justice Powell, voted to hold the rigid program in *Bakke* unlawful and unconstitutional but also voted to uphold flexible race consciousness under Title VI and the Fourteenth Amendment. Justice Powell, whose vote made a majority in *Bakke*, stated that the program would have been lawful if there had been findings of past discrimination against the medical school.

As a result of *Bakke*, is it now lawful and constitutional to use an affirmative action admissions program that uses race as a positive factor in admitting minority applicants?

Yes. As discussed, four of the nine judges on the Supreme Court, led by Justice Brennan, voted to uphold the affirmative action admissions program in *Bakke* as both lawful and constitutional, and thereby voted to uphold more flexible programs that merely take race into account. And Justice Powell said that flexible programs that take race into account would be constitutional. Educational institutions may seek to create diversity by giving positive consideration to such factors "as geographic origin or life spent on a farm,"[75] and similarly, "race or ethnic background may be deemed a 'plus' in a particular applicant's file."[76]

To emphasize the legality of race conscious affirmative action programs, Justice Powell cited with approval the Harvard College admissions program, a race conscious program that seeks to increase minority enrollment by giving positive consideration to applicants who are minority members. Since nearly all educational institutions with affirmative action admissions programs are similar to Harvard's, rather than to the rigid program of the University of California, the Supreme Court in *Bakke* did sanction affirmative action admissions programs in higher education.

Can you have affirmative action programs when there is not proof of past discrimination?

Yes, provided they comply with the guidelines set out in the *Bakke* decision.

NOTES

1. 347 U.S. 483 (1954).
2. *Id.*, at 495.
3. *See* cases cited in the footnotes to chapter 6, Public Accommodations.
4. 349 U.S. 294 (1955).
5. *Id.*, at 301.
6. *Cooper v. Aaron*, 358 U.S. 1 (1958); *see also Brown II*, 349 U.S. 294, 300 (1955).
7. *Goss v. Board of Educ.*, 373 U.S. 683, 689 (1963).
8. *McNeese v. Board of Educ.*, 373 U.S. 668, 676 (1963), *disapproving, e.g., Parham v. Dove*, 271 F.2d 132, 138 (8th Cir. 1959); *Covington v. Edwards*, 264 F.2d 780, 783 (4th Cir. 1959).
9. *Griffin v. County School Bd.*, 377 U.S. 218, 234 (1964).
10. *Rogers v. Paul*, 382 U.S. 198, 199 (1965).
11. *Green v. County School Bd.*, 391 U.S. 430, 439–41 (1968).
12. *Alexander v. Holmes County Bd. of Educ.*, 396 U.S. 19, 20 (1969); *see also Carter v. West Feliciana Parish School Bd.*, 396 U.S. 290, 291–93 (1970).

13. 402 U.S. 1 (1971).
14. *See Swann v. Charlotte-Mecklenburg Bd. of Educ.*, 402 U.S. 1, 15–19 (1971), interpreting several sections of Title IV of the Civil Rights Act of 1964, as amended, 42 U.S.C. § 2000c(b) and § 2000c-6, which prohibits reassignment of students merely to overcome racial imbalance. *See also Keyes v. School Dist. No. 1*, 413 U.S. 189 (1973); *North Carolina Bd. of Educ. v. Swann*, 402 U.S. 43 (1971); *McDaniel v. Varresi*, 402 U.S. 39 (1971).
15. *Swann v. Charlotte-Mecklenburg Bd. of Educ.*, 402 U.S. 1, 25 (1971).
16. 347 U.S. 483 (1954).
17. *Brown v. Board of Educ.*, 349 U.S. 294, 301 (1955).
18. *Green v. County School Bd.*, 391 U.S. 430, 439 (1968).
19. *Keyes v. School Dist. No. 1*, 413 U.S. 189, 200 (1973) (citations omitted), quoting from, respectively, *Brown II*, 349 U.S. 294, 301 (1955), and *Swann v. Charlotte-Mecklenburg Bd. of Educ.*, 402 U.S. 1, 15 (1971).
20. *See Swann v. Charlotte-Mecklenburg Bd. of Educ.*, 402 U.S. 1 (1971) and cases cited therein.
21. 402 U.S. 1 (1971).
22. *Id.*, at 1, 22–31. *See also Davis v. Board of School Commissioners*, 402 U.S. 33 (1971).
23. *Milliken v. Bradley*, 433 U.S. 267 (1977).
24. 413 U.S. 189, 201–2 (1973) (footnotes and citations omitted).
25. *Id.*, at 189, 212.
26. *E.g., NAACP v. Lansing Bd. of Educ.*, 559 F.2d 1042 (6th Cir.), *cert. denied*, 434 U.S. 997 (1977).
27. *Keyes v. School Dist. No. 1*, 413 U.S. 189 (1973). *See also Dayton Bd. of Educ. v. Brinkman*, 443 U.S. 526 (1979); *Columbus Bd. of Educ. v. Penick*, 443 U.S. 449 (1979).
28. *Keyes v. School District No. 1*, 413 U.S. 189, 208 (1973).
29. *Dayton Bd. of Educ. v. Brinkman*, 433 U.S. 406, 420 (1977). *Compare* cases in note 27, *supra*.
30. *See* notes 22 and 27, *supra*.
31. *See* note 23, *supra*.
32. *Pitts v. Freeman*, 887 F.2d 1438 (11 Cir. 1989); *See also U.S. v. Texas Educational Agency*, 647 F.2d 504 (5th Cir. Unit A May 1981); *Youngblood v. Board of Public Instruction of Bay County*, 448 F.2d 770 (5th Cir. 1971).
33. *Board of Educ. v. Dowell*, 111 S. Ct. 630 (1991).
34. *Keyes v. School District No. 1*, 540 F. Supp. 399, 403–4 D. Col. (1982).
35. *Board of Educ. v. Dowell*, 111 S. Ct. 630, 637 (1991). *See also* Milliken v. Bradley, 433 U.S. 267 (1977).

36. *Id. Board of Educ. v. Dowell*, 111 S. Ct. at 637–38.
37. *Id.*, at 638. *See also Swann v. Charlotte-Mecklenburg Bd. of Educ.*, 402 U.S. 1, 18 (1971); *Green v. County School Bd.*, 391 U.S. 430, 435 (1968).
38. *Swann v. Charlotte-Mecklenburg Bd. of Educ.*, 402 U.S. 1, 24 (1971).
39. *Id.*, at 25.
40. *Id.*, at 32.
41. *Id.*
42. 112 S. Ct. 1430 (1992).
43. *See* chapter 5, Housing.
44. *Milliken v. Bradley*, 418 U.S. 717, 724–34, 745 (1974) (plurality opinion of Burger, C.J.), *rev'g* 484 F.2d 215 (6th Cir. 1973).
45. 418 U.S., *Id.*, at 755 (plurality opinion of Burger, C.J.).
46. *Id.* (concurring opinion of Stewart, J.).
47. *Tinsley v. Superior Court of San Mateo*, 150 Cal. App. 3d 90, 197 Cal. Rptr. 643 (1983).
48. *Newburg Area Council v. Board of Educ. of Jefferson County*, 510 F.2d 1358 (6th Cir. 1974), *cert. denied*, 421 U.S. 931 (1975).
49. *Evans v. Buchananan*, 393 F. Supp. 428 (D. Del.), *sum. aff'd*, 423 U.S. 963 (1975), *guidelines for an interdistrict remedy imposed*, 416 F. Supp. 328 (D. Del.), *appeal dismissed*, 429 U.S. 973 (1976), *guidelines aff'd, en banc*, 555 F.2d 373 (3d Cir.), *cert. denied*, 434 U.S. 944 (1977).
50. 42 U.S.C. § 1983. *See also* § 207 of the Equal Educational Opportunities Act of 2974, 20 U.S.C. § 1706, which authorizes the filing of a lawsuit by any "individual denied an equal educational opportunity."
51. Section 718 of the Emergency School Aid Act, as amended by the Education Amendments of 1972, 20 U.S.C. § 1617. *See Bradley v. School Bd. of Richmond*, 416 U.S. 696 (1974). Attorneys' fees are also authorized for the "prevailing party" in § 1983 actions by the Civil Rights Attorneys' Fees Awards Act of 1976, 42 U.S.C. § 1988.
52. *Missouri v. Jenkins*, 491 U.S. 274 (1989).
53. Section 407 of the Civil Rights Act of 1964, as amended, 42 U.S.C. § 2000c-6.
54. Sections 207 and 211 of the Equal Educational Opportunities Act of 1974, 20 U.S.C. § 1706 and § 1710, respectively.
55. Title VI of the Civil Rights Act of 1964, as amended, 42 U.S.C. §§ 2000d *et seq.*
56. 411 U.S. 1 (1973).
57. *Id.*, at 11.
58. *Id.*, at 51.
59. *Id.*, at 37.
60. *Serrano v. Priest*, 5 Cal. 3d 584, 96 Cal. Rptr. 601, 487 P.2d 1241

(Cal. Sup. Ct. 1971), *subsequent opinion,* 18 Cal. 3d 728, 135 Cal. Rptr. 345, 557 P.2d 929 (Cal. Sup. Ct. 1976).

61. *Horton v. Meskill,* 172 Conn. 615, 376 A.2d 359 (Conn. Sup. Ct. 1977), *aff'd,* 31 Conn. Supp. 377, 332 A.2d 813 (Hartford Sup. Ct. 1974).
62. *Robinson v. Cahill,* 62 N.J. 473, 303 A.2d 273 (N.J. Sup. Ct. 1973).
63. 20 U.S.C. § 880b. The Bilingual Education Act, as amended, is codified at 20 U.S.C. §§ 880b, *et seq. See also* the Equal Education Opportunities Act of 1974, as amended, 20 U.S.C. § 1703.
64. 414 U.S. 563 (1974).
65. 42 U.S.C. §§ 2000d *et seq.*
66. 42 U.S.C. § 2000d.
67. *Lau v. Nichols,* 414 U.S. 563, 566 (1974).
68. *See also Serna v. Portales Mun. Schools,* 499 F.2d 1147 (10th Cir. 1974), *aff'g,* 351 F. Supp. 1279 (D.N.M. 1972); *Rios v. Read,* 73 F.R.D. 589 (E.D.N.Y. 1977); *ASPIRA of New York, Inc. v. Board of Educ. of New York,* 58 F.R.D. 62 (S.D.N.Y. 1973).
69. "At-risk" students are identified by determining whether a child's family receives public assistance, whether a child has limited English proficiency, or whether a child comes from a single parent family.
70. 42 U.S.C. § 1981.
71. *Runyon v. McCrary,* 427 U.S. 160 (1976).
72. *Id. See also* the discussion of the Thirteenth Amendment and of the Civil Rights Act of 1866 in chapter 1, Introduction and Overview, *supra.*
73. 42 U.S.C. § 2000d.
74. 438 U.S. 265 (1978).
75. *Id.,* at 317 (Powell, J.).
76. *Id.*

V

Housing

Of all the forms of racial discrimination discussed in this book, housing discrimination undoubtedly is the most widely practiced today. As a result, housing patterns are highly segregated and residential apartheid remains an American reality.

In many respects modern discriminatory housing practices are products of the past history of official segregation.[1] Among many examples, racially restrictive covenants (an agreement that bound the purchaser not to sell the property to a minority person of another race) in deeds and land contracts for the sale of housing were legally enforceable until 1948;[2] mortgage insurance and loan practices under Federal Housing Authority (FHA) and Veterans Administration (VA) policies, until the 1950s, officially encouraged the development and preservation of racially "homogeneous" neighborhoods; and public housing programs, until the early 1960s, provided housing for both racial minorities and whites, but on a segregated basis. In light of this longstanding pattern, it is not surprising that discriminatory practices by private realtors were, and still are, pervasive.

In the early 1960s, a presidential executive order commanded the termination of overt federal residential segregation practices.[3] Several years later, in 1968, two events increased the hope that private housing discrimination might be curbed as well. First, Congress passed Title VIII of the Civil Rights Act of 1968[4] (also known as the Fair Housing Act), specifically prohibiting racial discrimination in most private housing transactions. Second, the Supreme Court in *Jones v. Alfred H. Mayer Co.*[5] revived the Civil Rights Act of 1866[6] by deciding that it prohibits racial discrimination not only in public housing but also in the sale or rental of private property. Although integration was the goal, especially of the Fair Housing Act,[7] the "sweeping promise . . . that racial discrimination in housing would be permanently ended, has not been realized."[8]

By the late 1980s, it was clear that Title VIII, primarily dependent on private efforts, had insufficient enforcement and needed to be dramatically enhanced. Congress noted that:

Twenty years after the passage of the Fair Housing Act, discrimination and segregation in housing continue to be pervasive. The Department of Housing and Urban Development [HUD] estimates that 2 million instances of housing discrimination occur each year. In the most recent national study of housing discrimination, HUD concluded that a black person who visits 4 agents can expect to encounter at least one instance of discrimination 72 percent of the time for rentals and 48 percent of the time for sales.
. . .
Existing law has been ineffective because it lacks an effective enforcement mechanism. Private persons and fair housing organizations are burdened with primary enforcement responsibility.[9]

The Fair Housing Amendments Act of 1988[10] revitalized the fair housing laws.[11] It strengthened private enforcement by lengthening the statute of limitations, allowing punitive damages, and expanding the provisions for attorneys' fees. In addition, the 1988 act allows the attorney general to intervene in private cases, expands the role of the Justice Department, and extends the act's coverage to the handicapped and to families with children.[12]

What are the major federal prohibitions against discrimination in housing?
There are three major prohibitions. First, Title VIII of the Civil Rights Act of 1968,[13] as amended in 1988,[14] prohibits discriminatory real estate practices by government agencies or by private individuals. Second, the Civil Rights Act of 1866,[15] revived by the Supreme Court in 1968,[16] also prohibits discriminatory real estate practices by public officials and by private individuals. And third, the Fourteenth Amendment prohibits all forms of intentional housing discrimination practiced by state and local government agencies.

Are there differences in coverage and enforcement among Title VIII, the Civil Rights Act of 1866, and the Fourteenth Amendment?
Yes, there are important differences among the three federal

prohibitions which are discussed at some length later in this chapter. Briefly:

1. Title VIII broadly prohibits real estate discrimination, but it contains several coverage exemptions generally considered to be privacy exceptions. Persons who are discriminated against may use three different alternative procedural routes in enforcing Title VIII.
2. The Civil Rights Act of 1866 is the most sweeping prohibition against real estate discrimination; it contains no coverage exceptions. It is enforced only through lawsuits filed by individuals.
3. The Fourteenth Amendment prohibits only intentional discrimination by government agencies. It too is enforced only through lawsuits.

PROHIBITED REAL ESTATE PRACTICES

What types of discriminatory real estate practices are prohibited by Title VIII?

As amended in 1988, Title VIII provides legal procedures to help replace segregated housing with "truly integrated and balanced living patterns."[17] These laws prohibit a number of specific discriminatory practices on grounds of race, color, religion, sex, handicap, familial status, or national origin[18] including:

1. refusal "to sell or rent," refusal "to negotiate for the sale or rental," or simply to make "unavailable" a dwelling;[19]
2. discrimination in "the terms, conditions or privileges" or in "the provision of services or facilities" in connection with the sale or rental of a dwelling;[20]
3. publication of "any notice, statement, or advertisement" with respect to sale or rental indicating a racial limitation or preference;[21]
4. representation to any person "that any dwelling is not available for inspection, sale or rental when such dwelling is in fact so available;"[22]
5. any "attempt to induce," for profit, any person to sell or rent a dwelling based upon representations about the

probability of minority persons moving into the neighborhood (blockbusting);[23]

6. "to discriminate in any sale or rental to any person
because of a handicap"—persons with AIDS or who are
HIV positive qualify as handicapped under the 1988
act[24]—or to refuse to permit, at the expense of the handicapped person "reasonable modifications of existing
premises occupied or to be occupied . . . necessary to
afford such person equal opportunity to use and enjoy a
dwelling."[25]

These prohibitions give nondiscrimination rights primarily to
prospective buyers and renters. Another section of Title VIII
protects minority brokers and agents from the denial of access
to "membership or participation" in any multiple-listing service
or real estate organization.[26]

**Are any real estate transactions specifically exempted from
compliance with the foregoing nondiscrimination requirements of Title VIII?**

Yes, two major types of transactions are exempt. First, Title
VIII exempts the sale or rental of a single family dwelling sold
or rented by its owner so long as no real estate sales or rental
services are used and provided that the owner does not own
more than three such single family houses.[27] The second exemption, often referred to as the "Mrs. Murphy rooming house"
exemption, permits discrimination in the rental of rooms or
units in a dwelling containing living quarters for no more than
four families, so long as the owner actually occupies one of the
living quarters.[28] Even those sellers and renters exempted from
the above coverage, are prohibited from publishing or causing
to be published any notice, statement, or advertisement indicating a racial limitation or preference. Despite the two major
exceptions, "it is estimated that 80 percent of America's housing
is covered by Title VIII."[29]

In addition, there are some minor exceptions that have become more important as the act has aged. These exceptions
include exemptions for religious organizations and private
clubs;[30] limitations on a maximum number of occupants;[31] and
exclusion of a person that has been convicted of the illegal
manufacture or distribution of a controlled substance.[32]

Are other discriminatory real estate practices prohibited by Title VIII?

Yes. Title VIII also applies to banks, building and loan associations, insurance companies, and other businesses that make real estate loans; and it specifically prohibits them from engaging in any discriminatory loan denials (for "purchasing, contracting, improving, repairing or maintaining a dwelling") and any discrimination "in the fixing of the amount, interest rate, duration, or other terms or conditions of such loan or other financial assistance."[33]

In addition, Title VIII contains a catch-all provision making it unlawful to "intimidate" or to "interfere with" any person in connection with the exercise of rights protected by Title VIII.[34] This provision protects employees from being fired for having rented apartments to minority persons.[35] It also protects minority homeowners from racial intimidation and interference with the use of their home by neighbors. For example, a court applied this provision against white neighbors who firebombed a newly purchased home by an African-American woman after she moved into a predominately white neighborhood.[36] Finally, attempts to coerce a property owner to sell only to a particular racial group violate the Fair Housing Act.[37]

How does one prove discrimination in the sale of a lot or of a dwelling?

Proof of discrimination follows two basic principles. First, "to establish a prima facie case of racial discrimination, the plaintiff need prove no more than that the conduct of the defendant actually or predictably results in discrimination."[38] A federal court recently summarized an example of how a prospective minority buyer or renter would establish a prima facie case of discriminatory denial of housing:

> a plaintiff who claims that he as an individual has been the victim of a discriminatory denial of housing, may establish his prima facie case by proving the following facts:
> (1) that he is black;
> (2) that he applied for and was qualified to rent or purchase the housing;
> (3) that he was rejected; and
> (4) that the housing opportunity remained available.[39]

Second, after prima facie discrimination is shown, the burden shifts to the developer, seller, or agent "to articulate some legitimate nondiscriminatory reason" for rejecting the offer; he or she also must "demonstrate the absence of any acceptable alternative that will accomplish the same business goal with less discrimination."[40] The developer, seller, or agent then must come forward with evidence to "show that his actions were not motivated by considerations of race."[41] If the accused does not present any evidence, then a violation of the act is found and the complainant is entitled to legal relief.

For example, in one case prospective minority buyers proved that they had offered to purchase a lot from a developer, that similar offers were accepted from white buyers, that a substantial number of other lots had been sold to whites, and that the minority buyer's offer had been refused. This evidence shifted the burden of proving nondiscrimination onto the developer. The developer asserted that it did not sell lots to buyers but only to approved builders. This assertion, however, did not excuse the discrimination because the developer failed to give the minority buyer a list of approved builders, and in any event the approved builders were all white. The minority buyers were thus found to have been discriminated against in violation of Title VIII.[42]

Does Title VIII prohibit unintentional as well as intentional discrimination in real estate transactions?

Yes. Practices that have a discriminatory *effect* are unlawful under Title VIII, regardless of whether their use was intentionally discriminatory.[43] The *effects test* or *disparate impact theory* varies from circuit to circuit. Some circuits adopt a disparate impact theory, "a prima facie case is established by showing that the challenged practice of the defendant 'actually or predictably results in racial discrimination; in other words that it has a discriminatory effect.'"[44] Another circuit adopted a two-part test for determining whether a defendant can overcome the complainants prima facie case. The court in *Resident Advisory Board v. Rizzo*[45] advanced the following two-prong approach: first, the defendant must show that the reasons or actions were bona fide and legitimate; and second, the defendant must show that there was no other less discriminatory alternative. While the Supreme Court recently has eroded the effects test in other areas of discrimination law, it has declined to do so in the area of housing discrimination and Title VII.[46]

In order to establish a violation of Title VIII, must a person prove that race was the *sole* basis for a refusal to rent or sell?

No. A minority person does not need to prove that the refusal to sell or rent a dwelling was based solely on race. Instead, it need only be shown that race was a "significant factor" in the refusal.[47]

Are claims under Title VIII? possible only for minority persons?

No. Title VIII prohibits discriminatory practices because of race, color, religion, sex, national origin, or medical disability.[48] Therefore, whites and minorities who are discriminated against because of any of the above can bring a lawsuit for violation of Title VIII.

Are families, single people with children, and people who are unmarried protected by Title VIII?

Yes. Title VIII prohibits discrimination against families with children and discrimination based on family status.[49]

Is it also true that people with the HIV virus or AIDS are now protected by Title VIII?

Yes. Even if a person does not have the HIV virus or AIDS, but there is a perception that the person has or will get the HIV virus or AIDS, Title VIII applies.

Does a person have to be directly discriminated against to have a claim under Title VIII?

No. Title VIII has two primary goals: to promote integration and to end discrimination. If a party is denied the right to live in integrated housing because a particular group or individual is excluded based on race, religion, etc., there is cause for a claim for both the party excluded and those not excluded who are being denied an opportunity to live in integrated housing.[50]

Can a city do anything to stop practices that segregate housing?

Yes. Under Title VIII, a city has the right to sue on its own behalf to promote integration. In addition, most cities and states have separate laws prohibiting housing discrimination, which can give the city a right to sue either on behalf of those denied housing or on its own behalf. The Supreme Court recognizes that integrated housing benefits the entire community, and conversely, when housing is segregated, those excluded from the segregated housing, as well as those living in the segregated housing—and in the city itself—have all been injured.[51]

In proving discrimination under Title VIII, is it useful to have evidence of discrimination from testers?

Yes. *Testers* are minority persons and white persons, carefully matched in age, income, education, and other characteristics, who do not seek housing for themselves but who apply for a dwelling to "test" its availability. In proving a case of discrimination under Title VIII it is very helpful to have evidence from testers.[52] While minority testers and housing organizations are able to sue under Title VIII, white testers who have been offered housing may not sue.[53] The Supreme Court reasoned that only plaintiffs alleging "distinct and palpable injury" are eligible to sue under Title VIII. Since the white testers are offered housing, they must claim a specific injury in order to sustain their rights to sue.[54] Proof of discrimination against testers, although helpful, is not necessarily essential. As previously indicated, discrimination can be proved in part through the use of statistics.

What is the scope of the Civil Rights Act of 1866?

The Civil Rights Act of 1866, as opposed to Title VIII, is short and straightforward. One section of the older act, section 1982, states in one sentence that all citizens "shall have the same right . . . as is enjoyed by white citizens . . . to inherit, purchase, lease, sell, hold and convey real and personal property."[55] Section 1981 states that all persons "shall have the same right . . . to make and enforce contracts . . . as is enjoyed by white citizens."[56] Despite the breadth of its language, the 1866 act for a hundred years was presumed to apply only to government and not to private discrimination. However, two months after Title VIII was enacted by Congress, the Supreme Court in *Jones v. Alfred H. Mayer Co.* held for the first time that the act, specifically section 1982, also prohibits private discrimination.[57] In fact, the Court ruled that it "bars *all* racial discrimination, private as well as public, in the sale or rental of property."[58]

Does the Civil Rights Act of 1866 have exemptions similar to those in Title VIII?

No. While Title VIII exempts the sale or rental of certain single family homes, certain small rooming houses, religious organizations, and certain types of individuals, the 1866 act, by contrast, has no exemptions. Thus, some practices permitted by Title VIII are prohibited by the 1866 act and hence are unlawful.[59]

If the prohibitions against discrimination in the 1866 act are broader than in Title VIII, is Title VIII unnecessary?

No. Although it is ironic that the Supreme Court in *Jones v. Alfred H. Mayer Co.* revived the 1866 act only two months after Congress enacted Title VIII, the newer law does provide several advantages to discriminated-against persons that are not provided by the 1866 act. For example, Title VIII, unlike the 1866 act, prohibits discriminatory advertising,[60] authorizes an administrative remedy through the Department of Housing and Urban Development,[61] authorizes lawsuits by the attorney general,[62] and prohibits housing practices that have a discriminatory effect regardless of whether they were intentionally racially discriminatory.[63] Because of these differences, it is important to examine the methods of enforcement both of Title VIII and of the 1866 act.

REMEDIES AND PROCEDURES UNDER TITLE VIII AND UNDER THE CIVIL RIGHTS ACT OF 1866

Are there any enforcement procedures that must be followed under Title VIII or under the Civil Rights Act of 1866 in order to obtain the rights guaranteed by those federal statues?

Yes. Although Title VIII and the 1866 act together "prohibit all forms of discrimination, sophisticated as well as simple-minded,"[64] the federal guarantees usually are realized only through enforcement lawsuits. As stated by the Supreme Court in a Title VIII case called *Trafficante v. Metropolitan Life Ins. Co.*, federal court "complaints by private persons are the primary method of obtaining compliance" with Title VIII.[65]

Enforcement under Title VIII requires a private complainant to follow administrative procedures within certain time limitations. Enforcement under the 1866 act, on the other hand, simply requires a suit in court as soon as possible.

Who is authorized to enforce the guarantees of Title VIII?

There are three routes for enforcing the guarantees of Title VIII. First, aggrieved individuals may file complaints with HUD or seek administrative enforcement through state and local agencies.[66] This method was significantly amplified by the 1988 Amendments Act. The efficacy of this method can depend on the strength of local human rights and fair housing laws. Second, private individuals are authorized to enforce Title VIII through civil court cases.[67] Finally, the attorney general can enforce Title VIII in cases "of general public importance" or where a "pattern or practice" of discrimination is shown to exist.[68] Although housing lawsuits by the attorney general are rare, individuals should make their grievances known to the attorney general and urge that legal action be taken.

How does a private person proceed under Title VIII?

There are two separate methods of individual enforcement under Title VIII; each is authorized by a separate section of the statute providing different remedies. Method one, under sections 3610 through 3612, provides for administrative enforcement through the Department of Housing and Urban Development (HUD). Method two, under section 3613, is by filing a civil case in the courts.

What are the procedures and remedies for filing a complaint with HUD under sections 3610 through 3612?

The first method, under sections 3610 through 3612, allows an aggrieved person (complainant) to file a written complaint with HUD up to one year after a discriminatory housing practice has occurred. Upon receipt of a complaint, HUD is required to refer the complaint to certified state or local agencies before taking action on it if such an agency exists in the jurisdiction.[69] If there is no such agency, HUD will proceed with an investigation of the complaint. HUD will serve a notice on the respondent, or the accused discriminator, within 10 days advising the respondent of his or her rights and obligations under the law. The respondent must in turn file an answer within the next 10 days. Within 100 days of filing, the complaint will ordinarily be investigated by a HUD representative.[70] Should HUD fail to initiate the investigation within 100 days, it is required to inform the complainant of the reason for the delay. During the investigation period HUD will attempt to facilitate a conciliation agreement—which may include monetary relief—between the two parties.[71] By the end of the 100-day investigation period HUD will determine whether there is reasonable cause and issue a "charge" on behalf of the discriminated person.[72]

If reasonable cause is found, the complainant or the respondent may then elect to have the matter decided in a civil action in a U.S. district court. The attorney general is required to start and maintain the civil suit against the respondent. The complainant may choose to intervene and be represented by a private lawyer. Regardless of the complainant's actions, the case will be prosecuted by government attorneys and the prosecution costs will be paid by the government.

If the election to go to court is not made, HUD must pursue the case before an administrative law judge (ALJ) within 120 days of issuing a charge of discriminatory housing practice(s). Under the 1988 Amendments Act, HUD proceedings are granted broad subpoena powers, the ability to grant witness fees and issue criminal penalties for those who neglect to attend or testify or who submit misleading or false documents or statements.[73] In addition, the hearings use expedited rules of discovery and evidence.[74]

Within 60 days of the hearing the ALJ is to issue findings of fact and conclusions of law. If the ALJ finds a discriminatory housing practice he or she may award actual damages, compensatory damages, injunctive relief, and civil penalties that range from $10,000 to $50,000 fines, depending on the number of discriminatory housing practices committed within a certain time frame.[75] In one case, the ALJ required the defendant to pay $4,591.60 for actual damages and $40,000 in compensatory damages for embarrassment, humiliation, and emotional distress that an African-American couple endured because of discrimination. In addition, the ALJ imposed the maximum $10,000 civil fine.[76] An ALJ's finding may be appealed, but it must be filed within 30 days after a final order is entered.[77]

What about suing under section 3613 of Title VIII?

The second method of individual enforcement, suing directly in a U.S. district court under section 3613, must be initiated no later than two years after the alleged act of discrimination.[78] If the person with a discrimination claim cannot afford an attorney, the court may appoint an attorney for such a person.[79] If the court finds that a discriminatory housing practice has occurred or will occur, the court can order actual and punitive damages; injunctive relief including a temporary injunction, temporary restraining order, or other orders (including enjoining the defendant from engaging in the practice); or any other affirmative action held to be appropriate.[80]

What are the advantages and disadvantages of going to court under section 3613 as opposed to going through the administrative proceedings under sections 3610 through 3612 under Title VIII?

One advantage of going to court is that the statute of limitations is longer—two years for a civil case as opposed to one year for a HUD complaint. In other words, the complainant has two years to go to court and only one year to go to HUD after the discrimination incident has occurred. Perhaps the biggest advantage is that the court may award unlimited punitive damages. Unlike a HUD proceeding, a civil case can be held in front of a jury. Some complainants prefer juries because there is a possibility for higher damage awards—especially if the complainant is seen as sympathetic. Other complainants believe that jury trial awards are too erratic and that the HUD administrative law judges are more liberal.

The advantages of going to HUD include avoiding expensive legal fees, especially if the complainant does not receive a court appointed lawyer; having a HUD lawyer prosecute the complainant's case; and having statutorily hyphenated proceedings intended to take less time than court cases, which often take years to litigate due to court backlogs.

Are sections 3610 and 3612 wholly separate, or can a complainant proceed under both provisions at the same time?

A person who has been discriminated against in housing may proceed under both alternatives simultaneously because, as many courts have held: sections 3610 and 3612 provide complementary enforcement procedures under the Fair Housing Act.[81] The wisest course is to proceed under both sections—proceed administratively under section 3610 while exploring the option of filing a lawsuit under section 3613 within two years of the discrimination incident.

The right to sue under section 3613 is not affected by the administrative requirements of sections 3610 through 3612, because the two year time limit does *not* toll while pursuing a HUD administrative complaint.[82] The only limitation to pursuing both sections at the same time is that a complainant is barred from initiating a civil action if an ALJ has started the actual hearing on the case.[83]

Are courts authorized to appoint an attorney for a complainant who cannot afford a lawyer but who wishes to file suit under Title VIII?

Yes. A court is authorized to appoint an attorney upon "application by a person alleging a discriminatory housing practice or a person against whom such a practice is alleged."[84] There is no provision, however, for payment of attorneys' fees unless the plaintiff is deemed the prevailing party at the end of the lawsuit.[85] This restriction on payment as a practical matter makes courts hesitant to appoint an attorney for an indigent party and also makes it unlikely that attorneys will volunteer their services. Complainants, of course, may always act as their own counsel, but there are risks to doing so without adequate training.

What remedies are available to persons who have been discriminated against in housing in violation of the Civil Rights Act of 1866?

The remedies are very broad. For example, although the 1866 act itself specifies no remedies, the Supreme Court has held that court orders terminating the discrimination and awarding damages (including unlimited punitive damages) are available.[86] Courts also may award attorneys' fees to the prevailing party.[87]

Does a person have to choose whether to bring a housing discrimination lawsuit under Title VIII or under the Civil Rights Act of 1866?
No. Title VIII and the Civil Rights Act of 1866 provide independent remedies for discrimination in housing.[88] Aggrieved persons who file a lawsuit should claim violations of both statutes.

If a complainant fails to follow the procedural and time limitation requirements of Title VIII, can he or she still bring a lawsuit under the Civil Rights Act of 1866?
Yes. Failure to comply with the procedural requirements under either or both Title VIII alternatives does not affect a complainant's right to sue under the 1866 act to remedy housing discrimination.[89]

Are there procedural requirements that must be complied with before suing a housing discriminator under the Civil Rights Act of 1866?
The 1866 act itself contains no procedural requirements. However, the courts have uniformly held that a lawsuit under the 1866 act must be filed within the time period established by state law—a period that varies, depending upon the state, from one year to five or more years and is unaffected by any administrative filings under Title VIII or any other procedures.[90] Therefore, a complainant ordinarily should file a lawsuit under the 1866 act (and under Title VIII's direct litigation method) as soon as possible after the discriminatory action because the time is not extended for the period during which the administrative proceeding is pending.

EXCLUSIONARY ZONING AND OTHER GOVERNMENTAL DISCRIMINATION

Is discrimination still practiced in the public sector by state and local governments?
Unfortunately and quite obviously, yes. As noted at the

outset of this chapter, currently segregated residential patterns were created in part by federal, state, and local governments. Although most of the overtly segregative policies have disappeared, many have been replaced by more subtle policies of discrimination, especially exclusionary zoning policies that keep many suburban communities virtually all white.

What forms of overt discrimination in the public sector have been held unconstitutional or otherwise unlawful?

Generally, all forms of overt discrimination are prohibited. Probably the most blatant form of housing segregation ever confronted by the Supreme Court involved local ordinances that strictly prohibited blacks from living in white neighborhoods. As early as 1917, the Supreme Court, in a case entitled *Buchanan v. Warley,*[91] held that such ordinances violated the Fourteenth Amendment.

Another form of overt segregation involved enforcement by state courts of racially restrictive covenants (which require successive white purchasers of homes to sell ultimately only to other white purchasers). Believing these racially restrictive covenants to be an entirely private matter, the Supreme Court at first refused to find their state court enforcement unconstitutional.[92] However, in the 1948 case *Shelley v. Kraemer,*[93] the Court did decide that state judicial enforcement of racially restrictive covenants violated the Fourteenth Amendment. This decision, while it banned the enforcement, did not of itself ban restrictive covenants. In 1972, however, a federal court held that it was a violation of Title VIII for a local government even to file a deed with a racially restrictive covenant.[94]

Another form of overt segregation has been racial designation or "siting" of public housing, i.e., formally designating a public housing project as a black project or placing a housing project in the center of a black community. These practices have been held unlawful whether implemented by local housing authorities[95] or encouraged by the federal government.[96] In *Hills v. Gautreaux,*[97] where the federal government was shown to have participated in the segregated siting of public housing in minority areas within the city of Chicago, the Supreme Court held that HUD and the Chicago Housing Authority properly could be ordered to place public housing projects in white communities inside and outside of the city.

Have these various forms of overt housing segregation been reduced?

Yes. Overt segregation by government agencies has been reduced for a number of reasons. First, the Supreme Court has held several forms of overt discrimination unconstitutional.[98] Second, President Kennedy banned federally assisted discrimination in Executive Order 11063, in 1962.[99] Third, HUD has been required by Title VIII[100] and by *Gautreaux* to seek affirmative integration.[101]

This is not to say that the days of overt segregation are past. As late as 1977, a federal appeals court held that the City of Philadelphia had intentionally refused on grounds of racial discrimination to site a public housing project in a virtually all white part of town.[102] It is only to say, as one court has concluded, that "overtly bigoted behavior has become more unfashionable . . . not . . . that racial discrimination has disappeared."[103]

What is racially exclusionary zoning?

Zoning by its very nature has an exclusionary effect. For example, land that is zoned residential cannot be used for commercial development. In civil rights, exclusionary zoning refers to the use of low-density residential zoning (large expansive lots with big houses and few residents) to the almost total exclusion of other types of residential zoning (e.g., small lot, multi-dwelling multi-family zoning). The use of such exclusionary zoning, especially by a virtually all white community, has a discriminatory effect upon minorities since most minority members are poorer than whites and less able to buy or rent low-density housing.

Does racially exclusionary zoning deny minorities equal protection of the law in violation of the Fourteenth Amendment?

Yes, but it is almost impossible to prove it in court. Three major obstacles make proof of unconstitutional discrimination difficult.

1. The Supreme Court has been extremely deferential to local zoning. In a seminal decision, the Court in 1926 upheld local zoning as a valid exercise of the police power unless it was

clearly arbitrary and had no substantial relation to the public welfare.[104] The Court has adhered to this standard.[105]

2. The Supreme Court has narrowly defined those people who have "standing" to challenge exclusionary zoning under the Fourteenth Amendment. *Standing* refers to recognition by the Court for a party to bring and prosecute a case before it. Thus, for example, the Court has held that a minority person who is poor and who simply desires to live anywhere in a virtually all white suburban community, is not specifically harmed by that suburb's exclusionary zoning and hence has no standing to challenge it.[106] Instead, only a minority person who desires to live in a specific suburban housing development, which was not built because of zoning practices—has sufficient standing to challenge a community's exclusionary zoning.[107]

3. If the above two obstacles were not enough, the Supreme Court in *Arlington Heights v. Metropolitan Housing Development Corp.*,[108] a 1977 case, held that "proof of racially discriminatory intent or purpose is required to show a violation of the Equal Protection Clause."[109] Since there was no proof that the exclusionary zoning undertaken by the village of Arlington Heights was intentionally discriminatory, the zoning was upheld as constitutional, despite its discriminatory effect.[110] Similarly, in a 1971 case, the Supreme Court upheld a state requirement that all low-rent public housing had to be approved in a community referendum before the housing could be built; the referendum provision, the Court held, reflected devotion to democracy, not deference to discrimination.[111]

Is racially exclusionary zoning, regardless of the Fourteenth Amendment, prohibited by Title VIII of the Civil Rights Act of 1968?

Apparently, yes. Although the Supreme Court has not yet decided this issue, it has declined to review a number of lower court cases that have held that exclusionary zoning is prohibited by Title VIII.[112] The conclusion reached by the lower courts is warranted for a number of reasons.

1. Title VIII applies not just to private entities but also to government.[113]
2. Title VIII's prohibitions against making a dwelling unit "unavailable" on grounds of race and against

interfering with Title VIII rights cover exclusionary zoning.[114]

3. Title VIII prohibits practices that have a discriminatory effect, regardless of intent.[115]

4. Title VIII was enacted by Congress and has been interpreted by the Supreme Court liberally to confer standing upon aggrieved parties.[116]

As we have seen, the Supreme Court, in *Arlington Heights v. Metropolitan Housing Development Corp.*[117] held that Arlington Heights' exclusionary zoning did not violate the Fourteenth Amendment. However, the Court sent the case back to the court of appeals for a decision on whether the exclusionary zoning violated Title VIII. The court of appeals decided that the zoning was unlawful under Title VIII because of its discriminatory effect, and the Supreme Court declined review.[118] As a federal court recently stated, "we suspect that Title VIII will undoubtedly appear as a more attractive route to non-discriminatory housing, as litigants become increasingly aware that Title VIII rights may be enforced even without direct evidence of discriminatory intent."[119]

Must the procedural requirements of Title VIII be complied with when filing a lawsuit under Title VIII to stop exclusionary zoning?

Yes. Under Title VIII's section 3613 a person must file a lawsuit, if at all, within two years of the discriminatory zoning action (usually a refusal to rezone). In the 1988 Amendments Act, the agency enforcement provision, section 3610, was altered to require HUD to refer any matter involving the "legality of any State or local zoning" to the "Attorney General for appropriate action under section 3614 of this title, instead of issuing such charge."[120] In addition, HUD may order prompt Justice Department litigation in cases that require interim relief, like injunctions, to protect victims of discrimination.[121]

Are there other possible remedies for racially exclusionary zoning?

Yes. In several states, state courts have held racially exclusionary zoning to be unconstitutional under state constitutions on the grounds that it does not promote the general welfare of the state.[122] The first *Mount Laurel* case read affordable housing into the state constitution's welfare clause requiring developing New Jersey municipalities to use their zoning authority to guarantee that low cost housing would be built in municipalities in accordance with their fair share of the regions lower income communities' needs. Ideally, low income individuals were to be dispersed throughout the state forcing socioeconomic integration. The second *Mount Laurel* decision streamlined the procedures for challenging exclusionary zoning practices, built in "builders remedies" and developers incentives.[123] The third *Mount Laurel* decision upheld the New Jersey Fair Housing Act, passed in 1985 in response to the constitutional holdings of *Mount Laurel I and II.* While substantially weakened through the legislative process, the act maintains an obligation on suburbs to facilitate low income development. Other state-based approaches include restrictions on large lot zoning (Pennsylvania) and striking ordinances that exclude certain types of dwellings like mobile homes and multi-family units in (Pennsylvania and California).[124]

There seem to be several laws to promote integrated housing and to prohibit housing discrimination. Are they enough to end housing segregation and discrimination in the United States?

Unfortunately no. Housing is as segregated as it was twenty years ago. In a recent study by the government,[125] it was found that African Americans seeking housing will be discriminated against 40 percent of the time.[126] Although the laws discussed in this chapter are important, they will not alone end housing apartheid in the United States.[127]

What else is needed?

Housing opportunities in this country will not be free of discrimination until there is an affirmative effort by the government to end segregation. There need to be housing opportunities created throughout the country. The cost of housing cannot be allowed to be a pretext for excluding people based on their race or religion. Opposing exclusionary practices is not enough. There must be affirmative efforts to promote integration, such as inclusionary practices and more testers. The laws we have are an important beginning, but only a beginning.

NOTES

1. Our history of official housing segregation is summarized in U.S. Commission on Civil Rights, *Twenty Years after Brown: Equal Opportunity in Housing* (Government Printing Office, 1975). *See also* D. Falk and H. Franklin, *Equal Housing Opportunity: The Unfinished Federal Agenda* 9–13, 46 n.1 (Potomac Institute, 1976); J. Kushner, *Fair Housing Amendments Act: The Second Generation of Fair Housing*, 42 Vand. L. Rev. 1040 (1989).

2. In *Shelley v. Kraemer*, 334 U.S. 1 (1948), the Supreme Court held that state judicial enforcement of racially restrictive covenants unconstitutionally involved the state in discrimination in violation of the Fourteenth Amendment.

3. Overt segregation was barred from federal programs by President Kennedy's Executive Order 11063, entitled Equal Opportunity in Housing, 27 Fed. Reg. 11,527 (Nov. 1962).

4. 42 U.S.C. §§ 3601 *et seq.*

5. 392 U.S. 409 (1968).

6. Now codified in part as 42 U.S.C. § 1981 and 42 U.S.C. § 1982.

7. *See e.g. Jorman v. Veterans Admin.*, 579 F. Supp. 1407, (D.C. Ill. 1984); *Burney v. Housing Authority of Beaver County*, 551 F. Supp. 746 (D.C. Pa. 1982).

8. D. Falk and H. Franklin, *supra* note 1, at 161.

9. H. R. Rep. No. 100-711, 100th Cong., 2d Sess. *reprinted in* 1988 U.S.C.C.A.N. 2173, 2176–77.

10. Pub. L. No. 100-430, 102 Stat. 1619 (1900) (amending 42 U.S.C. §§ 3601–19 (1982)).

11. J. Kushner, *Fair Housing Amendments Act of 1988: The Second Generation of Fair Housing*, 42 Vand. L. Rev. 1049, 1051, 1087–98 (1989).

12. H. R. Rep. No. 100-711, 100th Cong., 2d Sess. *reprinted in* 1988 U.S.C.C.A.N. 2173, 2178–82.

13. 42 U.S.C. §§ 3601 *et seq.*

14. 42 U.S.C. §§ 3601 *et seq.* (West Supp. 1991).

15. Codified in part as 42 U.S.C. § 1981 and 42 U.S.C. § 1982.

16. *Jones v. Alfred H. Mayer Co.*, 392 U.S. 409 (1968).

17. 114 Cong. Rec. 3422 (1968)(remarks of Senator Walter F. Mondale, an author of Title VIII).

18. 42 U.S.C. §§ 3604–6 (West Supp. 1991).

19. 42 U.S.C. § 3604(a). *See Heights Community Congress v. Hilltop Realty, Inc.*, 774 F.2d 135, (6th Cir. 1985), *cert. denied*, 475 U.S. 1019, (statements or acts that would have discriminatory effect and are made with intent to racially steer violate § 3604(a) of the act); *See also Dillon v. AFBIC Development Corp.*, 597 F.2d 556 (5th Cir. 1979).

20. 42 U.S.C. § 3604(b). *See United States v. Pelzer Realty Co.*, 484 F.2d 438 (5th Cir. 1973), *cert. denied*, 416 U.S. 936 (1974).

21. 42 U.S.C. § 3604(c). *See United States v. Hunter*, 459 F.2d 205 (4th Cir. 1972), *cert. denied*, 409 U.S. 934 (1972); *Ragin v. The New York Times Co.*, 923 F.2d 995 (2d Cir. 1991); *Spann v. Carley Capital Group*, 734 F. Supp. 1 (D.D.C. 1988)(real estate advertisements that only use white human models are covered by the Fair Housing Act § 3604(c) making it unlawful to publish advertisement indicating racial preference); *Housing Opportunities Made Equal v. Cincinnati Enquirer, Inc.* 731 F. Supp. 801 (S.D. Ohio 1990).

22. 42 U.S.C. § 3604(d). This section gives a valid discrimination claim to a "tester" (a person who does not seek housing for oneself but who tests the availability of or restrictions on a dwelling on grounds of race). *See Havens Realty Corp. v. Coleman*, 455 U.S. 363 (1982) and cases cited therein; *Bellwood v. Gladstone Realtors*, 441 U.S. 91 (1979); *See also McDonald v. Verble*, 622 F.2d 1227, (6th Cir. 1980); *Davis v. Mansards*, 587 F. Supp. 334 (D.C. Ind. 1984); *cf., Evers v. Dwyer*, 358 U.S. 202 (1958).

23. 42 U.S.C. § 3604(e). *See United States v. Bob Lawrence Realty, Inc.*, 474 F.2d 115 (5th Cir. 1973).

24. *Baxter v. City of Belleville, Ill.*, 720 F. Supp. 720, (S.D. Ill., 1989)(finding persons with AIDS to be handicapped under the 1988 act); *Association of Relatives and Friends of AIDS Patients v. Administration de Reglamentos y Permisos*, 740 F. Supp. 95, (D. Puerto Rico, 1990); *Stewart B. McKinney Foundation, Inc. v. Town Plan and Zoning Com'n of Town of Fairfield*, 790 F. Supp. 1197 (D. Conn. 1992) (finding persons who are HIV positive to be handicapped under the 1988 act).

25. 42 U.S.C. § 3604(f)(1–3).

26. 42 U.S.C. § 3606.

27. 42 U.S.C. § 3603(b)(1). *See Singleton v. Gendason*, 545 F.2d 1224 (9th Cir. 1976)(exemption is not available when commercial services are used).

28. 42 U.S.C. § 3603(b)(2).

29. D. Falk and H. Franklin, *supra* note 1, at 57.

30. 42 U.S.C.A. § 3607(a)(West Supp. 1991); *See e.g. U.S. v. Columbus Country Club*, 915 F.2d 877 (3d Cir. 1990)(U.S. Appeals pending) (a religious club that maintains summer lodging does not qualify as a dwelling within the act's religious organization exemption).

31. 42 U.S.C.A. § 3607(b)(1)(West Supp. 1991).

32. 42 U.S.C.A. § 3607(b)(4)(West Supp. 1991).

33. 42 U.S.C. § 3605. *See U.S. v. American Institute of Real Estate Appraisers of Nat. Ass'n. of Realtors*, 442 F. Supp. 1072 (D.C. Ill.

1977)(promulgation of standards causing appraisers and lenders to treat race and national origin as a negative factor in determining value of homes and in evaluating soundness of loans violates the act); *Laufman v. Oakley Bldg. & Loan Co.*, 408 F. Supp. 489 (S.D. Ohio 1976)(redlining prohibited by this section).

34. 42 U.S.C. § 3617. *See Laufman v. Oakley Bldg. & Loan Co.*, 408 F. Supp. 489 (S.D. Ohio 1976); *Cf. Metropolitan Hous. Dev. Corp v. Village of Arlington Heights*, 558 F.2d 1283 (7th Cir. 1977), *cert. denied*, 434 U.S. 1025 (1978).

35. *See Smith v. Stechel*, 510 F.2d 1162 (9th Cir. 1975)(firing of apartment manager for not following policy of discouraging minority applicants violates Title VIII); *Wilkey v. Pyramid Const. Co.*, 619 F. Supp 1453, (D.C. Conn. 1985)(part-time secretary fired for encouraging prospective tenants protected by Title VIII).

36. *Stirgus v. Benoit*, 720 F. Supp. 119, (N.D. Ill. 1989). *See also Seaphus v. Lilly*, 691 F. Supp. 127 (N.D. Ill. 1988)(acts of violence and property damage inducing minority residents to move are prohibited by § 3617 of Title VIII).

37. *Delano Village Companies v. Orridge*, 553 N.Y.S.2d 938, (N.Y. Supp. 1990).

38. *United States v. City of Black Jack*, 508 F.2d 1179, 1184–85 (8th Cir. 1976)(citations and footnotes omitted).

39. *Robinson v. 12 Lofts Realty, Inc.*, 610 F.2d 1032, 1038 (1979). *See also Williams v. Matthews Co.*, 499 F.2d 819 (8th Cir. 1974), *cert. denied*, 419 U.S. 1021 (1974). *Cf. McDonnell-Douglas Corp. v. Green*, 411 U.S. 792, 802 (1973)(outlining principles of establishing prima facie discrimination case under Title VII employment context).

40. *Williams v. Matthews Co.*, 499 F.2d at 827–28 (8th Cir. 1974). *See also Resident Advisory Bd. v. Rizzo*, 564 F.2d 126, 149 (3d Cir. 1977) *cert. denied*, 435 U.S. 908 (1978); *United States v. West Peachtree Tenth Corp.*, 437 F.2d 221 (5th Cir. 1971).

41. *Robinson v. 12 Lofts Realty, Inc.*, 610 F.2d 1032, 1039 (1979).

42. *Williams v. Matthews Co.*, *supra* note 40.

43. *See* Resident Advisory Bd. v. Rizzo, 564 F.2d 126, 146–48 (3d Cir. 1977), *cert. denied*, 435 U.S. 908 (1978); *Metropolitan Hous. Dev. Corp. v. Village of Arlington Heights*, 558 F.2d 1283, 1286–90 (7th Cir. 1977), *cert. denied*, 434 U.S. 1025 (1978); *Smith v. Anchor Building Corp.*, 536 F.2d 231, 233 (8th Cir. 1976); *United States v. City of Black Jack*, 508 F.2d 1179, 1185 (8th Cir. 1974) *cert. denied*, 422 U.S. 1042 (1975); *United States v. Pelzer Realty Co.*, 484 F.2d 438, 443 (5th Cir. 1973), *cert. denied*, 416 U.S. 936 (1974).

These decisions are in accord with Supreme Court decisions interpreting Title VII of the Civil Rights Act of 1964, *Dothard v. Rawlinson*,

433 U.S. 321 (1977); *Griggs v. Duke Power Co.*, 401 U.S. 424 (1971); and interpreting Title VI of the Civil Rights Act of 1964, *Lau v. Nichols* 414 U.S. 563 (1974).

44. *Huntington Branch, NAACP v. Town of Huntington*, 844 F.2d 926, 934 (2d Cir. 1988) *aff'd. per curiam*, 109 S. Ct. 276 (1988)(quoting from *United States v. City of Black Jack*, 508 F.2d 1179, 1184–85 (8th Cir. 1974), *cert. denied*, 422 U.S. 1042 (1975)).

45. 564 F.2d 126, (3d Cir. 1977), *cert. denied*, 435 U.S. 908 (1978).

46. *See Town of Huntington, New York v. Huntington Branch, NAACP*, 488 U.S. 15 (1988)(affirming the Second Circuit's use of disparate impact analysis but refusing to reach the question of whether the "effects" test is appropriate in Title VIII cases). *cf. Wards Cove Packing Co. v. Atonio*, 490 U.S. 642 (1989)(for Title VII cases racial imbalance in one segment of employer's work force is insufficient to establish a prima facie case of disparate impact of employment discrimination; burden of persuasion remains with the plaintiff).

47. *U.S. v. Parma, Ohio*, 494 F. Supp. 1049 (D.C. Ohio, 1980), *aff'd* 661 F.2d 562, *rehearing denied* 456 U.S. 926; *See also Metropolitan Housing Development Corp. v. Village of Arlington Heights*, 558 F.2d 1283, 1977, *cert denied*, 434 U.S. 1025, *on remand* 469 F. Supp. 836; *Burris v. Wilkins*, 544 F.2d 891 (5th Cir. 1977); *Williams v. Matthews Co.*, 499 F.2d 819 at 826 (8th Cir 1974); *U.S. v. Pelzer Realty Co.*, 484 F.2d 438, 443 (5th Cir. 1973) *cert. denied*, 416 U.S. 936 (1974); *Wang v. Lake Maxinhall Estates, Inc.*, 531 F.2d 832, 836 n.112 (7th Cir. 1976); *Huertas v. East River Housing Corp.*, 674 F. Supp. 440 (S.D.N.Y. 1987); *Bishop v. Pecsok*, 431 F. Supp. 34, 37 (N.D. Ohio 1976); *cf. Smith v. Sol D. Adler Realty Co.*, 436 F.2d 344 (7th Cir. 1970) (same standard under Civil Rights Act of 1866).

48. 42 U.S.C. § 3604 as amended.

49. *Id.*

50. *Gladstone Realtors v. Bellwood*, 441 U.S. 91 (1979).

51. *Id.*

52. *E.g., United States v. Youritan Construction Co.*, 509 F.2d 623 (9th Cir. 1975), *aff'd*, 370 F. Supp. 643 (N.D. Cal. 1973); *Johnson v. Jerry Pals Real Estate*, 485 F.2d 528 (7th Cir. 1973); *Hamilton v. Miller*, 477 F.2d 908 (10th Cir. 1973) (state laws which prohibit "testing" are themselves unlawful under Title VIII); *United States v. Wisconsin*, 395 F. Supp. 732 (W.D. Wis. 1975).

53. *Havens Realty Corp v. Coleman*, 455 U.S. 363 (1982). *But see Village of Bellwood v. Gorey & Assoc.*, 664 F. Supp. 320 (N.D. Ill. 1987)(non-resident testers may allege personal interest in dispute with direct,

palpable injuries and thus have standing to sue under Fair Housing
Act and civil rights statute).

54. *Havens Realty Corp. v. Coleman*, 455 U.S. 363, 368 (1982).
55. 42 U.S.C. § 1982. *See Smith v. Sol D. Adler Realty Co.*, 436 F.2d 344 (7th Cir. 1970).
56. 42 U.S.C. § 1981.
57. 392 U.S. 409, 420 (1968).
58. *Id.*, at 413 (emphasis in original).
59. *E.g.*, *Morris v. Cizek*, 503 F.2d 1303 (7th Cir. 1974)(the 1866 act prohibits discrimination in the lease of an apartment in a small apartment house exempted from Title VIII). *Compare* 42 U.S.C. § 3603(b)(2).
60. 42 U.S.C.A. § 3604(c)(West Supp. 1991). *See* note 21, *supra*.
61. 42 U.S.C.A. §§ 3608–11 (West Supp. 1991).
62. 42 U.S.C.A. § 3614 (West Supp. 1991).
63. *See* cases cited in notes 42 and 46, *supra*, supporting the proposition that Title VIII prohibits practices with a discriminatory effect. It is unclear whether proof of discriminatory intent is necessary to prove a violation of the 1866 act.
64. *Williams v. Matthews Co.*, 499 F.2d 819, 826 (8th Cir. 1974), *cert. denied*, 419 U.S. 1021 (1974), and cases cited therein.
65. 409 U.S. 205, 209 (1972).
66. 42 U.S.C.A §§ 3610–12 (West Supp. 1991).
67. 42 U.S.C.A § 3613 (West Supp. 1991).
68. 42 U.S.C.A. § 3614(a)(West Supp. 1991).
69. 42 U.S.C.A. § 3610(f)(1)(West Supp. 1991). HUD has recognized half of the states and many localities as having laws substantially equivalent to Title VIII. They are listed in 24 C.F.R. § 115.12.
70. 42 U.S.C.A. § 3610(a)(B)(ii–iii)(West Supp. 1991).
71. 42 U.S.C.A. § 3610(b)(West Supp. 1991).
72. 42 U.S.C.A. § 3610(g)(West Supp. 1991).
73. 42 U.S.C.A. § 3611 (West Supp. 1991).
74. 42 U.S.C.A. § 3611(d) (West Supp. 1991).
75. 42 U.S.C.A. § 3612(g)(3)(West Supp. 1991).
76. *Secretary, H.U.D. v. Blackwell*, 908 F.2d. 864, 872–73 (11th Cir. 1990). *See also Douglas v. Metro Rental Services, Inc.*, 827 F.2d 252 (7th Cir. 1987)(complainant awarded $43,000 damages); *Marable v. Walker* 704 F.2d 1219 (11th Cir. 1983) (complainant awarded $20,000 punitive damages and $10,000 compensatory damages); *U.S. v. Pelzer Realty Co.*, 537 F.2d 841 (5th Cir. 1976); *Saunders v. General Services Corp.*, 659 F. Supp. 1042 (E.D. Va. 1986).
77. 42 U.S.C.A. § 3612(i)(2)(West Supp. 1991).

78. 42 U.S.C.A. § 3613(a)(1)(A)(West Supp. 1991).
79. 42 U.S.C.A. § 3613(b)(West Supp. 1991).
80. 42 U.S.C.A. § 3613(c)(West Supp. 1991).
81. *TOPIC v. Circle Realty*, 532 F.2d 1273, 1275 (9th Cir.1976); *see also, Bellwood v. Gladstone Realtors*, 569 F.2d 1013, 1018-20 (7th Cir. 1978), *aff'd*, 441 U.S. 91 (1979) and cases cited therein.
82. 42 U.S.C.A. § 3613(a)(1)(B)(West Supp. 1991).
83. 42 U.S.C.A. § 3613(a)(3)(West Supp. 1991).
84. 42 U.S.C.A. § 3613(b)(West Supp. 1991).
85. 42 U.S.C.A. § 3613(c)(2) (West Supp. 1991).
86. *See Sullivan v. Little Hunting Park*, 396 U.S. 229, 239 (1969); *See also Jones v. Alfred H. Mayer Co.*, 392 U.S. 409 (1968); *Gore v. Turner*, 563 F.2d 159, 164 (5th Cir. 1977); *Bishop v. Pecsok*, 431 F. Supp. 34 (N.D. Ohio 1976) ($1500 compensatory damages and $5000 punitive damages); *Parker v. Shonfeld*, 409 F. Supp. 876 (N.D. Cal. 1976) ($10,000 compensatory damages and $10,000 punitive damages).
87. 42 U.S.C. § 1988, as amended by the Civil Rights Attorneys Fees Awards Act of 1976. *See Gore v. Turner*, 563 F.2d 159, 163 (5th Cir. 1977).
88. *Jones v. Alfred Mayer Co.*, 392 U.S. 409 (1968). *See Dillon v. AFBIC Development Corp.*, 597 F.2d 556 (5th Cir. 1979).
89. *Meyers v. Pennypack Woods Home Ownership Ass'n*, 559 F.2d 894, 899–900 (3d Cir. 1977); *Warren v. Norman Realty Co.*, 513 F.2d 730, 732–33 (8th Cir.), *cert. denied*, 423 U.S. 855 (1975); *Hickman v. Fincher*, 483 F.2d 855, 856–57 94th Cir. 1973); *cf. Johnson v. Railway Express Agency*, 421 U.S. 454 (1975); *Goodman v. Lukens Steel*, 482 U.S. 656 (1987) (questioning *Meyers*' refusal to apply state two year statute of limitations to § 1981 claims).
90. *Id.*
91. 245 U.S. 60 (1917).
92. *Corrigan v. Buckley*, 271 U.S. 323 (1926).
93. 334 U.S. 1 (1948).
94. *Mayers v. Ridley*, 465 F.2d 630 (D.C. Cir. 1972).
95. *Gautreaux v. Chicago Hous. Auth.*, 265 F. Supp. 582 (N.D. Ill. 1967), 296 F. Supp. 907 (N.D. Ill. 1969) and 304 F. Supp. 736 (N.D. Ill. 1969), *aff'd*, 436 F.2d 306 (7th Cir. 1970), *cert. denied*, 402 U.S. 922 (1971); *cf.*, *Otero v. New York City Hous. Auth.*, 484 F.2d 1122 (2d Cir. 1973) and cases cited therein.
96. *See Gautreaux v. Romney*, 448 F.2d 731 (7th Cir. 1971); *Shannon v. HUD*, 436 F.2d 809 (3d Cir. 1970).
97. 425 U.S. 284 (1976). *See also Dayton Board of Education v. Brinkman* 4333 U.S. 406 (1977)(expanded notions of remedy followed).

98. *See* notes 87 and 89, *supra*.
99. *See* note 3, *supra*.
100. 42 U.S.C. §§ 3608(d) and (e)(5) require HUD to administer its housing programs "affirmatively" to further the purposes and policies of Title VIII. *See N.A.A.C.P., Boston Chapter v. Secretary, H.U.D.*, 817 F.2d 149 (1st Cir. 1987); *Otero v. New York City Hous. Auth.*, 484 F.2d 1122, 1133–34 (2d Cir. 1973) and cases therein. *But see Anderson v. City of Alphrette, Ga.*, 737 F.2d 1530 (C.A. Ga. 1984)(narrow interpretation of H.U.D.'s affirmative duty).
101. *See, generally*, 24 C.F.R. pt. 1.
102. *Resident Advisory Bd. v. Rizzo*, 564 F.2d 126 (3d Cir. 1977), *cert. denied*, 435 U.S. 908 (1978).
103. *Metropolitan Hous. Dev. Corp. v. Village of Arlington Heights*, 558 F.2d 1283, 1290 (7th Cir. 1977), *cert. denied*, 434 U.S. 1025 (1978).
104. *Euclid v. Ambler Realty Co.*, 272 U.S. 365 (1926).
105. *Compare Belle Terre v. Boraas*, 416 U.S. 1 (1974), *with Moore v. East Cleveland*, 431 U.S. 494 (1977).
106. *Warth v. Seldin*, 422 U.S. 490 (1975); *see also Hartford v. Glastonbury*, 561 F.2d 1032 (2d Cir. 1977) (*en banc*), *cert. denied*, 434 U.S. 1034 (1978); *Evans v. Lynn*, 537 F.2d 571 (2d Cir. 1976), *cert. denied*, 429 U.S. 1066 (1977).
107. *Arlington Heights v. Metropolitan Hous. Dev. Corp.*, 429 U.S. 252 (1977).
108. *Id.*
109. *Id.*, at 265.
110. Earlier lower court decisions holding that proof of discriminatory intent was unnecessary to show that exclusionary zoning violated the equal-protection clause of the Fourteenth Amendment were overruled by the Supreme Court not just in *Arlington Heights* but also in *Washington v. Davis*, 426 U.S. 229, 244 n.12 (1976).
111. *James v. Valtierra*, 402 U.S. 137 (1971); *compare Hunter v. Erickson*, 393 U.S. 385 (1969).
112. *Resident Advisory Bd. v. Rizzo*, 564 F.2d 126 (3d Cir. 1977), *cert. denied*, 434 U.S. 908 (1978); *Metropolitan Hous. Dev. Corp. v. Village of Arlington Heights*, 558 F.2d 1283 (7th Cir. 1977), *cert. denied*, 434 U.S. 1025 (1978); *United States v. City of Black Jack*, 508 F.2d 1179 (8th Cir. 1974), *cert. denied*, 422 U.S. 1042 (1975).
113. *Id. See also Mayers v. Ridley*, 465 F.2d 630, 635 (D.D.C. 1972) (Wright, J. concurring).
114. 42 U.S.C. § 3604(a) and § 3617. *See* cases cited in note 89, *supra*.
115. *See* note 25, *supra*.
116. *Gladstone Realtors v. Bellwood*, 441 U.S. 91 (1979). *Trafficante v.*

Metropolitan Life Ins. Co., 409 U.S. 205 (1972); *but see TOPIC v. Circle Realty*, 532 F.2d 1273 (9th Cir. 1976), *cert. denied*, 429 U.S. 859 (1977).

117. 429 U.S. 252 (1977).

118. *Metropolitan Hous. Dev. Corp. v. Village of Arlington Heights*, 558 F.2d 1283, 1290-94 (7th Cir. 1977), *cert. denied*, 434 U.S. 1025 (1978).

119. *Resident Advisory Bd. v. Rizzo*, 564 F.2d 126, 146 (3d Cir. 1977), *cert. denied*, 435 U.S. 908 (1978).

120. 42 U.S.C.A. § 3610(g)(2)(C) (West Supp. 1991).

121. 42 U.S.C.A. § 3610(e)(2)(West Supp. 1991)("Whenever the Secretary has reason to believe that a basis may exist for the commencement of proceedings . . . for proceedings by any governmental licensing or supervisory authorities, the Secretary shall transmit the information upon which such belief is based to the Attorney General, or to such authorities, as the case may be.")

122. *E.g., Southern Burlington County NAACP v. Mount Laurel*, 336 A.2d 713 (N.J. 1975)(hereinafter *Mount Laurel I*) (state constitution's welfare clause requires every municipality in New Jersey to accommodate its fair share of the *regional* housing needs of low- and moderate-income families); *Southern Burlington County NAACP v. Township of Mount Laurel*, 456 A.2d 390 (N.J. 1983) (hereinafter *Mount Laurel II*) (imposing an affirmative duty on communities to assure that their fair share of low and moderate income housing would be constructed); *Hills Dev. v. Township of Bernards*, 510 A.2d 621 (N.J. 1986) (hereinafter *Mount Laurel III*) (upholding New Jersey Fair Housing Act on voluntary compliance to provide affordable housing). *See* H. McDougall, *From Litigation to Legislation in Exclusionary Zoning Law*, 22 Harv. C.R.-C.L. L. Rev. 623, 625 (1987) ("The lesson of New Jersey is that the legislature will not act without pressure from the judiciary."); J. Payne, *Title VIII and Mount Laurel: Is Affordable Housing Fair Housing?* 6 Yale L. & Pol. Rev. 361 (1988); *See also*, D. Falk and H. Franklin, *supra* note 1, at 104–21.

123. H. McDougall, *From Litigation to Legislation in Exclusionary Zoning Law*, 22 Harv. C.R.-C.L. L. Rev. 623, 627–30 (1987).

124. *Id.*, at 631–35.

125. Housing Discrimination Study, Prepared by Margery Austin Turner, Raymond J. Struyk, John Yinger, The Urban Institute and Syracuse University, August 1991.

126. N. Y. Times, Sun., Nov. 3, 1991, Section 10, p. 1, col. 2.

127. M. F. Potter, *Racial Diversity in Residential Communities: Societal Housing Patterns and a Proposal for "Racial Inclusionary Ordinance,"* 63 S. Cal. L. Rev. 1151, 1190–1206 (1990).

VI

PUBLIC ACCOMMODATIONS

The modern civil rights movement, which toppled the more overt forms of racial discrimination, had its beginning in an effort to integrate public accommodations—city buses in Montgomery, Alabama. On 1 December 1955, Mrs. Rosa Parks, a black woman, refused to yield her seat on a city bus to a white passenger. Following her arrest for violating an ordinance requiring segregation in public transportation, a citywide boycott of buses was organized by a twenty-seven-year-old minister named Martin Luther King, Jr. In the years that followed, his tactic of direct, nonviolent action was replicated in countless lunch counter sit-ins, freedom rides, marches, boycotts, and demonstrations and helped change the laws and customs of a nation.

What is a "public accommodation"?

A *public accommodation* is any establishment or entity that serves the public or is open to the public, such as a hotel, restaurant, library, train, bus, or tennis court. A less obvious example would be the Boy Scouts, which one court has held is a place of public accommodation even though it does not operate a unitary, definite "place" of business but conducts its activities in a large number of temporary locations.[1]

What federal laws protect against racial discrimination in public accommodations?

The most important federal laws that prohibit racial discrimination in public accommodations are the Thirteenth Amendment, which bars the imposition of "badges and incidents of slavery" and protects the equal right to contract; the Fourteenth Amendment, which prohibits official discrimination; statutes implementing the Thirteenth and Fourteenth Amendments and imposing civil and criminal penalties upon those who interfere with access and use of public accommodations;[2] the Interstate Commerce Act of 1887, which forbids common carriers from imposing "unreasonable discrimination" upon their patrons;[3] the Civil Aeronautics Act, which prohibits discrimination in air travel;[4] Title II of the Civil Rights Act of 1964, the modern public accommodations law protecting the equal enjoyment of most business establishments without regard to race, color, religion, or historical origin;[5] and Title III of the Civil Rights Act of 1964, prohibiting discrimination in the use of any public facility operated, owned, or managed by a state or its political subdivisions, other than a school or college.[6]

THE THIRTEENTH AND FOURTEENTH AMENDMENTS AND THE CIVIL RIGHTS ACT OF 1866

What kinds of discrimination in public accommodations are prohibited by the Thirteenth and Fourteenth Amendments?

The Fourteenth Amendment prohibits all forms of state imposed or sanctioned racial segregation in places of public accommodation regardless of whether the facilities are actually owned or operated by the state.[7] Purely private acts of segregation, however, in which there has been no significant state involvement, do not violate the equal protection clause of the Fourteenth Amendment.

The Thirteenth Amendment, unlike the Fourteenth, applies to private as well as official acts. Although it was initially construed as banning only slavery and physical restraint, the Supreme Court more recently has ruled that the Thirteenth Amendment prohibits the imposition of "badges and incidents of slavery," such as the refusal of private realtors to sell or lease real estate to blacks,[8] and protects the equal right to contract for services and accommodations.[9]

Were the Thirteenth and Fourteenth Amendments effectively enforced after their enactment to prohibit discrimination in public accommodations?

No. Both the Thirteenth and Fourteenth Amendments contain provisions authorizing congressional implementation through appropriate legislation.[10] Under this constitutional authority, Congress enacted in 1875 the nation's first public accommodations law,[11] intended to guarantee to all persons, without regard to race or color, the full and equal enjoyment of the accommodations, advantages, facilities, and privileges of inns, public conveyances, theaters, and other places of public amusement. Eight years later, in a decision known as *The Civil Rights Cases*,[12] the Supreme Court declared the act unconstitutional. The Court had before it five cases involving the denial to blacks of the use of privately owned hotels and theaters and the ladies' car of a railroad company. A majority of justices concluded that the Thirteenth Amendment prohibited slavery, not racial discrimination, and that the Fourteenth Amendment was a limitation on state, not private, action. The discrimination involved in the facilities, although perhaps a "civil injury" under state law, was not prohibited by the Constitution. The decision thus denied Congress the authority to implement the Thirteenth or Fourteenth Amendments to ban segregation in privately owned places of public accommodations.

Was there any response by the states to *The Civil Rights Cases*?

Yes. Partially in response to *The Civil Rights Cases* but more importantly as part of the "redemption" of white rule after Reconstruction, many of the states adopted so-called Jim Crow statutes requiring segregation of the races in places of public accommodation. No detail of life was too small to fall under the regulation of Jim Crow. Jim Crow laws required segregation in schools, churches, housing, transportation, jobs, prisons, cemeteries, and public buildings. Courts in Atlanta used a Jim Crow Bible to swear in Negro witnesses, and Birmingham had an ordinance making it a crime "for a Negro and a white person to play together or be in company of each other" at checkers or dominoes.[13]

Was Jim Crow ever tested in court?

Yes. In 1896 the Supreme Court decided *Plessy v. Ferguson*,[14] a case involving a Jim Crow law from the state of Louisiana. Plessy, who was seven-eighths white and one-eighth Negro, was a passenger in June 1892 on the East Louisiana Railway from New Orleans to Covington. He purchased a first class ticket and took a seat in the car reserved for white passengers. The conductor, however, directed that Plessy take a seat in the Jim Crow car, which by state law was required to be "equal but separate." Plessy refused to move. He was arrested and charged with the crime of going "into a coach or compartment to which by race he does not belong." Plessy argued that the law was unconstitutional and that in any event "the mixture of colored blood was not discernible in him." His arguments were rejected, and the Court, adhering to the narrow interpretation of the Constitution it had set down in *The Civil Rights Cases*, held that "separate but equal" accommodations for blacks on railway cars, even though required by state law, were constitutional because they existed for the "preservation of the public peace and good order."[15] The Court thus approved official racial segregation in places of public accommodation and allowed the states the right to adopt Jim Crow as the law of their land.

Plessy v. Ferguson was not to be the last word spoken by the Court on the constitutionality of Jim Crow. In 1954 in *Brown v. Board of Education*,[16] a case as dramatic for race relations as *Plessy v. Ferguson*, the Supreme Court effectively reversed itself and laid Jim Crow to rest.

Brown was the culmination of a line of cases in which the Court had found the maintenance of separate educational facilities and programs for blacks to be unconstitutional because they were in fact unequal.[17] The Court did not expressly overrule *Plessy v. Ferguson*, but it held categorically that "in the field of public education the doctrine of 'separate but equal' has no place."[18]

What practices have been held unconstitutional under *Brown* and the Fourteenth Amendment?

Over the next twenty years the decision was used to ban officially sanctioned racial segregation in such places of public accommodation as buses,[19] parks,[20] hospitals,[21] swimming pools and bath houses,[22] city golf courses,[23] airport restaurants,[24] courtroom seating,[25] municipal auditoriums,[26] prisons and jails,[27] and in virtually every other form in which it came before the courts.

Is it always easy to draw a line between state imposed or sanctioned discrimination in public accommodations prohibited by the Fourteenth Amendment and purely private discrimination beyond its reach?

No. There is no specific formula for determining state action.[28] Instead, the courts sift and weigh all the facts involved, including whether the operation of a facility is essentially a public function[29] and whether the state has any obligation or responsibility or confers or receives any benefit in its operation. If there is a "sufficient" degree of state involvement, the facility, even if privately owned, is subject to the prohibition against racial discrimination contained in the Fourteenth Amendment.

In one case, for example, the Supreme Court held that a privately operated coffee shop located in a parking building owned by the city of Wilmington, Delaware, was in partnership with the state so that the coffee shop's refusal to serve blacks was state action prohibited by the Fourteenth Amendment.[30] The Court based its conclusion upon the facts that the building was publicly owned and maintained, the parking lot was dedicated to public use, while operation of the cafe conferred mutual benefits to the city, patrons of the parking lot, and the operators of the cafe. Under the circumstances, there was sufficient state involvement to trigger the Fourteenth Amendment.

In a later case, however, the Court held that the refusal of a Moose Lodge in Harrisburg, Pennsylvania to serve a black was not prohibited by the Constitution.[31] The complainant, Leroy Irvis, contended that because the Pennsylvania liquor board had issued the lodge a licensed to serve alcohol the refusal to serve him was state action, prohibited by the equal protection clause of the Fourteenth Amendment. A majority of the Court disagreed. It found the lodge to be private because it was a member of a national fraternal organization, the building in which its activities were conducted was owned by it, there were well-defined requirements for membership, and only members and their guests were permitted in any lodge of the order. Even though the lodge had a license from the state to serve alcoholic beverages, that fact did not constitute sufficient state involvement or support in the operation of the lodge to make its racially exclusive membership policies unconstitutional. The Court did, however, enjoin enforcement of a state regulation that required the lodge to comply with the provisions of its bylaws and constitution containing racially discriminatory provisions.[32]

Racial discrimination in the operation of privately owned facilities, however, is always unconstitutional under *Brown v. Board of Education* and the Fourteenth Amendment if it is carried out under state or local Jim Crow laws or as part of official policy.[33] Under such circumstances, the state may be said to have compelled the discrimination. The Supreme Court has even held that a Florida Board of Health regulation requiring separate toilet and lavatory rooms for the races in privately owned restaurants involved the state in the promotion of segregation to such an extent that the trespass convictions of civil rights demonstrators who had protested a local restaurant's segregationist policies violated the Fourteenth Amendment.[34]

Can a state or municipality close down a place of public accommodation rather than operate it on a desegregated basis?

Yes and no. The Supreme Court has held that a state may not close public schools and meanwhile contribute to the support of private, segregated white schools.[35] Such a course merely continues segregation in violation of the Fourteenth Amendment. However, in another case, the Court held it to be no violation of the Fourteenth Amendment for the city of Jackson, Mississippi, to close its municipal swimming pools rather than operate them on a desegregated basis.[36] The Court reasoned that the closing of the pools to all citizens, black and white, did not deny to either group equal treatment under the Constitution. The decision has been severely criticized on the grounds that the Fourteenth Amendment prohibits all forms of purposeful discriminatory state action, including opposition to the desegregation of public facilities, which was admittedly present in the case.

Aside from the public accommodations law of 1875, was there any other Reconstruction era legislation barring private discrimination in public accommodations?

Yes. The Civil Rights Act of 1866 contained two provisions, now known as 42 U.S.C. §§ 1981 and 1982, barring, among other things, discrimination in public accommodations. Section 1982 provides that all citizens "shall have the same right . . . as is enjoyed by white citizens . . . to inherit, purchase, lease, sell, hold and convey real and personal property."[37] Section 1981 states that all persons "shall have the same right . . . to make and enforce contracts . . . as is enjoyed by white citizens."[38]

Have sections 1981 and 1982 been used extensively to remedy discrimination in public accommodations?

No, but the law is changing and the use of the two statutes has increased. Both sections 1981 and 1982 were presumed for more than a hundred years to apply only to state action, while Jim Crow, as we have seen, was long regarded as constitutional. The statutes thus had no impact on private discrimination in public accommodations. In 1968, however, the Supreme Court ruled that section 1982, based in part upon the Thirteenth Amendment, prohibited private discrimination in real estate transactions[39] and in 1975 that section 1981 prohibited private discrimination in the making of contracts.[40] The effect of these decisions has been to allow use of the Reconstruction era statutes to prohibit owners and managers from discriminating in contracting with minorities for the use of privately owned public accommodations.

What kinds of practices are subject to challenge under sections 1981 and 1982?

A wide variety of racially discriminatory practices are subject to challenge under sections 1981 and 1982, including the refusal of a hunting and fishing club to admit a black to its membership;[41] the refusal of a beauty salon operator to wash and set the hair of a black patron;[42] a lounge operator's discriminatory application of a facially neutral "drinks only" policy to exclude blacks;[43] the refusal of a bartender to sell soft drinks to blacks attending a private party held in the meeting hall of a local fraternal organization;[44] and the refusal of a public cemetery to sell burial plots to blacks.[45]

Do sections 1981 and 1982 contain any express or implied limitations excluding certain kinds of discriminatory practices from coverage?

Neither statute contains any express limitations in coverage, while the Supreme Court has never ruled whether the statutes are limited by implication. The argument has been raised in several cases in the Supreme Court that the scope of section 1981 and 1982 is impliedly limited by the right of privacy, so that certain discriminatory practices, such as those in the home or a similar intimate setting, are simply beyond the power of the government to regulate. In those cases, however, the Court concluded that the setting in which the discrimination was practiced was not in fact private and thus had no occasion to rule on implied privacy limitations that might be contained in the statutes.

In one of the cases the Court held that the refusal of a community corporation, which operated a park and playground, to approve assignment of a membership share to a black was unlawful under section 1982 since membership was generally open to all persons—except blacks—living within a certain geographic area.[46] The corporation was not in fact a private social club, only a racially exclusive club. The Court reached the same result under section 1982 in a similar case decided four years later involving a community swimming pool association.[47] In one of its most recent section 1981 cases, the Supreme Court held that the statute prohibited a private, commercially operated, nonsectarian school from refusing to contract with and admit blacks.[48] Lower courts have similarly refused to apply a privacy or associational exemption to the statutes where the discrimination was practiced in a public setting, e.g., in a fraternal organization which the court found was "simply a drinking club."[49]

Is it necessary to prove that the discrimination was intentional to establish a violation of sections 1981 and 1982?

Yes, if the discrimination is challenged under section 1981. The Supreme Court has held (although it acknowledged Congress could have provided otherwise) that section 1981, like the equal protection clause of the Fourteenth Amendment, can be violated only by acts that are intentionally discriminatory.[50] In another case, however, the Court expressly declined to consider whether a showing of discriminatory intent was also a required element of a violation of section 1982.[51]

How are the Thirteenth and Fourteenth Amendments and sections 1981 and 1982 enforced to end discrimination in places of public accommodation? What remedies do they provide?

The Thirteenth and Fourteenth Amendments are enforced primarily through lawsuits brought by private individuals pursuant to implementing legislation, such as sections 1981 and 1982, enacted by Congress.[52] Remedies include orders terminating discrimination and awarding damages[53] and attorneys' fees.[54] The federal government also has authority to prosecute violations of criminal statutes protecting Thirteenth and Fourteenth Amendment rights,[55] including equal access to public accommodations.

Are there procedural requirements that must be complied with before suing to enforce Thirteenth and Fourteenth Amendment equal accommodation rights?

No. Yet the courts have held that a lawsuit must be filed within the time period established by state law[56]—a period that varies, depending upon the state, from one year to five or more. Therefore, a complainant ordinarily should file a lawsuit as soon as possible after the discriminatory action.

THE INTERSTATE COMMERCE ACT

What is the Interstate Commerce Act? Does it prohibit racial discrimination?

Congress enacted the Interstate Commerce Act[57] in 1887 under the commerce clause of the Constitution.[58] The act established the Interstate Commerce Commission (ICC) whose duty it is to license and regulate rail, bus, and other carriers. The act specifically prohibits common carriers engaged in interstate commerce from giving undue preference to any person or subjecting any person to unreasonable discrimination.[59]

Is discrimination affecting only transportation within a state also prohibited by the act?

No. Discrimination that is purely local and has no impact upon commerce between the states or with foreign countries is not subject to regulation by the Interstate Commerce Act.[60] The Supreme Court has yet to find challenged action to be purely local.

Is state action a requirement for a violation of the act?

No. The act prohibits discrimination in interstate commerce by private as well as public carriers and whether or not the discrimination is caused by state or local laws or the carrier's own practices.

154   *The Rights of Racial Minorities*

What kinds of practices have been found discriminatory under the Interstate Commerce Act?

As might be expected, during the early years of its existence the Interstate Commerce Act was held to permit Jim Crow facilities for the races in interstate commerce, whether required by state statute or carrier rule.[61] In 1941, however, the Supreme Court ushered in a new era in interstate transportation in a case involving a black Congressman from Chicago, Arthur W. Mitchell.[62] Mitchell, who held a first class ticket, was required to accept second class accommodations pursuant to state Jim Crow laws when the train on which he was a passenger crossed over the state line from Tennessee into Arkansas. The ICC dismissed the congressman's complaint, but the Supreme Court reversed. The Court refused to decide whether Arkansas's segregation statutes were lawful, but held that the denial to Mitchell of equality of accommodations because of his race was a violation of the Interstate Commerce Act.

Following the *Mitchell* case, the Court in 1946 confronted Jim Crow in interstate commerce head on and struck down a Virginia statute requiring separate but equal facilities for the races on motor buses. Justice Frankfurter in a concurring opinion observed that "imposition upon national systems of transportation of a crazy-quilt of state laws would operate to burden commerce unreasonably, whether such contradictory and confusing state laws concern racial commingling or racial segregation."[63] In other cases, the courts have struck down discrimination in the provision of services and facilities by the Southern Railway Company,[64] the Atlantic Coast Line Rail Road,[65] and bus terminals in Montgomery, Alabama.[66]

As for the ICC, it issued rulings in two major cases on 7 November 1955, terminating segregation in interstate rail travel[67] and on buses.[68] As a consequence of the various decisions of the courts and the ICC, the Interstate Commerce Act is now regarded as imposing the same standard as far as race is concerned as the Fourteenth Amendment and as barring "discriminations of all kinds."[69]

Do the nondiscrimination provisions of the act apply to such facilities as restaurants and terminals that cater to interstate passengers?

Yes. The act bans discrimination in terminals and restaurants that are an integral part of the carrier's service for interstate passengers, and it is immaterial whether such facilities are actually owned or operated by the carrier itself. The Supreme Court has held that a carrier cannot escape its statutory duty to treat all interstate passengers alike either through segregation in facilities it owns or use of the facilities of others who practice segregation.[70]

How are the antidiscrimination provisions of the act enforced?

The antidiscrimination provisions of the act are enforced administratively in proceedings before the ICC and by lawsuits brought in the federal district courts. Any person or governmental entity adversely affected by a carrier practice may file a discrimination complaint with the secretary of the ICC in Washington, D.C.[71] The ICC is required to investigate, and if it finds a violation, it is required to take action to correct it. The ICC may also begin an investigation on its own initiative.

As an alternative to filing an administrative complaint, those discriminated against, as well as the attorney general and the ICC itself, may file a suit in federal district court for injunctive relief and damages.[72] Damages, costs, and attorneys' fees are authorized,[73] and those who disobey ICC orders are subject to civil fines.[74]

There is no requirement that administrative remedies be exhausted before filing a lawsuit, but if a complaint is filed with the ICC, then the federal courts have jurisdiction only to review the record on the action taken by the ICC, as opposed to hearing the matter from the beginning on its merits.[75]

THE CIVIL AERONAUTICS ACT

Is discrimination in air travel also prohibited by law?

Yes. The Civil Aeronautics Act[76] contains a provision patterned after the Interstate Commerce Act prohibiting racial discrimination in air travel. One of the first cases applying this law was brought by the popular black singer Ella Fitzgerald. She charged that she was discriminated against because of her race when she was denied a reserved seat on a flight from Honolulu to Sydney, Australia, where she was scheduled to give a performance.[77] The act has also been used to prohibit segregation in airport terminal facilities.[78]

Are the Civil Aeronautics Act and the Interstate Commerce Act frequently used today to remedy discrimination in air travel and interstate commerce?

No. The importance of both acts has diminished with the decline of discrimination in air and interstate travel and, as we shall see, with enactment of the Civil Rights Act of 1964.

TITLE II OF THE CIVIL RIGHTS ACT OF 1964

What is Title II of the Civil Rights Act of 1964 and what does it provide?

Title II of the Civil Rights Act of 1964[79] is the nation's first modern public accommodations law. It was enacted by Congress, not pursuant to the Thirteenth and Fourteenth Amendments but to its power to regulate commerce under article I, section 8, clause 3 of the Constitution. Title II provides that all persons shall be entitled to the full and equal enjoyment of goods, services, facilities, privileges, advantages, and accommodations of any place of public accommodation without discrimination or segregation on the grounds of race, color, religion, or national origin. Four classes of business establishments are covered by the act if the establishment serves the public, is a place of public accommodation and its operations affect commerce, or if discrimination by it is supported by state action. The covered establishments are:

1. any inn, hotel, motel, or other establishment that provides lodging to transient guests;
2. any restaurant or similar facility principally engaged in selling food for consumption on the premises or any gasoline station;
3. any theater, sports arena, or other place of exhibition or entertainment; and
4. any establishment that is physically located within the premises of a covered establishment or any establishment within the premises on which is physically located

a covered establishment and serving patrons of such covered establishment.

Discrimination or segregation required by state or local law is expressly prohibited,[80] and no persons may deny or interfere with the right of access and use of any covered facility by any other person.[81]

Does Title II unreasonably interfere with the rights of ownership of private property?

No. In *Heart of Atlanta Motel v. United States*,[82] the Supreme Court held Title II to be constitutional, rejecting the argument that it deprived individuals of their liberty and property interests. The Court noted that 32 states and numerous cities had enacted similar laws and that their constitutionality had repeatedly been upheld. Not only was public accommodations legislation common, but there was no merit in the claim that prohibition of racial discrimination in public facilities interfered with personal liberty. Congress acted in light of the dramatic evidence before it of the difficulties blacks encountered in travel and to ease the burdens that discrimination by race or color placed upon interstate commerce. Under the circumstances, the Court concluded, Title II was reasonably adapted to an end permitted by the Constitution.

May a member of a racial minority be denied access to a place of public accommodation because other patrons might object and the owner lose business?

No. The protection of Title II cannot be yielded to the prejudices of patrons or the claimed nonracial economic interests of owners and managers. The exclusion of persons from public accommodations because of their race, whatever the asserted justifications, is prohibited.[83]

How is the determination made whether an establishment's operations "affect commerce" and are thus covered by Title II?

Commerce is defined by Title II basically as trade or travel among the states, the District of Columbia, and any foreign country or territory or possession of the United States.[84] Inns, motels, and similar facilities are deemed to affect commerce if they provide lodging to transient guests. Restaurants, lunch counters, and gasoline stations are covered by Title II if they serve interstate travelers or if a substantial portion of what they sell has moved in commerce. Motion picture houses and other places of entertainment affect commerce if their films, performers, or other sources of entertainment have moved in commerce. Finally, any establishment located within the premises of a facility that affects commerce, or any establishment within the premises on which is located a facility that affects commerce, is itself covered by Title II.

Must an establishment have a substantial effect upon interstate commerce to be covered by Title II?

No. The success of Title II depends upon the regulation of all establishments that contribute to the problem of racial discrimination in interstate commerce. Accordingly, the fact that an establishment's effect upon interstate commerce is trivial does not remove it from coverage. Thus a barbecue restaurant in Birmingham, eleven blocks from an interstate highway, was covered by the act since nearly half of the food it served was purchased outside the state and moved through interstate commerce.[85] The requisite interstate commerce connection has also been made to bring a billiard parlor within Title II as a place of entertainment where its snooker and pool tables and cues were manufactured out of state.[86]

What kinds of practices and facilities have been held to be covered by Title II?

Practices and facilities held by the courts to be covered by Title II include: segregation in hotels, motels,[87] YMCA facilities,[88] trailer parks,[89] restaurants, health and beauty spas,[90] bars and package stores,[91] and hospitals;[92] "freedom of choice" seating in dining rooms;[93] a local ordinance prohibiting service at bars to persons in military uniform enacted to impede integration efforts at a nearby military installation;[94] denial of the use of facilities to blacks at a remote fishing camp,[95] a hunting club,[96] an amusement park,[97] a recreational complex containing boating and swimming facilities,[98] skating rinks,[99] a tournament held on a municipal golf course,[100] a golf course,[101] beach club,[102] bowling alleys,[103] movie theaters;[104] refusal to serve a white woman at a lunch counter because she was in the company of blacks;[105] refusals at beach apartments,[106] a drive-in restaurant,[107] lunch counters,[108] snackbars,[109] a gasoline station and its rest rooms,[110] nightclubs and cabarets,[111] a country club operated by a profit-making corporation,[112] pool rooms,[113] racetracks,[114] and a swimming club.[115]

Are there any exemptions from coverage contained in Title II?

Yes. Excluded from Title II are private clubs not in fact open to the public and the so-called Mrs. Murphy's boarding house—that is, any rooming house with not more than five rooms for rent and which is actually occupied by the proprietor as a residence.[116]

May an establishment that serves the general public call itself a "private club" to escape Title II coverage and practice racial discrimination?

No. A place of public accommodation may not defeat Title II coverage by the simple expedient of calling itself a private club or even by adopting some of the formal trappings of a private club. In determining if a facility is private, the courts look at all the facts and circumstances surrounding its operation. How and why was it created? Is it run for a profit? Who owns it? How has it been operated in the past? Does it have members? If so, how are they chosen? Do they pay dues? Are nonmembers allowed to use the facilities?[117]

In one case the Supreme Court was asked to decide if the Lake Nixon Club, a 232-acre amusement park with swimming, boating, golf, and dancing facilities located outside Little Rock, Arkansas, was a private club. Patrons were required to pay a twenty-five cent membership fee and were issued membership cards for entry on the premises. The Court reviewed the facts, including facts that the privately owned park had always been operated on a racially segregated basis and that whites were routinely given, and blacks denied, membership. Lake Nixon Club was found to be simply "a business operated for a profit with none of the attributes of self-government and membership-ownership traditionally associated with private clubs."[118]

In a similar case, the Court held a neighborhood swimming pool was not a private facility or club since the association that owned it granted a preference in membership to anyone living within a three-quarter-mile radius of the pool, except blacks.[119] Aside from the geographical requirement, the only condition for membership was race. The pool was no more private under Title II than the Lake Nixon Club.

Who has the burden of proving whether a club is or is not private within the meaning of the private club exemption in Title II?

Those complaining of discrimination have the initial burden of establishing a prima facie case of a violation of Title II—that is, they must show that an establishment is covered by the act and that it discriminates on the basis of race. Thereafter, the burden shifts to the establishment to prove by significant or clear and convincing evidence that it is in fact truly private.[120]

How is Title II enforced?

Title II depends for enforcement upon both private and federal lawsuits, as well as administrative conciliation by the Community Relations Service established by Title VIII of the Civil Rights Act of 1964. Any person aggrieved by racial discrimination in access to or use of public accommodations is authorized to bring a suit for injunctive relief in the federal courts.[121] If the court deems it proper, an attorney may be appointed to represent the complainant and the payment of fees and other court costs may be waived. The attorney general is allowed, with the permission of the court, to intervene if the case is deemed to be of general public interest. The attorney general is also authorized to bring suit for injunctive relief against discriminatory practices where there is "reasonable cause" to believe that a pattern and practice of resistance to Title II exists.[122]

To encourage individuals injured by racial discrimination to seek judicial relief under Title II and further the purposes of the act, Congress has provided that "prevailing parties" are entitled to recover costs and reasonable attorneys' fees.[123] Damages are not authorized. The provision of costs and fees has not only facilitated access by the poor and disadvantaged to the courts but has deterred discrimination in the operation of public accommodations.

Are the enforcement procedures contained in Title II the sole means of remedying discrimination in public accommodations?

No. Title II provides that nothing in the act shall preclude any person from asserting a right under another statute or ordinance or from pursuing another remedy for the vindication or enforcement of such right.[124] Thus a person discriminated against may bring suit under Title II or, for example, under sections 1981 and 1982.

Since Title II and sections 1981 and 1982 provide independent remedies for discrimination in public accommodations,[125] an aggrieved person who files a lawsuit should claim violations of both Title II and sections 1981 and 1982.

Are there advantages to filing a lawsuit under Title II as opposed to sections 1981 and 1982?

There are advantages under both because the remedies provided, and often the scope of coverage, are different. Sections 1981 and 1982 authorize recovery of damages; Title II does not. Title II, however, provides for enforcement by the attorney general and conciliation by the Community Relations Service; sections 1981 and 1982 contain no similar provisions. As for scope of coverage, Title II requires effect upon interstate commerce, while sections 1981 and 1982 do not. Section 1981 requires proof of intentional discrimination; Title II does not.

Are there steps that must be taken before an individual can file a lawsuit to enforce Title II?

Yes, in some instances. Title II provides that no lawsuit may be brought under the statute in a state, or political subdivision of a state, that has an agency authorized to grant or seek relief from discrimination in public accommodations before the expiration of 30 days after written notice, by registered mail or in person, of the act or practice has been given to such agency.[126] The purpose of the provision is to give states and local governments an initial opportunity to remedy discrimination.[127] However, if they fail to do so within the 30-day period, the aggrieved individual is free to bring suit in the federal district court without having to comply with any other remedy that may be provided by law.[128] The notice requirements do not apply to pattern-and-practice suits brought by the attorney general.[129]

How does the Community Relations Service enforce Title II?

The Community Relations Service (CRS) is a federal agency established by Title VIII of the Civil Rights Act of 1964.[130] Its function is to provide assistance to communities in resolving disputes relating to discriminatory practices based on race, color, or national origin. After a lawsuit has been filed to enforce Title II, the court may refer the matter to the CRS for up to 60 days, if the court believes there is a reasonable possibility of attaining a voluntary resolution of the discrimination.[131] The court may extend the referral for an additional 60 days, not to exceed a cumulative total of 120 days.

Does the Community Relations Service play an active role in resolving complaints of discrimination in public accommodations?

No. References to the CRS are infrequent due to the relative decline in the number of lawsuits filed under Title II and because the CRS has no authority, other than through conciliation, to resolve disputes.[132]

Can a member of a racial minority who seeks access to a facility covered by Title II be prosecuted for trespass under state law?

No. Persons threatened with prosecution under state trespass laws stemming from their peaceful exercise of the right of equal accommodation in establishments covered by Title II have a right not even to be brought to trial on such charges.[133] Accordingly, any charges that might be brought may be removed to the federal courts and there dismissed.[134] The right of removal under Title II is an important one and is a substantial deterrent to efforts by local officials to use state criminal prosecutions to defeat implementation of Title II under the guise of protecting property rights.

Can a person be prosecuted criminally for discriminating in the operation of public accommodations?

Title II contains no criminal provisions for the punishment

of persons who merely refuse to serve others because of race. Injunctive relief is the sole remedy available under the act. However, persons who conspire against or assault others seeking access to public accommodations can be prosecuted by the federal government under 18 U.S.C. §§ 241 and 245 for interfering with the protected rights of citizens.[135]

TITLE III OF THE CIVIL RIGHTS ACT OF 1964

What is Title III of the Civil Rights Act of 1964?

Title III of the Civil Rights Act of 1964 is a special public accommodations law that authorizes the attorney general to bring suit in the name of the government to end discrimination in the use of a public facility operated, owned, or managed by a state or its political subdivisions, other than a school or college.[136]

Are there limitations on the attorney general's authority to bring suit under Title III?

Yes. Before filing suit under Title III, the attorney general must (1) have received a complaint in writing signed by an individual to the effect that he is being discriminated against on the basis of race, color, religion, or national origin in the use of a public facility; (2) believe the complaint is meritorious; (3) certify that the signer is unable to bring a suit on his own behalf; and (4) certify that a lawsuit will materially further the orderly progress of desegregation in public facilities.

How does the attorney general determine whether a person is unable to bring a lawsuit on his own?

Title III provides that a person may be deemed unable to bring a lawsuit on his own behalf if the expense of litigation is too great, if the person cannot obtain effective legal representation, or if the institution of a lawsuit would jeopardize the personal safety, employment, or economic standing of such person or his family or property.

Does Title III affect the right of private individuals to sue for discrimination in public accommodations?

No. Title III specifically provides that nothing in the act shall adversely affect the right of any person to sue in court against discrimination in public accommodations.[137]

How has Title III been used? What is its significance today?

Title III has been used primarily to desegregate prisons and jails.[138] Its main significance is that it allows the attorney general to bring suit to enforce the Fourteenth Amendment in places of public accommodation, and of equal importance, spares private parties the burden and expense of litigation. Those discriminated against in use of state owned or operated facilities should always make a written complaint to the Attorney General, United States Department of Justice, Washington, D.C. 20530.[139]

STATE LAWS PROHIBITING DISCRIMINATION IN PUBLIC ACCOMMODATIONS

Do states also have laws that prohibit discrimination in public accommodations?

Yes. The District of Columbia, most states, and many cities now have laws prohibiting discrimination on the basis of race or color in places of public accommodation. To determine whether a jurisdiction has a public accommodations law, consult the state or local legal or public information office or one of the agencies or sources of legal assistance listed in the appendixes to this book.

Have these state laws been effectively enforced?

Yes and no. Some state courts have proved hostile to local public accommodations laws and have given them restrictive application to exclude such apparently public facilities and organizations as restaurants,[140] dentists' offices,[141] golf courses,[142] apartments, hotels,[143] the Jaycees,[144] the Boy Scouts,[145] and saloons.[146] The reasons for exclusion have included the facts that the statutes have been strictly construed and because they were said to limit the use of private property.

The Supreme Court, however, has given such laws a broad construction and has upheld them against claims that they interfered with individual privacy and expressive associational rights protected by the First Amendment. In one case, the

Court held that a Minnesota law that made it unlawful to discriminate in access to public accommodations "because of race, color, creed, religion, disability, natural origin or sex" was constitutional and prohibited the Jaycees from excluding women from its membership. The Court reasoned that the Jaycees are neither small nor select, there are no criteria for judging applicants for membership, and numerous nonmembers regularly participate in organizational activities. Accordingly, the Jaycees lack the distinctive characteristics (of a family or small neighborhood club, for example) that might afford constitutional protection to its members' decision to exclude a protected group. The Court also held that the state had a compelling interest in eradicating "acts of invidious discrimination . . . wholly apart from the point of view such conduct may transmit" and that the Minnesota law abridged no more speech or associational freedom than was necessary to accomplish that purpose.[147]

In a similar case from California, the Court held that the state's public accommodations law (the Unruh Act) prohibited the Rotary Club from excluding a protected group (women) from its membership.[148] The Court has also upheld a New York City law prohibiting discrimination in public accommodations in a case brought by a consortium of private clubs.[149]

Regardless of how the courts may have ruled on a particular state or local public accommodations law, a person who has been discriminated against in public accommodations in any of the jurisdictions that have such laws should file a written notice, by registered mail or in person, with the appropriate nondiscrimination agency in order to assert later on his or her rights under Title II.

NOTES

1. *Welsh v. Boy Scouts of America*, 742 F. Supp. 1413 (N.D. Ill. 1990).
2. *E.g.*, 42 U.S.C. §§ 1981, 1982, 1983, and 1985, and 18 U.S.C. §§ 241, 242, and 245.
3. 24 Stat. 380, 49 U.S.C. §§ 3(1) and 316(d), revised, 96 Stat. 2413, 49 U.S.C. § 10741(b).
4. 49 U.S.C. § 1374(b).
5. 42 U.S.C. § 2000a *et seq.*

166   *The Rights of Racial Minorities*

6. 78 Stat. 246, codified as 42 U.S.C. § 2000b *et seq.*
7. *Burton v. Wilmington Parking Auth.*, 365 U.S. 715 (1961).
8. *Jones v. Alfred H. Mayer Co.*, 392 U.S. 409 (1968), construing 42 U.S.C. § 1982, derived from the Civil Rights Act of 1866, 14 Stat. 27.
9. *Tillman v. Wheaton-Haven Recreation Association, Inc.*, 410 U.S. 431 (1973); *Johnson v. Railway Express Agency*, 421 U.S. 454 (1975), and *Runyon v. McCrary*, 427 U.S. 160 (1976), construing 42 U.S.C. § 1981, derived from the Civil Rights Act of 1866, 14 Stat. 27.
10. Thirteenth Amendment, § 2; Fourteenth Amendment, § 5.
11. 18 Stat. 335.
12. 109 U.S. 3 (1883).
13. C. Vann Woodward, *The Strange Career of Jim Crow* 104 (New York: Oxford University Press, 1957).
14. 163 U.S. 537, 16 S. Ct. 1138 (1896).
15. *Id.*, 16 S. Ct. at 1143.
16. 347 U.S. 483 (1954).
17. The cases include *Gaines v. Canada*, 305 U.S. 337 (1938); *Sweatt v. Painter*, 339 U.S. 629 (1950); and *McLaurin v. Oklahoma State Regents*, 339 U.S. 637 (1950).
18. 347 U.S. at 495.
19. *Gayle v. Browder*, 352 U.S. 903 (1956) (*per curiam*); *Boman v. Birmingham Transit Company*, 280 F.2d 531 (5th Cir. 1960).
20. *City of New Orleans v. Barthe*, 376 U.S. 189 (1964).
21. *Simkins v. Moses H. Cone Hospital*, 323 F.2d 959 (4th Cir. 1963).
22. *Clark v. Thompson*, 313 F.2d 637 (5th Cir. 1963).
23. *City of Greensboro v. Simkins*, 246 F.2d 425 (4th Cir. 1957).
24. *Turner v. City of Memphis, Tenn.*, 369 U.S. 250 (1962); *Smith v. Birmingham*, 226 F. Supp. 838 (N.D. Ala. 1963).
25. *Johnson v. State of Virginia*, 373 U.S. 61 (1963); *Wood v. Vaughan*, 321 F.2d 480 (4th Cir. 1963).
26. *Schiro v. Bynum*, 375 U.S. 395 (1964).
27. *Lee v. Washington*, 390 U.S. 333 (1968).
28. *Bell v. Maryland*, 378 U.S. 226 (1964).
29. *Marsh v. Alabama*, 326 U.S. 501 (1946).
30. *Burton v. Wilmington Parking Authority*, 365 U.S. 715 (1961).
31. *Moose Lodge No. 107 v. Irvis*, 407 U.S. 163 (1972).
32. The *Moose Lodge* case is probably limited to its facts involving a truly private club. In cases involving the refusal of otherwise public restaurants to serve women, the courts have held that the granting of a liquor license *was* state action and that the discriminatory policies of the restaurants were prohibited by the Fourteenth Amendment. *Seidenberg v. McSorley's Old Ale House, Inc.*, 317 F. Supp. 593

(S.D.N.Y. 1970); *Bennett v. Dyer's Chop House, Inc.*, 350 F. Supp. 153 (N.D. Ohio 1972).

33. *Peterson v. City of Greenville*, 373 U.S. 244 (1963); *Lombard v. Louisiana*, 373 U.S. 267 (1963). In a related case, the court held that an agreement between a grill and city police to enforce the grill's policy of serving only men made the policy unlawful state action prohibited by the Fourteenth Amendment. *Johnson v. Heinemann Candy Co., Inc.*, 402 F. Supp. 714 (E.D. Wisc. 1975).

34. *Robinson v. Florida*, 378 U.S. 153 (1964).

35. *Griffin v. County School Board*, 377 U.S. 218 (1964).

36. *Palmer v. Thompson*, 403 U.S. 217 (1971).

37. 42 U.S.C. § 1982.

38. 42 U.S.C. § 1981.

39. *Jones v. Alfred H. Mayer Co.*, 392 U.S. 409 (1968).

40. *Johnson v. Railway Express Agency*, 421 U.S. 454 (1975).

41. *Durham v. Red Lake Fishing and Hunting Club, Inc.*, 666 F. Supp. 954 (W.D. Tex. 1987).

42. *Perry v. Command Performance*, 913 F.2d 99 (3d Cir. 1990).

43. *Wyatt v. Security Inn Food & Beverage, Inc.* 819 F.2d 69 (4th Cir. 1987).

44. *Watson v. Fraternal Order of Eagles*, 915 F.2d 235 (6th Cir. 1990).

45. *Terry v. Elmwood Cemetery*, 307 F. Supp. 369 (N.D. Ala. 1969).

46. *Sullivan v. Little Hunting Park*, 396 U.S. 229 (1969).

47. *Tillman v. Wheaton-Haven Recreation Association, Inc.*, 410 U.S. 431 (1973).

48. *Runyon v. McCrary*, 427 U.S. 160 (1976).

49. *Watson v. Fraternal Order of Eagles*, 915 F.2d 235, 244 (6th Cir. 1990).

50. *General Building Contractors Association v. Pennsylvania*, 458 U.S. 375 (1982).

51. *City of Memphis v. Greene*, 451 U.S. 100 (1981).

52. *E.g.*, 42 U.S.C. §§ 1981, 1982, 1983, and 1985.

53. *Sullivan v. Little Hunting Park*, 396 U.S. 229 (1969).

54. 42 U.S.C. § 1988.

55. 18 U.S.C. §§ 241, 242, and 245.

56. *Johnson v. Railway Express Agency*, 421 U.S. 454 (1975).

57. 24 Stat. 380, 49 U.S.C. § 1 *et seq.*, revised, 96 Stat. 2413, 49 U.S.C. § 101 *et seq.*

58. Article 1, Section 8, Clause 3.

59. 49 U.S.C. § 10741.

60. *Cf. Bob-Lo Excursion Co. v. Michigan*, 333 U.S. 28 (1948).

61. *Council v. Western & A.R.R.*, 1 I.C.C. 339 (1887). *Cf. also, Chesa-*

peake & Ohio Railway Co. v. Kentucky, 179 U.S. 388 (1900) and *Plessy v. Ferguson*, 163 U.S. 537 (1896).

62. *Mitchell v. United States*, 313 U.S. 80 (1941).
63. *Morgan v. Virginia*, 328 U.S. 373, 387 (1946).
64. *Henderson v. United States*, 339 U.S. 816 (1950).
65. *Solomon v. Pennsylvania R. Co.*, 96 F. Supp. 709 (D.C.N.Y. 1951).
66. *Lewis v. The Greyhound Corporation*, 199 F. Supp. 210 (M.D. Ala. 1961).
67. *NAACP v. St. Louis-San Francisco Ry. Co.*, 297 I.C.C. 335 (1955).
68. *Keys v. Carolina Coach Co.*, 64 M.C.C. 769 (1955).
69. *Boynton v. Virginia*, 364 U.S. 454 (1960).
70. *Boynton v. Virginia*, 364 U.S. 454, 457 (1960); *United States v. Lassiter*, 203 F. Supp. 20 (W.D. La. 1962), *aff'd*, 371 U.S. 10 (1962).
71. 49 U.S.C. § 11701. *See, NAACP v. St. Louis-San Francisco Ry.*, 297 I.C.C. 335, 346 (1955).
72. *Wright v. Chicago, Burlington & Quincy Railroad Co.*, 223 F. Supp. 660 (N.D. Ill. 1963); *Lyons v. Illinois Greyhound Lines*, 192 F.2d 533 (7th Cir. 1951); *Lassiter v. United States*, 371 U.S. 10 (1962), and *United States v. Jackson*, 318 F.2d 1 (5th Cir. 1963).
73. 49 U.S.C. § 11705.
74. 49 U.S.C. § 11901.
75. *Mitchell v. United States*, 313 U.S. 80 (1941).
76. 49 U.S.C. § 1374(b).
77. *Fitzgerald v. Pan American World Airways*, 229 F.2d 499 (2d Cir. 1956).
78. *United States v. City of Montgomery*, 201 F. Supp. 590 (M.D. Ala. 1962).
79. 78 Stat. 243, Title II, codified as 42 U.S.C. § 2000a *et seq.*
80. 42 U.S.C. § 2000a-1.
81. 42 U.S.C. § 2000a-2.
82. 379 U.S. 241 (1964).
83. *United States v. Gulf State Theaters*, 256 F. Supp. 549 (N.D. Miss. 1966).
84. 42 U.S.C. § 2000a(c).
85. *Katzenbach v. McClung*, 379 U.S. 294 (1964).
86. *United States v. Williams*, 376 F. Supp. 750 (M.D. Fla. 1974).
87. *Heart of Atlanta Motel v. United States*, 379 U.S. 241 (1964).
88. *Smith v. YMCA*, 462 F.2d 634 (5th Cir. 1972).
89. *Dean v. Ashling*, 409 F.2d 754 (5th Cir. 1969).
90. *Rousseve v. Shape Spa for Health and Beauty, Inc.*, 516 F.2d 64 (5th Cir. 1975).
91. *United States v. Degorio*, 473 F.2d 1041 (5th Cir. 1973).

92. *United States v. Medical Society of South Carolina*, 298 F. Supp. 145 (D.S.C. 1969).
93. *United States v. Gramer*, 418 F.2d 692 (5th Cir. 1969).
94. *United States v. Cantrell*, 307 F. Supp. 259 (E.D. La. 1969).
95. *United States v. Skidmore*, 1 R.R.L. Sur. 267 (M.D. Fla. 1969).
96. *Durham v. Red Lake Fishing and Hunting Club, Inc.*, 666 F. Supp. 954 (W.D. Tex. 1987).
97. *Miller v. Amusement Enterprises*, 394 F.2d 342 (5th Cir. 1968).
98. *Scott v. Young*, 421 F.2d 143 (4th Cir. 1970).
99. *Evans v. Seamen*, 452 F.2d 749 (5th Cir. 1971).
100. *Wesley v. Savannah*, 294 F. Supp. 698 (S.D. Ga. 1969).
101. *United States v. Central Carolina Bank and Trust Co.*, 431 F.2d 972 (4th Cir. 1970).
102. *United States v. Beach Associates, Inc.*, 286 F. Supp. 801 (D. Md. 1968).
103. *Fazzio Real Estate Co. v. Adams*, 396 F.2d 146 (5th Cir. 1968).
104. *Twitty v. Vogue Theatre Corp.*, 242 F. Supp. 281 (M.D. Fla. 1965).
105. *Adickes v. S. H. Kress & Co.*, 398 U.S. 144 (1970).
106. *United States v. Beach Associates, Inc.*, 286 F. Supp. 801 (D. Md. 1968).
107. *Newman v. Piggie Park Enterprises*, 390 U.S. 400 (1968).
108. *Hamm v. Rock Hill*, 379 U.S. 306 (1964).
109. *Daniel v. Paul*, 395 U.S. 298 (1969).
110. *Presley v. Monticello*, 395 F.2d 675 (5th Cir. 1968).
111. *Robertson v. Johnston*, 249 F. Supp. 618 (E.D. La. 1966).
112. *Bell v. Kenwood Golf and Country Club*, 312 F. Supp. 753 (D. Md. 1970).
113. *United States v. Williams*, 376 F. Supp. 750 (M.D. Fla. 1974).
114. *Bonomo v. Louisiana Downs, Inc.*, 337 So. 2d 553 (La. App. 1976).
115. *Tillman v. Wheaton-Haven Recreation Association, Inc.*, 410 U.S. 431 (1973).
116. 42 U.S.C. §§ 2000a(b)(1) and (e).
117. *United States v. Lansdowne Swim Club*, 713 F. Supp. 785, 796 (E.D. Pa. 1989), *aff'd*, 894 F.2d 83 (3d Cir. 1990).
118. *Daniel v. Paul*, 395 U.S. 298, 301 (1969).
119. *Tillman v. Wheaton-Haven Recreational Association, Inc.*, 410 U.S. 431 (1973).
120. *Anderson v. Pass Christian Isles Golf Club*, 488 F.2d 855 (5th Cir. 1974).
121. 42 U.S.C. § 2000a-3(a).
122. 42 U.S.C. § 2000a-5(a).

170   *The Rights of Racial Minorities*

123. *Id.*, at § 2000a-3(b), applied in *Newman v. Piggie Park Enterprises,* 390 U.S. 400 (1968).
124. 42 U.S.C. § 2000a-6(b).
125. *Tillman v. Wheaton-Haven Recreation Association, Inc.*, 367 F. Supp. 860 (D. Md. 1973), *rev'd on other grounds*, 517 F.2d 1141 (4th Cir. 1975).
126. 42 U.S.C. § 2000a-3(c).
127. *Harris v. Ericson*, 457 F.2d 765 (10th Cir. 1972).
128. 42 U.S.C. § 2000a-6(a).
129. *Harris v. Ericson*, 457 F.2d 765 (10th Cir. 1972).
130. 42 U.S.C. § 2000g.
131. 42 U.S.C. § 2000a-3(d).
132. 42 U.S.C. § 2000g-2.
133. 42 U.S.C. § 2000a-2.
134. *City of Greenwood v. Peacock*, 384 U.S. 808 (1966) and *Georgia v. Rachel*, 384 U.S. 780 (1966), construing the removal provisions of 28 U.S.C. § 1443.
135. *United States v. Johnson*, 390 U.S. 563 (1968).
136. 78 Stat. 246, codified as 42 U.S.C. § 2000b *et seq.*
137. 42 U.S.C. § 2000b-2.
138. *E.g., United States v. Wyandotte County*, 480 F.2d 969 (10th Cir. 1973).
139. The attorney general also has authority under 42 U.S.C. § 2000h-2 to intervene in any suit to enforce the equal protection of the Fourteenth Amendment.
140. *State v. Brown*, 112 Kan. 814, 212 P. 663 (1923).
141. *Coleman v. Middlestaff*, 147 Cal. App. 2d 833, 305 P.2d 1020 (1957).
142. *Delaney v. Central Valley Golf Club*, 289 N.Y. 577, 43 N.E.2d 716 (1942).
143. *Alsberg v. Lucerne Hotel Co.*, 46 Misc. 617, 92 N.Y.S. 851 (1905).
144. *United States Jaycees v. Massachusetts Commission Against Discrimination*, 391 Mass. 594, 463 N.E.2d 1151 (1984).
145. *Schwenk v. Boy Scouts of America*, 275 Or. 327, 551 P.2d 465 (1976).
146. *Gibbs v. Arras Bros.*, 222 N.Y. 332, 118 N.E. 857 (1918).
147. *Roberts v. United States Jaycees*, 468 U.S. 609, 628 (1984).
148. *Board of Directors of Rotary International v. Rotary Club*, 481 U.S. 537 (1987).
149. *New York State Club Association v. City of New York*, 487 U.S. 1 (1988).

VII

Federally Assisted Discrimination

Government assistance is often given to institutions or organizations that practice racial discrimination. Sometimes, for example, free textbooks are provided to public or private schools that exclude or assign pupils on the basis of race; tax exemptions are granted to all-white private clubs; or money is given to support the programs of private and public entities that discriminate. Not only is the underlying discrimination in these instances unlawful or contrary to national public policy, but the provision of government assistance to the discriminatory is a separate, independent violation of the law.

One of the remedies for unconstitutional provision of government assistance is simply to terminate the financial aid. Indeed, even threatened termination of aid frequently eliminates the underlying discrimination itself. As a federal judge has stated, "Stopping the flow of lifeblood [federal money] to a body [recipient of that money] is certainly more fatal than enjoining that body from certain activity."[1] This chapter explores the advantages and methods of pursuing various remedies against governmentally assisted discrimination, including seeking termination of federal funding.

Is government assistance to organizations and institutions engaged in discrimination very widespread?

Yes. Government assistance to institutions and organizations, many of which are engaged in discrimination, is a common phenomenon. There are three main types of government assistance. First, tax abatement: private clubs and not-for-profit organizations receive substantial government assistance in the form of tax exempt status and income tax deductibility of contributions. Second, direct grants: public and private schools receive funding from the Department of Education (DOE); state and local governments receive public housing funds from the Department of Housing and Urban Development (HUD); hospital and health care facilities receive substantial grants from the Department of Health and Human Services (DHS) and so forth. Third, contracts: private companies and institutions of

higher education receive large government contracts to build
government buildings, undertake government research, and
similar undertakings.

**Is it unconstitutional for government agencies to provide
assistance to organizations or institutions engaged in discrimination?**

Yes. It is unconstitutional under the Fourteenth Amendment
for a state government, and unconstitutional under the Fifth
Amendment for the federal government, to provide assistance
to entities that discriminate. There are, however, several problems in enforcing the law. First, provision of assistance is unconstitutional only if it can be proved that the government is
knowingly and intentionally assisting discrimination. Second,
the only effective means of terminating the unconstitutional
assistance is through a lawsuit against the government.

**Has Congress enacted any laws prohibiting federal govern-
ment agencies from providing assistance to organizations or
institutions engaged in discrimination?**

Yes. Congress has enacted a variety of such laws. The theory
behind this principle was explained by President John Kennedy
in 1963: "Simple justice requires that public funds to which all
taxpayers of all races contribute, not be spent in any fashion
which encourages, entrenches, subsidizes or results in racial
discrimination."[2]

The most important of the federal laws prohibiting federal
agencies from providing assistance to discriminatory organizations and institutions is Title VI of the Civil Rights Act of 1964.[3]
A similar law is the Justice System Improvement Act of 1979,[4]
which applies to the millions of dollars of law enforcement
funding provided by the federal government.[5]

Although these laws have the same objectives and although
the methods of federal enforcement are generally similar, there
are important differences in the ways they are implemented.
Accordingly, each law is discussed separately in this chapter.

THE FIFTH AND FOURTEENTH AMENDMENTS

**What are the Fifth and Fourteenth Amendment prohibi-
tions against government assisted discrimination?**

The Fourteenth Amendment's equal protection clause,

which applies to state and local governments, prohibits them from engaging in intentional discrimination. The Fifth Amendment's due process clause, which applies to the federal government, has been interpreted to prohibit the federal government from engaging in intentional discrimination.[6]

Although the amendments generally are perceived only as prohibiting direct discrimination, they have been interpreted by the courts as prohibiting intentional participation in discrimination by others. This makes sense, of course, since government should not be able to discriminate indirectly when it is prohibited from discriminating directly.

What types of state assistance to discrimination are prohibited by the Fourteenth Amendment?

Generally, all forms of state assistance provided to recipients that the state knows are discriminatory are prohibited by the Fourteenth Amendment. For example, in 1973 the Supreme Court held that the state of Mississippi had violated the Fourteenth Amendment by providing free textbooks to students attending discriminatory private schools.[7] Similarly, courts have held unconstitutional state provision of tuition grants to students attending discriminatory private schools,[8] as well as state provision of tax exempt status to discriminatory private organizations.[9]

What types of federal assistance to discrimination are prohibited by the Fifth Amendment?

The same types of assistance as are prohibited when given by states under the Fourteenth Amendment: generally, all forms of federal assistance provided to recipients that a federal agency knows, or should know, are discriminatory are prohibited by the Fifth Amendment.[10] For example, the courts have held unconstitutional federal funding of discriminatory public housing,[11] and the federal provision of tax exempt status to discriminatory private schools[12] and private clubs.[13] Similarly, a court has held unconstitutional any recognition by the National Labor Relations Board of a discriminatory construction union.[14]

Can a nonprofit private school that practices racial discrimination because of its religious beliefs be denied tax exempt status?

Yes. When the government grants a tax exemption, i.e., excuses an entity from paying income tax and allows persons making a contribution to the entity to take a tax deduction, all taxpayers are affected and may be said to be vicarious "donors" to the entity. Under the circumstances, a tax exemption is justified only if it confers a public benefit. Practicing racial discrimination does not confer a public benefit and is contrary to national public policy. For that reason, the Internal Revenue Service and the courts have denied tax exempt status to entities that practice racial discrimination for whatever reason, including religious beliefs. In one case, for example, the Supreme Court upheld the denial of tax exempt status to Bob Jones University because it prohibited interracial dating and marriage among its students.[15]

Does the denial of tax exempt status to a school or other entity that practices racial discrimination based upon its religious beliefs violate the religious freedom provisions of the First Amendment?

No. Although the denial of tax benefits can certainly have a negative effect on the operation of a school or other entity, it will not prevent it from practicing its religious beliefs. Moreover, the government has a fundamental, overriding interest in eradicating racial discrimination that outweighs whatever burden denial of tax benefits places on the exercise of religion.

How are the Fifth and Fourteenth Amendment prohibitions against unconstitutional government assistance enforced?

Theoretically, each government agency that provides assistance is responsible for ensuring that it does not unconstitutionally aid discriminatory recipients. In practice, however, there is very little constitutional self-enforcement by assisting government agencies. Accordingly, the only effective remedy has been to sue the government agencies that are providing assistance to discriminatory recipients.

Are there any problems facing a person who wants to sue a government agency that is providing assistance to a discriminatory recipient?

Yes. Since such a lawsuit is a big case, an initial problem will be finding a lawyer who is willing to handle this type of litigation. Additionally, there are two significant legal problems. First, when suing under the Fifth and Fourteenth Amendments, the person suing has to prove that the agency being sued has engaged in intentional discrimination.[16] Second, while some lawsuits against federal agencies have been successful,[17] others have been dismissed on the grounds that the persons discriminated against by the recipients were not harmed by the agency providing the assistance and hence did not have legal standing to challenge the agency.[18]

In view of the problems with forcing government agencies to obey their Fifth and Fourteenth Amendment obligations, are there any other methods of terminating federal government assistance to discriminatory recipients and challenging their unlawful practices?

Yes. The other methods involve filing lawsuits directly against the recipients and filing administrative charges of discrimination with the federal agencies providing the assistance. Most federal agencies are governed by civil rights laws that authorize or require the agencies to terminate assistance to discriminatory recipients. The filing of an administrative charge may lead to threatened suspension of funds and ultimately to elimination by the recipient of its discrimination.

TITLE VI OF THE CIVIL RIGHTS ACT OF 1964

What is Title VI of the Civil Rights Act of 1964?

Title VI is one of the group of statutory provisions in the Civil Rights Act of 1964. It provides that no person shall be discriminated against on the basis of race, color, or national origin under any program or activity receiving federal financial assistance. As Senator Hubert H. Humphrey explained when Congress was enacting Title VI, "The purpose of Title VI is to make sure that funds of the United States are not used to support racial discrimination."[19] The ultimate sanction under Title VI is to terminate the violator's federal funding.[20]

How broad is the coverage of Title VI?

Fairly broad. Title VI applies to all federal agencies that make grants (there are approximately thirty) and prohibits discrimination in "any program or activity" receiving federal financial assistance.[21] In *Grove City College v. Bell*[22] the Supreme Court gave a very narrow definition to the "program or activity" language of a similar statute (Title IX of the Education Amendments of 1972) that had been patterned after Title VI and held that discrimination in a particular program or activity of a college didn't subject the institution as a whole to the nondiscrimination provisions of the law. Congress responded to *Grove City* by enacting the Civil Rights Restoration Act of 1987[23] to provide that discrimination is prohibited by Title VI throughout entire institutions or agencies if any part receives federal financial assistance.

For educational institutions, where federal aid is extended anywhere within a college, university, or public system of higher education, the entire institution or system is covered. If federal aid is extended anywhere in an elementary or secondary school system, the entire system is covered.

For state and local governments, only the department or agency that receives the aid is covered. Where an entity of state or local government receives federal aid and distributes it to another department or agency, both entities are covered.

For private corporations, if the federal aid is extended to the corporation as a whole, or if the corporation provides a public service such as social services, education, or housing, the entire corporation is covered. If the federal aid is extended to only one plant or geographically separate facility, only that plant is covered.

For other entities established by two or more of the above-described entities, the entire entity is covered if it receives any federal aid.

Are there any exemptions from coverage of Title VI?

Yes. Despite its breadth, there are two significant exceptions. First, Title VI applies only to federal financial assistance. Specifically exempted are contracts of insurance or guarantees.[24] Thus, for example, banking programs involving federally insured bank deposits are not covered by Title VI. Second, also exempted are employment practices in any program or activity receiving federal aid unless a primary objective of the financial assistance is to provide employment.[25]

How is Title VI enforced?

There are two basic methods of enforcing Title VI: (1) suits by the attorney general and private parties who have been harmed by the discrimination brought directly against the recipients of federal funds;[26] and (2) administrative proceedings by federal agencies for termination of funding or other relief under 42 U.S.C. § 2000d-1.

Some discriminated-against individuals have also sued the funding federal agency, seeking to enjoin it from continuing to support discriminatory entities or programs. These suits have sometimes been successful,[27] but increasingly the courts have dismissed them on a variety of procedural grounds, e.g., the plaintiffs lacked standing, they failed to exhaust administrative remedies, the court lacked power to grant the relief requested,[28] or the court lacked jurisdiction to order a federal agency to terminate its funding.[29]

Which federal agencies are required to enforce the nondiscrimination provisions of Title VI?

Title VI applies to every federal department and agency empowered to extend financial assistance through a grant, a loan, or a contract.[30] For example, Title VI applies to the Department of Education, which provides education grants; it applies to the Department of Housing and Urban Development, which provides grants for public housing and for community improvements; it applies to the Department of Transportation, which provides funding for highways and mass transit; it applies to the Department of Health and Human Services, which supports hospitals and health care facilities; and so forth. Each federal department and agency that extends financial assistance is responsible for its own Title VI enforcement. Coordination of the overall Title VI enforcement effort is provided by the Office for Civil Rights of the Department of Justice.[31] The grant-making agencies covered by Title VI, and the regulations they have promulgated to administer the statute, are listed in appendix A.

Is it necessary to show that a recipient of federal funds was engaged in intentional discrimination to establish a violation of Title VI, or is it sufficient to show that the recipient's practice had a discriminatory effect?

Despite conflicting indications in earlier cases,[32] a majority of the members of the Supreme Court held in *Guardians Association v. Civil Service Commission of City of New York*,[33] that it is not necessary to prove intentional discrimination to prove a violation of Title VI. Practices that have the effect of discrimination also violate the statute.

What remedies are available to the plaintiffs in lawsuits brought under Title VI against recipients of federal funds?

In lawsuits brought by private parties, the prevailing plaintiffs are entitled to declaratory and injunctive relief, e.g., an order declaring the discrimination unlawful and, at least where the discrimination was intentional, compensatory relief such as backpay and damages.[34] In suits by the attorney general, the government is also entitled to declaratory and injunctive relief prohibiting the discrimination and terminating the violator's federal funding. The court can also force the violator to repay the misspent funds.[35]

Must a litigant exhaust any administrative remedies before bringing a Title VI claim in federal court?

No. Despite earlier decisions to the contrary, the courts have held that a litigant need not exhaust any administrative remedies prior to bringing a suit against a recipient of federal funds to enforce Title VI.[36]

How do federal agencies enforce Title VI?

There are two basic methods by which federal agencies enforce Title VI. First, an administrative charge against a recipient filed by or on behalf of a person or class alleging discrimination prompts a federal agency investigation of the alleged discrimination. Second, the agency itself, on its own initiative or in response to a large number of charges, may start a thorough compliance review of the recipient's practices. With either method, the federal agency investigates the recipient and makes a finding of discrimination (noncompliance with Title VI) or of no discrimination (compliance with Title VI).

Since most federal agencies do not initiate Title VI enforcement on their own accord, it is very important that administrative charges of discrimination be filed with the federal agencies. Unfortunately, it usually is very difficult to figure out which discriminatory institutions are receiving federal financial assistance from which federal agencies, and thus it is difficult to know which is the appropriate federal agency to receive the administrative charge. Some situations, however, are easier than others.

For example, all public schools and nearly all public and private institutions of higher education receive substantial federal financial assistance from the Department of Education. Accordingly, a person who has been discriminated against by a school should send an administrative charge of discrimination to the Office for Civil Rights of the U.S. Department of Education in Washington, D.C., or to any regional office of the department.

Similarly, all public housing authorities and all local community development agencies receive federal financial assistance from the Department of Housing and Urban Development. Accordingly, a person who has been discriminated against by a housing authority or a community development agency should send an administrative charge of discrimination to the Office of Fair Housing and Equal Opportunity of the U.S. Department of Housing and Urban Development in Washington, D.C., or to any regional office of HUD.

Because federal agencies provide so many different kinds of federal financial assistance, we have listed in appendix A the names and addresses of the principal federal agencies providing federal financial assistance and thus engaging in Title VI enforcement. A person who has been discriminated against should look in appendix A for the appropriate federal agency and then mail an administrative charge of discrimination to that federal agency.

What are the requirements for filing an administrative charge of discrimination with a federal agency under Title VI?

As noted, federal agency enforcement of Title VI almost always starts with an individual's filing an administrative charge of discrimination. An administrative charge under Title VI is not a formal legal document. There is no prescribed form; a letter is sufficient. The letter should fully describe the nature of the discrimination and name the institution (and its address) and the individuals that have committed the discrimination. The letter should be signed, but it need not be sworn to. And it should be mailed to the appropriate federal agency as soon as possible and not later than 180 days after the discrimination occurred.

What happens once an agency determines that a recipient has engaged in discrimination?

After an agency makes a determination of discrimination, it must take several steps. First, it must seek to obtain voluntary compliance with Title VI from the recipient.[37] This means that the recipient must be given an opportunity to stop its discrimination, rather than having its federal assistance stopped. Second, if voluntary compliance is not achieved, the agency then must start administrative hearings to terminate the federal assistance, or the agency may refer the matter to the Department of Justice for a lawsuit against the recipient.[38] Third, if the agency decides to terminate funding, it must file with the committees of the House and Senate having legislative jurisdiction over the program or activity a report of the circumstances and grounds for the proposed action. Termination becomes effective 30 days after the filing of the report. Although termination or the threat of termination of funds has been effective, particularly in the area of school discrimination, termination is not the only remedy authorized by the statute, and the courts have held that termination is not required.[39] Other remedies, as noted, include referring the case to the attorney general to seek injunctive relief against continuation of the discrimination.

Once a person files a complaint with a federal agency, the agency has the responsibility to enforce Title VI. There is nothing else for the individual to do. It might be helpful, however, to write a letter to the agency once in a while to remind the federal officials that action is expected.

Can a recipient appeal a decision to terminate its funds?

Yes. A recipient of federal funds can appeal the decision of an agency to terminate its funding by filing a petition for review in the court of appeals.[40]

Do the federal agencies extending financial assistance have good reputations for enforcing Title VI?

Their reputations are uneven. Enforcement of Title VI has

often been ineffective because the various federal agencies charged with enforcement have been an integral part of the discriminatory system. Not only have they resisted civil rights goals, but they have often viewed such goals to be against their agency's self-interest or have argued that they had no authority to end the discrimination. One court, for example, strongly criticized HUD for failing to prohibit segregation and of having an attitude of "amiable apartheid" in funding racially segregated public housing.[41]

Given the uneven record of civil rights enforcement by federal agencies providing financial assistance, is it really worth the time and effort to file administrative charges against discriminatory recipients?

Yes. The administrative procedure for terminating federal assistance is still recommended as a means for individuals to assert their civil rights to equal treatment under the law. And the filing of an administrative charge is a very easy step to take since it only involves sending a simple letter.

Are there any advantages to litigation as opposed to seeking an administrative remedy for a violation of Title VI?

Yes. Title VI does not provide a mechanism by which a claimant can actually participate in the administrative process. Moreover, even a finding of a violation by an administrative agency may not include relief for the individual claimant. For example, in a case involving a Gwinnett County, Georgia high school student who filed a complaint of sexual harassment against a teacher under Title IX of the Education Amendments of 1972, which was patterned after Title VI, the Department of Education's Office of Civil Rights (OCR) conducted an investigation and concluded that the school district had violated the student's rights. Nonetheless, after the resignation of the offending teacher and the implementation of a school grievance procedure, OCR determined that the district had come into compliance with Title IX and terminated its investigation. The student later filed a private suit seeking damages for the violation of her rights. The lower courts held that damages were not available, but the Supreme Court reversed and sent the case back to the district court for a trial on the merits of the plaintiff's damages claim.[42] Thus, litigation may under some circumstances be a better route than filing an administrative complaint.

What kind of practices have been held to be covered by Title VI?

Title VI has been held to prohibit a wide variety of practices, including the granting of federal tax benefits to organizations that exclude minorities from membership,[43] and discrimination by the recipients of federal funds in public housing,[44] municipal employment,[45] public schools,[46] farm labor employment programs,[47] state welfare programs,[48] urban renewal,[49] the provision of municipal services,[50] special education programs,[51] processing loan applications by a building and loan association,[52] membership practices of a rural recreation association,[53] and processing the application of a local theater company for federal funds under the Comprehensive Employment and Training Act (CETA).[54]

THE JUSTICE SYSTEM IMPROVEMENT ACT OF 1984

What is the Justice System Improvement Act of 1984?

The Justice System Improvement Act of 1984 (JSIA),[55] the successor to the Omnibus Crime Control and Safe Streets Act of 1968, as amended, is an act of Congress that created a number of federal programs and agencies, including the National Institute of Justice (NIJ), the Bureau of Justice Statistics (BJS), and the Bureau of Justice Assistance (BJA), to assist and improve national, state, and local law enforcement. In furtherance of these goals, the NIJ, BJS, and BJA are authorized to make grants (in the millions of dollars) to private and public entities, such as state law enforcement and rehabilitation agencies, police departments, and correctional facilities.

Does the JSIA prohibit discrimination in programs or activities funded under the act?

Yes. The JSIA, in addition to being subject to Title VI, is an example of a statute that contains separate provisions for enforcing nondiscrimination in federally assisted programs. The act, at 42 U.S.C. § 3789d(c), provides that no person shall be discriminated against or denied employment on the basis of race, color, religion, national origin, or sex, in any program or activity funded in whole or in part under the act.

How are the nondiscrimination provisions of the JSIA enforced?

Section 3789d(c) is enforced administratively by the Office of Justice Programs (OJP), a coordinating agency created by the JSIA, and by lawsuits brought by the attorney general and aggrieved private parties.

How does the Office of Justice Programs enforce the act?

Administrative enforcement by the OJP is fairly complex. Briefly, however, once the OJP learns that a recipient is engaging in discrimination, either as a result of its own investigation or a finding by a federal or state court or administrative agency, it is required to notify the chief executive of the state or unit of local government involved within 10 days and request the chief executive to secure compliance. If at the conclusion of 90 days compliance has not been secured, the OJP must notify the attorney general and cause to have suspended further payment of JSIA funds to the discriminatory program or activity. The suspension is effective for 120 days but may become permanent if the OJP finds after notice and opportunity for hearing that the recipient is not in compliance with section 3789d(c).[56]

The OJP is also required to suspend funding within 45 days after the attorney general files a lawsuit alleging a violation of section 3789d(c), unless the defendant secures a preliminary injunction from the court ordering a resumption of payment.[57]

Under what circumstances can payment of suspended funds be resumed?

Payment of suspended funds can be resumed if (1) the affected state or local unit of government enters into a compliance agreement with the OJP and the attorney general; (2) the recipient has been judged to be in compliance by a federal or state court or administrative agency; or (3) the OJP concludes after a hearing that noncompliance has not been determined.[58]

Can the recipient take any action to seek to avoid termination of its funding?

Yes. Prior to the suspension of funds, but within the ninety-day period after notification of noncompliance, the affected entity may request an expedited preliminary hearing before an administrative law judge. If the judge determines that the state or unit of local government would likely prevail at a full hearing on the merits, she shall defer suspension of funds.

The recipient may also request a full hearing before the OJP. If the OJP makes a finding of compliance, payment of the suspended funds is resumed. If the finding is of noncompliance, the OJP must notify the attorney general, cause to have terminated the payment of funds, and, where appropriate, seek the repayment of expended funds.[59] Any state or local unit of government aggrieved by a final determination of the OJP may appeal to the federal circuit court.[60]

How does the attorney general enforce the JSIA?

Whenever the attorney general has reason to believe that a recipient is engaging in a pattern or practice of discrimination, he may bring a civil action in the federal district court. The court is authorized to grant injunctive relief against continuation of the discrimination, including suspension, termination, or repayment of the JSIA funds.[61]

How do private parties enforce the nondiscrimination provisions of the act?

Any person aggrieved by a recipient of funds under the JSIA may file a lawsuit in federal district court. In addition to injunctive relief, a prevailing plaintiff is entitled to recover reasonable attorneys' fees.[62]

Must a private party exhaust any administrative remedies before filing suit?

Yes. Prior to filing a lawsuit an aggrieved party is required to file an administrative complaint with the OJP or other appropriate administrative enforcement agency.[63] Administrative remedies are deemed exhausted, however, upon the expiration of 60 days, or sooner if the OJP or agency makes a determination on the merits of the complaint. There is no prescribed form for the administrative charge of discrimination; a letter is sufficient. It should fully describe the nature of the discrimination and should state the name and address of the agency that has engaged in the discrimination. The letter need not be sworn to, but it should be signed. Filing is accomplished by mailing the letter to the Office of Justice Programs of the U.S. Department of Justice in Washington, D.C.

Do the civil rights enforcement provisions of the JSIA differ from those in Title VI?

Yes. The civil rights enforcement provisions of the JSIA are different from those in Title VI, in that they require investigations, determinations of noncompliance or compliance, and suspension and termination of funding—all within set time periods. There is also no exemption, as there is in Title VI, for employment discrimination.

Before finding a violation of the JSIA, does the OJP have to make a finding of intentional discrimination?

No. The JSIA prohibits discrimination that has a discriminatory effect, as well as that which has a discriminatory purpose.[64]

Have the OJP and its predecessors done a good job investigating charges and making determinations of discrimination?

Not particularly. During the early years of its existence the predecessor of the OJP did a poor job of enforcing the antidiscrimination provisions of the law. It was for that reason that Congress amended the act to require termination of federal funding to discriminatory recipients. Prior to the amendment, the enforcing agency never applied for sanctions, had never held a compliance hearing, and never promulgated procedures for such a hearing.[65]

NOTES

1. *United States v. Chicago*, 549 F.2d 415, 448 (7th Cir. 1977) (Pell, J., dissenting), *cert. denied*, 434 U.S. 875 (1978).
2. 109 Cong. Rec. 11161 (June 19, 1963).
3. 42 U.S.C. §§ 2000d *et seq.*
4. 42 U.S.C. § 3711 *et seq.*, successor to the Omnibus Crime Control and Safe Streets Act of 1968, as amended.
5. The Revenue Sharing Act of 1972, which also had stringent nondiscrimination provisions, was repealed in 1986. 100 Stat. 327, Pub. L. No. 99-272.

6. Although the Bill of Rights (which applies to the federal government) nowhere contains a guarantee of equal protection of the laws, the courts consistently have applied equal-protection principles through the due process clause of the Fifth Amendment. *E.g., Bolling v. Sharpe,* 347 U.S. 497 (1954).

7. *Norwood v. Harrison,* 413 U.S. 455 (1973).

8. *Coffey v. State Educational Finance Commission,* 296 F. Supp. 1389 (S.D. Miss. 1969) and cases cited at 1390 n.1.

9. *Pitts v. Department of Revenue for Wisconsin,* 333 F. Supp. 662 (E.D. Wis. 1971).

10. *National Black Police Association, Inc. v. Velde,* 712 F.2d 569, 580–83 (D.C. Cir. 1983).

11. *Hills v. Gautreaux,* 425 U.S. 284 (1976).

12. *Green v. Kennedy,* 309 F. Supp. 1127 (D. D.C. 1970) (three-judge court) and *Green v. Connally,* 330 F. Supp. 1150 (D.D.C.) (three-judge court), *aff'd sub nom., Coit v. Green,* 404 U.S. 997 (1971).

13. *McGlotten v. Connally,* 338 F. Supp. 448 (D.D.C. 1972) (three-judge court).

14. *NLRB v. Mansion House Center Management Corp.,* 473 F.2d 471 (8th Cir. 1973).

15. *Bob Jones University v. United States,* 461 U.S. 574 (1983).

16. *E.g., Village of Arlington Heights v. Metropolitan Housing Development Corp.,* 429 U.S. 252 (1977); *Washington v. Davis,* 426 U.S. 229 (1976).

17. *NAACP, Western Region v. Brennan,* 350 F. Supp. 1006 (D.D.C. 1973); *Young v. Pierce,* 628 F. Supp. 1037 (E.D. Tex. 1985); *Hills v. Gautreaux,* 425 U.S. 284 (1976).

18. *Simon v. Eastern Kentucky Welfare Rights Organization,* 426 U.S. 26, 40–6 (1976); *Allen v. Wright,* 468 U.S. 737 (1984). *See also Abramson v. Bennett,* 707 F. Supp. 13, 17 (D.D.C. 1989).

19. 110 Cong. Rec. 6544.

20. *Regents of the University of California v. Bakke,* 438 U.S. 265, 284 (1978)(Powell, J.).

21. 42 U.S.C. § 2000d.

22. 465 U.S. 555 (1984).

23. 102 Stat. 28, 42 U.S.C. § 2000d-4a.

24. 42 U.S.C. § 2000d-4.

25. 42 U.S.C. § 2000d-3; *Valentine v. Smith,* 654 F.2d 503 (8th Cir. 1981).

26. *Guardians Association v. Civil Service Commission of City of New York,* 463 U.S. 582 (1983).

27. *Adams v. Richardson,* 356 F. Supp. 92 (D.D.C.), *aff'd,* 480 F.2d 1159 (D.C. Cir. 1973)(requiring the Department of Education to initiate enforcement proceedings under § 2000d-1 against North Carolina's

higher education system); *NAACP, Western Region v. Brennan*, 360
F. Supp. 1006 (D.D.C. 1973)(ordering Department of Labor officials
to remedy discrimination in federally funded state operated farm labor
employment services); *Young v. Pierce*, 628 F. Supp. 1037 (E.D. Tex.
1985)(allowing plaintiffs to sue HUD for knowingly maintaining a
system of racially segregated public housing in 36 East Texas counties).

28. *Abramson v. Bennett*, 707 F. Supp. 13, 16, 17 (D.D.C. 1989).
29. *National Black Police Association, Inc. v. Velde*, 712 F.2d 569, 576-77 (D.D.C. 1983).
30. 42 U.S.C. § 2000d-1.
31. Exec. Order No. 12250. The attorney general's coordinating regulations are at 28 C.F.R. § 42.401 *et seq.*
32. *Cf. Lau v. Nichols*, 414 U.S. 563, 568 (1974), with *Regents of the Univ. of California v. Bakke*, 438 U.S. 265 (1978). *See also, e.g.*, Department of Health and Human Services' implementing regulation, 45 C.F.R. § 80.3(b)(2).
33. 463 U.S. 582 (1983).
34. *Consolidated Rail Corporation v. Darrone*, 465 U.S. 624, 630 (1984); *Franklin v. Gwinett County Public Schools*, 112 S. Ct. 1028, 1035 (1992).
35. *Guardians Association v. Civil Service Commission of City of New York*, 463 U.S. 582, 603 n.24 (1983).
36. *Neighborhood Action Coalition v. Canton, Ohio*, 882 F.2d 1012, 1015 (6th Cir. 1989) and cases cited; *Young v. Pierce*, 628 F. Supp. 1037 (E.D. Tex. 1985).
37. 42 U.S.C. § 2000d-1.
38. *Id.*
39. *National Black Police Association, Inc. v. Velde*, 712 F.2d 569, 576–77 (D.D.C. 1983).
40. 42 U.S.C. § 2000d-2; *Gardner v. State of Alabama*, 385 F.2d 804 (5th Cir. 1967).
41. *Young v. Pierce*, 628 F. Supp. 1037, 1056 (E.D. Tex. 1985).
42. *Franklin v. Gwinnett County Public Schools*, 112 S. Ct. 1028 (1992).
43. *McGlotten v. Connally*, 338 F. Supp. 448 (D.D.C. 1972).
44. *Hills v. Gautreaux*, 425 U.S. 284 (1976); *Young v. Pierce*, 628 F. Supp. 1037 (E.D. Tex. 1985).
45. *Association Against Discrimination in Employment v. The City of Bridgeport*, 479 F. Supp. 101 (D. Conn. 1979).
46. *Serva v. Portales Municipal Schools*, 499 F.2d 1147 (10th Cir. 1974).
47. *NAACP, Western Region v. Brennan*, 360 F. Supp. 1006 (D.D.C. 1973).
48. *Gardner v. State of Alabama*, 385 F.2d 804 (5th Cir. 1967); *Player v. State of Alabama*, 400 F. Supp. 249 (M.D. Ala. 1975).

49. *Garrett v. City of Hamtramck*, 503 F.2d 1236 (6th Cir. 1974).
50. *Neighborhood Action Coalition v. Canton, Ohio*, 882 F.2d 1012 (6th Cir. 1989).
51. *S-1 By and Through P-1 v. Turlington*, 646 F. Supp. 1179 (S.D. Fla. 1986).
52. *Laufman v. Oakley Building & Loan Co.*, 408 F. Supp. 489 (S.D. Ohio 1976).
53. *Hawthorne v. Kenbridge Recreation Association, Inc.*, 341 F. Supp. 1382 (E.D. Va. 1972).
54. *Hudson Valley Freedom Theater, Inc. v. Heinbach*, 671 F.2d 702 (2d Cir. 1982).
55. 42 U.S.C. § 3711, *et seq.*
56. 42 U.S.C. § 3789d(c)(2).
57. 42 U.S.C. § 3789d(c)(2)(E); *United States v. County of Milwaukee*, 449 F. Supp. 949 (E.D. Wisc. 1978); *United States v. City of Los Angeles*, 595 F.2d 1386 (9th Cir. 1979).
58. 42 U.S.C. § 3789d(c)(2)(D).
59. 42 U.S.C. § 3789(c)(2)(F) and (G).
60. 42 U.S.C. § 3789d(c)(2)(H).
61. 42 U.S.C. § 3789d(c)(3).
62. 42 U.S.C. § 3789d(c)(4).
63. 42 U.S.C. § 3789d(c)(4)(A); *Nash v. City of Oakwood, Ohio*, 541 F. Supp. 220 (S.D. Ohio 1982).
64. *United States v. Commonwealth of Virginia*, 620 F.2d 1018, 1024–25 (4th Cir. 1980).
65. *National Black Police Association, Inc. v. Velde*, 712 F.2d 569 (D.D.C. 1983).

VIII
Jury Selection and Trials

Racial discrimination in the administration of justice has been chronic. Not only have physical facilities such as courtrooms and prisons and jails been segregated, but minorities were traditionally deemed not competent to serve on juries, were denied employment in law enforcement, and because of limited opportunities for education, had virtually no chances to become members of the bar, judges, or prosecutors. The inevitable consequence of racially exclusive justice was that minorities were not simply denied the protection of the law, they were frequently its victims.

This chapter will focus primarily on discrimination in jury selection and trials, for it is through the institution of trial by jury that citizens have an opportunity to exercise direct control over the administration of justice and ensure its fairness.

What are the basic federal laws that protect minorities against discrimination in the administration of justice?

Minorities are protected against discrimination in the administration of justice by the Sixth Amendment, which guarantees a fair and impartial trial; by the Fourteenth Amendment, which prohibits intentional discrimination by public officials; by a Reconstruction-era statute making it a crime to exclude any person from jury service because of race or color;[1] by the Federal Jury Selection and Service Act of 1968, which prohibits racial discrimination in federal jury selection;[2] and by a provision of the Civil Rights Act of 1968 making it a crime willfully to interfere with any person who has served as a juror.[3]

CONSTITUTIONAL PROTECTION AGAINST DISCRIMINATION IN THE ADMINISTRATION OF JUSTICE

How are juries chosen?

Jury selection varies from state to state, but generally involves several common, distinct steps. Selection officials, often called *jury commissioners*, meet periodically and compile master lists of persons in the jurisdiction eligible to serve on juries. Eligibility is variously defined but includes those who meet age, residency, and other requirements and are free of any specified disability, such as felony conviction, insanity, or physical infirmity. Selection laws also allow exemptions that may be claimed by individuals who have hardships or hold critical employment. In compiling the master lists, the commissioners typically consult voter rolls, telephone directories, and other like sources or even add the names of personal acquaintances. The names on the master lists are then placed in separate boxes or wheels for grand and trial juries, from which they are drawn and placed on lists, or *venires*, as jurors are needed for particular terms of court. Finally, the parties to a lawsuit are permitted to "strike" a juror from the venire by asking the court to excuse persons for prejudice or other cause or by excusing a predetermined number peremptorily for no stated cause at all.

Does the Constitution protect against racial discrimination in jury selection?

Yes. Perhaps no right of minorities has been more constitutionally protected, at least in theory, than the right to be free of racial discrimination in jury selection. As early as 1880, the Supreme Court reversed the conviction of a black man by a West Virginia court because state law had disqualified blacks from sitting on his jury. The disqualification was found to be stigmatizing to the defendant and "a stimulant to that race prejudice which is an impediment to securing . . . equal justice" in violation of the Fourteenth Amendment.[4]

Discrimination in jury selection also offends the Sixth and Fourteenth Amendments right to representative juries drawn from a cross section of the community and the right of all citizens to be considered on a basis of equality for jury duty.[5] Not only are those eligible for jury service found in every stratum of society, but the jury is a democratic institution deriving its legitimacy from the fact that it is representative of the community. To allow the exclusion of racial minorities would tend to establish the jury as an instrument of the racially privileged and to that extent would undermine it as an institution of democratic government. In addition, discrimination in jury selection destroys the appearance of fairness and casts into doubt the integrity of the entire judicial process.[6]

Is there any difference in the scope of protection against discrimination in jury selection provided by the Sixth and the Fourteenth Amendments?

Yes. Both the Sixth and the Fourteenth Amendments guarantee the right to a jury selected from a fair cross section of the community.[7] Proof of a racially discriminatory purpose, however, is required for a Fourteenth, but not a Sixth, Amendment violation. In addition, the Sixth Amendment applies only to criminal trial juries, while the Fourteenth Amendment is broader in scope and covers all forms of intentional discrimination in jury selection. The Fourteenth Amendment may also be enforced in civil proceedings by minorities who have been excluded from jury service.

How does a criminal defendant establish a violation of the fair cross-section requirement of the Sixth Amendment?

To establish a violation of the Sixth Amendment's fair cross-section requirement, a defendant must show that the excluded group is "distinctive," that the group's representation on the venires from which juries are selected is not fair and reasonable in relation to the number of such persons in the community, and that the underrepresentation is due to systematic exclusion of the group in jury selection, i.e., it is inherent in the particular jury selection process used. When a defendant establishes these facts the exclusion is deemed unconstitutional, unless the state can justify the infringement by proving that attaining a fair cross section would be incompatible with a significant state interest.[8]

Must the defendant be a member of the excluded group to raise a Sixth Amendment fair cross-section claim?

No. The Sixth Amendment entitles every defendant to object to a venire that is not designed to represent a fair cross section of the community, whether or not the excluded group is one to which the defendant belongs.[9]

How is a violation of the Fourteenth Amendment in jury selection established?

A challenger can prove a violation of the Fourteenth Amendment in jury selection by direct evidence of intentional discrimination or by establishing a *prima facie* case (or presumption of) discrimination by statistical evidence showing the substantial underrepresentation of a distinct class among those summoned for jury duty over time. The assumption is that if the disparity is sufficiently large, it likely did not occur because of accident or chance, but race or other class-related factors played a part in selection. Evidence that selection procedures are susceptible of abuse or are not racially neutral can support the presumption of discrimination raised by the statistical evidence. The burden then shifts to the defendant to rebut the challenger's case and show that no discrimination in fact occurred.[10]

What kinds of intentional discrimination have been found to violate the Fourteenth Amendment?

The early jury cases, such as the one from West Virginia, involved total exclusion, but later decisions make clear that any purposeful discrimination against minorities in jury selection violates the Fourteenth Amendment. Examples of discriminatory practices found to be unconstitutional include the token inclusion or restriction of the number of minorities on lists of persons eligible for jury duty;[11] the selection of jurors from segregated tax digests;[12] placing the names of black and white jurors on different colored tickets so that race could be identified prior to juror selection;[13] assigning blacks to special jury panels;[14] and placing blacks at the end of jury lists so that they would be called last, if at all.[15]

Has the same degree of underrepresentation been required to establish a probable fair cross-section violation of the Sixth as well as the Fourteenth Amendments?

Yes. The courts have generally applied the same standards for underrepresentation to jury composition challenges whether brought under the Sixth or the Fourteenth Amendment.[16] An argument can be made, however, that different standards should apply. Since statistical disparity is relevant in Fourteenth Amendment cases as circumstantial evidence of discriminatory intent, where direct evidence of intent is present any required disparity or impact should be minimal. In Sixth Amendment cases, where intent is irrelevant, a disparity too small to raise an inference of discriminatory intent may none the less be large enough to violate the fair cross-section goal.

How large must a disparity in minority representation on juries be to establish a probable violation of the fair cross-section standard of the Constitution?

In one leading case, *Swain v. Alabama*,[17] the Supreme Court indicated that a disparity as great as 10 percent between blacks in the population and blacks summoned for jury duty would not prove a prima facie case of unconstitutional underrepresentation under the Fourteenth Amendment. Conversely, the case has generally been read to mean that disparities in excess of 10 percent *would* establish a probable violation of the fair cross-section standard under either the Sixth or Fourteenth Amendments.[18]

Swain has been criticized both for tolerating a relatively large disparity and for the formula it used for calculating underrepresentation. This is called the *absolute deficiency* standard, by which the percent of blacks summoned was merely subtracted from the percentage of blacks in the population presumptively eligible for jury duty. This standard may be an acceptable measure where the percent of the group in the general population is relatively large. However, it does not give a true measure of underrepresentation when the excluded group is small. For example, if the excluded group were 20 percent of the population and 10 percent of those summoned for jury duty, the absolute deficiency would be only 10 percent, whereas in fact the group would be underrepresented by one-half. Where the group was 10 percent or less of the population, its total exclusion would apparently not violate the literal application of the *Swain* standard.

To meet the limitations of the absolute deficiency standard, some courts have used a *comparative deficiency* test for measuring underrepresentation, by which the absolute disparity is divided by the proportion of the population comprising the specified category.[19] Using the 20 percent population/10 percent summoned example above, the comparative deficiency test would yield a 50 percent underrepresentation of minorities. The courts that have used the comparative deficiency standard have not adopted a maximum tolerable deviation similar to the one in *Swain*.

Another technique for measuring underrepresentation that has won some judicial support is the *absolute impact standard*, which focuses on persons who serve on juries rather than percentages in the abstract. Using this technique, the absolute disparity is multiplied by the number of persons on a given venire or panel. For instance, if the absolute disparity is 10 percent and a grand jury panel is made up of 24 persons, the absolute impact is a reduction of 2.4 minority grand jurors on any average panel. Using this analysis, the courts have rejected jury composition challenges where the procedures used did not alter the composition of an average grand or trial jury by more than one or two minority jurors.[20]

The Supreme Court has also referred to, without adopting, another method of evaluating underrepresentation in jury selection, the *statistical probability* test.[21] The test measures representativeness by calculating the probability of a disparity occurring by chance in a random drawing from the population. If the probability is low, the conclusion is warranted that the disparity did not occur by chance but was caused by intentional discrimination. The statistical probability test involves relatively complicated calculations of probabilities and standard deviations and must generally be done by an expert statistician.[22]

In summary, the courts have not adopted a single mathematical formula or standard for measuring underrepresentation in all jury selection cases. Instead, they have looked at the particular facts of each case, taking into account the size of the minority group relative to the general population and other relevant factors, in order to develop a distortion-free picture of the group's participation in jury selection and to determine whether a prima facie case of exclusion or a violation of the fair cross section standard has been made.[23]

Is it easy for local officials to rebut a prima facie showing of intentional discrimination in jury selection?

No. Once a prima facie case of discrimination is established, selection officials then have the burden of proving that selection procedures were racially neutral. Mere protestations of good faith that no discrimination, intentional or otherwise, was practiced are not sufficient to rebut a prima facie case. Otherwise, the right to equal service upon juries would be illusory, for public officials can hardly be expected to admit to violations of the law. Neither the administrative convenience of jury commissioners nor their subjective notions about who might be willing to serve have been found adequate to overcome a prima facie case on the theory that officials have a duty not to pursue a course that operates in fact to exclude minorities.[24] Rebuttal might be made, however, by showing that the under-represented group was not proportionately available or eligible for jury duty because of age or similar disqualification.

Is the fact that some jury selection officials are members of a racial minority enough to overcome a prima facie case of discrimination?

No. Because human behavior and motivation are complex, the courts will not presume as a matter of law that members of racial minorities will not discriminate against other members of their own group. In *Castaneda v. Partida*,[25] for example, a jury discrimination case from Texas, the Supreme Court ruled that a prima facie case of exclusion of Mexican Americans was not rebutted, even though three of the five jury commissioners were Mexican American, the judge who appointed the commissioners and later presided over the defendant's trial was Mexican American, both grand and trial juries included Mexican Americans, and a majority of local elected officials were Mexican American. The Court refused to assume without evidence that where a minority was in fact the "governing majority" no discrimination could exist and concluded that the only way discriminatory intent could be rebutted was "with evidence in the record about the way in which the commissioners operated and their reasons for doing so."[26]

Which racial minorities are protected from discrimination in jury selection?

In order to claim the protection of the Fourteenth Amendment in jury selection, the group in question must establish that it is a recognizable, distinct class, singled out for different treatment under the laws, as written or applied. Applying this test, the Supreme Court has found African Americans and Mexican Americans to be clearly identifiable racial classes.[27]

Lower federal and state courts have found other racial groups entitled to equal protection status including Puerto Ricans,[28] "non-Caucasians,"[29] Native Americans,[30] and those with "Spanish-sounding names."[31]

Are jury laws constitutional if they require the selection of persons for jury duty who are "upright and intelligent" or of "good character and sound judgment"?

Yes. The charge has been made that subjective standards for jury selection allow officials to give effect to their beliefs that racial minorities are generally inferior to whites and less likely to measure up to the statutory requirements, but the Supreme Court has held such laws to be constitutional.[32] The Court reasoned that the statutes do not refer to race and are capable of being administered on a nondiscriminatory basis. While the use of such laws in fact to exclude minorities is plainly prohibited, the statutes themselves are not unconstitutional merely because they vest a certain amount of discretion in selection officials.

May jury commissioners impose their own standards, in addition to or different from those set out by applicable statutes, in selecting jurors?

No. Selection officials may not use standards different from those prescribed by law in selecting jurors, even though their motives may be to choose "the best" jurors or excuse people for whom service would be inconvenient.[33] They are required, rather, to comply strictly with applicable laws, both as to selection procedures and substantive standards.

May jury commissioners use source lists for jurors, such as voter registration or tax lists, which underrepresent minorities?

Yes and no. No source list may be used for juror selection which itself is discriminatory or which fails reasonably to reflect a cross section of the population.[34] Thus, the use of segregated tax digests in drawing grand and trial jurors has been held to be unconstitutional.[35] By the same token, use of voter registration lists from which minorities have been excluded should also be unconstitutional. Where the right of registration is fully open, however, the courts have consistently approved the use of voter lists either as the sole or primary source for jurors, even though they underrepresent minorities and even in jurisdictions in which there has been a long history of discrimination in registering and voting.[36] The courts have thus far concluded that there is no violation of the fair cross-section requirement where there is merely underrepresentation of a cognizable group by reason of its failure to register to vote.[37] An additional justification for use of voter lists has been the practical one that, in spite of their deficiencies, they are among the most broadly based lists available. That justification does not, however, explain why multiple or supplementary lists should not be required where voter lists are in fact underrepresentative.

Must individual grand and trial juries exactly reflect the various minority groups in the population?

No. As long as juries are drawn from a source that is fairly representative of the community, there is no additional requirement under the Constitution that jurors actually chosen for particular cases must exactly mirror the community and reflect all the various racial groups in the population.[38]

Is discrimination in jury selection still a significant problem?

Yes. In many jurisdictions, minorities remain underrepresented in the jury system. Because selection procedures are complex, they allow for the exploitation, deliberate or otherwise, of the historic disadvantages of the minority community, such as lower rates of voter registration and the entire heritage of separate but equal. Discrimination can occur at any step in the selection process, whether in choosing source lists, determining eligibility or granting exemptions, compiling master lists, or even as we have seen in selecting names from the box or wheel and assigning persons to particular venires. Although the law of nondiscrimination in jury selection has always been plain, the continuing and steady stream of jury litigation is tribute to the enduring problem of racial discrimination in this crucial phase of the administration of justice.

How are constitutional challenges raised to discrimination in jury selection?

Challenges to discriminatory jury selection practices may be raised in affirmative civil suits under the Fifth or Fourteenth

Amendments by those who have been excluded from jury service because of their minority status,[39] by potential parties in civil cases who desire representative cross sectional juries,[40] as well as by criminal defendants at their trials or in post-conviction proceedings. Although no court has apparently so held, members of majority groups included on jury lists should also have standing to complain of exclusion of racial minorities because of the unequal burden of jury service such practices cast upon them.

What is the remedy for discrimination in jury selection?

The prevailing parties in affirmative civil suits are entitled to declaratory and injunctive relief prohibiting continuing discrimination and requiring selection officials to recompile constitutional jury lists that adequately represent a cross section of the community.[41] Attorneys' fees are authorized for prevailing parties against state defendants.[42] Criminal defendants who prove racial discrimination in selection of their juries are entitled to have the indictments against them dismissed and their convictions, if any, reversed.[43] They may, however, be reindicted and retried but only by procedures that conform to constitutional requirements.[44]

In recompiling jury lists to remedy past discrimination, how close must the percentages be between minority members eligible to serve on juries and those actually on the master jury lists?

The Supreme Court has not adopted a specific mathematical formula but has said that in correcting past underrepresentation, the courts have not merely the power but the duty to render a decree that will so far as possible eliminate the discriminatory effects of the past.[45] Lower federal courts in implementing this directive have rejected the argument based upon *Swain v. Alabama* that a 10 percent disparity is tolerable in a remedial list, drawing a distinction between proving discrimination in the first instance and measuring the adequacy of a remedy for discrimination once it has been found to exist. Accordingly, selection officials are held to a very high standard of comparability between population percentages and those on jury lists in correcting past underrepresentation.[46] Unless there is some compelling reason why such a high degree of comparability cannot be achieved, there seems no reason to tolerate any deviation at all.

Is a criminal defendant required to show actual prejudice to be entitled to a new trial where racial minorities have been excluded or underrepresented in trial jury selection?

No. The Supreme Court has held that due process and equal protection are denied by circumstances that create the likelihood or the appearance of bias in the trial of a case.[47] Moreover, illegal jury-selection procedures cast such doubt on the integrity of the whole judicial process that convictions secured in violation of constitutional selection norms may not stand, irrespective of a showing of actual prejudice in a particular case.[48]

Is discrimination in grand jury selection rendered harmless by a defendant's subsequent trial and conviction by a properly constituted trial jury?

No. Because of the overriding need to eliminate discrimination in the charging process, as well as the difficulty of determining its effect on any given defendant, the Supreme Court has adhered to its long-standing rule that discrimination in the selection of the grand jury is not cured by a subsequent trial before a properly constituted trial jury.[49] The defendant's remedy in such a case is reindictment and retrial by grand and trial juries that have been selected in conformity with the Constitution.

Is discrimination in the selection of the foreman of the grand jury grounds for a new trial?

No. While discrimination in the selection of grand jury foremen is forbidden by the Constitution, the Supreme Court has held that the discrimination is harmless and does not entitle a defendant to reindictment or a new trial.[50] A majority of justices took the view that the grand jury foreman's role was ministerial and that discrimination in the selection of that position could have little effect upon the defendant's due process right to fairness. Three of the justices dissented on the grounds that in view of the great potential for harm in an unconstitutional jury selection system, the strong interests of the defendant in avoiding that harm, and the unique position of influence held by the foreman, any doubt should be resolved in favor of applying standards that are too stringent rather than too lax.

Is there a particular time during a criminal proceeding when the issue of discrimination in grand and trial jury selection must be raised?

Yes. Great care should be taken in criminal cases to raise the issue of discrimination promptly and in the manner prescribed by federal or state law. In federal prosecutions, Rule 12(b)(2) of the Federal Rules of Criminal Procedure requires that all challenges to the grand jury be raised by motion prior to trial. If the motion is made after trial, the defendant is deemed to have waived objection except for "cause shown." *Cause* is a technical term that means that the defendant had a legally valid excuse for not objecting. In addition to showing cause, the defendant must also show the case was actually prejudiced by the discrimination in grand jury selection.[51]

Most states have procedural rules comparable to Rule 12(b)(2) requiring criminal defendants to make contemporaneous objections to any defects in their trials. These state rules have been upheld by the Supreme Court with the result that any error in the trial, including discrimination in grand and trial jury selection, is deemed waived as a matter of state and federal law unless the defendant can show both "cause and prejudice" for the failure to make a timely objection.[52]

Is it difficult to show "cause and prejudice" for failing to raise the issue of jury discrimination in a timely manner?

Yes, but not impossible. The courts have indicated that the requisite cause for failing to object to jury discrimination in a timely manner would exist where the defendant's attorney was incompetent or physically incapacitated, where the underlying facts or the legal basis for a challenge were reasonably unknown, where state officials interfered in some way with the defendant's ability to comply with the contemporaneous objection requirement, or to prevent a miscarriage of justice, e.g., the conviction of one who is actually innocent.[53]

Prejudice has been held to flow from the fact of intentional discrimination in jury selection and from the likelihood that the outcome of the trial would have been different but for the claimed error.[54]

Are such courtroom practices as segregated seating and refusing to use courtesy titles when addressing blacks permissible?

No. Segregation in seating and other discriminatory courtroom practices such as referring to black witnesses and defendants solely by their first names violate equal protection under the Fourteenth Amendment.[55]

May a decision to prosecute ever be based on a person's race?

No. The courts have repeatedly held that while the prosecution has broad discretion, it may never decide to prosecute based on a defendant's race.[56]

May race ever be considered in determining guilt or sentence?

Not if race is being considered in an invidious or discriminatory manner. Historically, state laws made race a factor in assessing guilt or in determining sentence. During the days of Jim Crow, it was generally a crime to integrate common carriers, prisons, and jails.[57] But in no situation was race more crucial in determining guilt or sentence than in violations of laws regulating sexual conduct and marriage. Alabama, for example, had one statute that punished fornication between members of the same race by imprisonment for six months but had another statute punishing fornication between members of different races by imprisonment for two to seven years. The statutory scheme was initially upheld in 1883 by the Supreme Court on the grounds that all persons, black or white, who committed violations were punished the same.[58] Eighty-one years later, however, the Court concluded that such a narrow view of equal protection had been "swept away" and invalidated a Florida statute that made it a crime for an interracial couple to live in and occupy the same room at night.[59] The Court found no compelling justification for the racial classification and held it to be invidious discrimination forbidden by the Fourteenth Amendment. Subsequently, the Court struck down Virginia's miscegenation statutes (which made interracial marriage a crime) on the grounds that mere equal application of a racial classification was not enough to remove it from the reach of the Fourteenth Amendment and that the definition of criminal conduct could not be made to turn on the color of a person's skin.[60] Many state criminal statutes embodying discriminatory racial classifications remain on the statute books, but there is little doubt that they would be declared unconstitutional if challenged today.

Is a sentence unconstitutional if the defendant shows by statistical evidence that racial considerations may have entered into the discretionary deliberations of the jury?

No. The problem of racial discrimination in discretionary sentencing, as opposed to racial classifications written into the law, has been very difficult to remedy. Race has often made the difference in sentences handed down in cases involving black defendants and white victims. One of the most documented instances of the discriminatory imposition of sentencing is use of the death penalty against blacks for the crime of rape. Although more than half of all convicted rapists were white, of 455 men executed for rape since 1930, 405 (nearly 90 percent) were black.[61] (In 1977 the Supreme Court ruled that the death penalty for rape was disproportionate and excessive in violation of the cruel and unusual punishment clause of the Eighth Amendment.[62]) Blacks have also been disproportionately executed for other nonhomicidal crimes, such as robbery, assault by a life prisoner, and burglary. Of 3,984 persons executed for all crimes since 1930, 2,113 were black—more than 50 percent of the total and five times the proportion of blacks in the population.[63] While the rate of crime among blacks is higher than among other groups, numerous studies have documented that the higher execution rate of blacks is also due to the operation of racial factors in the capital sentencing scheme.[64] No court, however, has ever held that such a statistical showing of discrimination would render unconstitutional the death penalty in a given case.[65]

In a 1987 case from Georgia, *McClesky v. Kemp*,[66] involving a black defendant who had been given a death sentence for killing a white police officer, the statistical evidence showed that defendants charged with killing white victims were 4.1 times as likely to receive a death sentence as defendants charged with killing blacks. Black defendants were also 1.1 times as likely to receive a death sentence as other defendants. Despite this evidence, which the Court accepted as true, a majority held that the death sentence was not unconstitutionally imposed. According to the Court, in order to prevail the defendant would have to show that the jury in his case acted with a discriminatory purpose or that the state enacted or maintained the death penalty because of an anticipated racially discriminatory effect. Since the defendant showed only that there was a risk that his sentence had been imposed for racial reasons, he failed to prove unconstitutional discrimination. Four of the Justices dissented and questioned "the depth of moral commitment among the living" in approving a capital sentencing system that was admittedly affected to some extent by racial bias.[67]

STATUTORY PROTECTION AGAINST DISCRIMINATION IN JURY SELECTION

Do any federal criminal statutes specifically protect minorities from discrimination in jury selection?

Yes. An early federal criminal statute, enacted in 1875, makes it a crime for any person charged with any duty in selecting or summoning jurors to exclude persons from jury service in any state or federal court because of race or color.[68] The penalty for violation of the act is a fine of not more than $5,000.

A second criminal statute enacted as part of the Civil Rights Act of 1968 makes it a crime for any person to interfere willfully with another who has served as a juror. Those convicted of violating the statute may be fined not more than $1,000 or imprisoned not more than one year or both; and if bodily injury results they may be fined not more than $10,000 or imprisoned not more than ten years or both; and if death results they may be subjected to imprisonment for any term of years or for life.[69]

Have the criminal laws against jury discrimination been effectively enforced?

No. In spite of the volume of jury litigation in the courts and the admitted discrimination that has occurred against minorities, there has been only one reported prosecution under the 1875 act, that of a Virginia state judge in 1878 who refused to consider blacks for jury duty in his court. In that case, the Supreme Court sustained the indictment and found the act to be a proper exercise of congressional power under the Fourteenth Amendment to protect the right to an impartial jury trial by jurors "indifferently selected" without discrimination because of their color.[70]

Are there any federal civil statutes designed specifically to protect minorities from discrimination in jury selection?

Yes. The Federal Jury Selection and Service Act of 1968 (Federal Jury Act) declares it to be national policy that all litigants have the right to grand and trial juries in the federal courts selected at random from a fair cross section of the community and that all citizens have the opportunity for consideration for jury service. In furtherance of that policy, the act prohibits exclusion of any person from service upon grand and trial juries in federal courts on account of race, color, religion, sex, national origin, or economic status. Each federal trial court is required to devise a written plan for random selection of jurors designed to achieve the statutory objective of representativeness. No plan may be put into operation until it has been reviewed and approved by a panel of the members of the judicial council of the circuit and the chief judge of the district whose plan is being reviewed or his or her designee.[71]

What general provisions must be included in jury plans required to be adopted by the Federal Jury Act?

The selection plans devised under the Federal Jury Act must provide for establishment of a jury commission or authorize the clerk of court to manage the jury selection process. They must specify whether jurors are to be selected from voter registration lists or lists of actual voters and whether any other additional source of names is to be used to ensure that a representative cross section of the community is chosen. Detailed procedures must be specified to ensure random selection of a fair cross section, including provision for the excuse of individuals for whom service would entail "undue hardship or extreme inconvenience" and exemption of those "in the public interest," such as members of fire or police departments or the armed forces.[72] Through use of qualification forms mailed to those who have been randomly selected, a "qualified jury wheel" must be prepared containing the names of all those determined to be eligible and not excused or exempted from jury duty.[73] Persons are required to be publicly drawn at random from the qualified jury wheel, assigned to grand and trial jury panels, and summoned for service.

Can persons be required to give their race in responding to federal juror questionnaires?

No. The Federal Jury Act provides, however, that the forms sent to prospective jurors elicit such information as address, age, occupation, etc., as well as race. The purpose of gathering racial data is solely to aid in the enforcement of nondiscrimination in jury selection and has no bearing on an individual's qualification for jury service. Accordingly, each juror questionnaire must contain words clearly informing the person that the furnishing of any information with respect to race or national origin is not a prerequisite to qualification for jury service and need not be furnished if the person finds it objectionable to do so.[74]

Is there a constitutional, as opposed to a statutory, requirement that juries be randomly selected in addition to representing a cross section of the community?

No. Random selection is required for federal juries by the Federal Jury Act, but there is no separate, constitutional requirement that either federal or state juries be randomly selected.[75]

Is the fair cross-section standard of the Federal Jury Act the same as that of the Sixth and Fourteenth Amendments?

Yes. The courts have held that the test for determining a violation of the fair cross-section standard of the statute is the same as that for determining violations of the analogous provisions of the Constitution.[76]

How is the Federal Jury Act enforced?

The Federal Jury Act is enforced by parties to federal trials and by the attorney general. Either may file motions in civil or criminal cases to dismiss or stay the proceedings on the grounds of "substantial failure" to comply with the provisions of the act.[77] The motion must be accompanied by a sworn statement of facts describing the failure to comply and must be filed before the voir dire (examination of jurors) begins or within seven days after the noncompliance was discovered or could have been discovered by the exercise of diligence, whichever is earlier. Great care must be taken to follow the procedures prescribed, for they are the only means by which a party may challenge a jury on the ground that it was not selected in conformity with the act. The absolute insistence by the courts on strict and complete compliance with procedural requirements has inevitably resulted in hardships to individual litigants who did not know until after their trials that selection officials had not complied with the act.[78]

Are all failures of selection officials to comply with the Federal Jury Act and local selection plans deemed substantial and thus unlawful?

No. Mere technical violations of the act or those that involved good faith efforts to comply and that do not affect the random nature or objectivity of the selection process and that do not frustrate the goals of the act are not regarded as "substantial."[79] Thus, a grand jury selection in which the drawing took place in a room in the clerk's office that, though open to the public, contained only clerk personnel was not deemed a substantial failure to comply with the act's requirement that jurors be "publicly" drawn from the jury wheel.[80]

What kinds of failures in compliance with the Federal Jury Act have been regarded as substantial?

In one case, a district court in Georgia had a rule that if there was an unexpected shortage of trial jurors drawn from the qualified jury wheel, the deficiency could be made up by asking jurors who had served at the previous term of court to volunteer for additional service. The court of appeals declared the policy to be in violation of the Federal Jury Act on the ground that a volunteer was quite the opposite of a person selected at random.[81]

In another case, the failure of selection officials in Guam to require prospective jurors to answer questions in the juror questionnaire was deemed a substantial failure to comply with the act, requiring dismissal of an indictment. The procedures used were found to create a serious risk that jurors selected were not proficient enough in English to understand the proceedings and did not represent a fair cross section of the community.[82]

In addition to showing substantial noncompliance with the Federal Jury Act, must a challenger also show prejudice or show that the violation tended to exclude some racial group?
No. Once it has been established that selection officials failed substantially to conform to the requirements of the Federal Jury Act, it is not necessary that the challenger show actual or specific prejudice to his or her case. Congress, in passing the act, was more concerned that regular procedures be established to ensure that juries were representative than that individual challengers show actual prejudice arising from statutory violations. Thus, a departure from the statutory scheme that affects randomness is a distinct violation independent of its impact in a particular case.[83]

Does the fact that a jury selection plan has been approved by the judicial council of a federal court of appeals foreclose challenge to the plan or the representativeness of jury lists?
No. Approval of a jury selection plan by a federal judicial council does not validate the plan. Not only does the Federal Jury Act itself provide procedures by which a party may attack the validity of a plan, making such an attack proper, but serious constitutional issues would be presented by substituting judicial council approval for judicial determination in a live case presented by adversary parties.[84]

What are the remedies for noncompliance with the Federal Jury Act?
The only remedy for noncompliance provided by the Federal Jury Act is a court order staying the proceedings pending selection of a new grand or trial jury or dismissing the indictment, whichever is appropriate.[85]

Are the challenge procedures in the Federal Jury Act also the sole means of attacking constitutional infirmities in jury selection?
No. The Federal Jury Act specifically provides that nothing in the act shall preclude any person or the United States from pursuing any remedy, civil or criminal, that may be available

for the vindication or enforcement of any law prohibiting discrimination on account of race, color, religion, sex, national origin, or economic status in the selection of persons for service on grand or trial juries. Failure to comply with the statute does not, therefore, preclude resort to other remedies to enforce the Constitution's ban on race discrimination.[86]

ADDITIONAL PROTECTIONS AGAINST RACIALLY BIASED TRIALS

Does a defendant have the right to question prospective jurors prior to trial to determine if they might be racially biased?

Yes, where there is a significant likelihood that racial prejudice might affect the trial or where other special circumstances are present. The right, called the right of *voir dire*, derives from a defendant's entitlement under the Sixth Amendment and under the due process clause of the Fourteenth Amendment to a fair and impartial jury.[87] The right is not absolute. In one case the defendant claimed that South Carolina police officers had framed him on a narcotics charge in retaliation for his civil rights activities. Under the circumstances, the Supreme Court held it was an error not to allow questions to be asked of prospective jurors specifically directed to racial prejudice.[88] In another case the Court found special circumstances requiring voir dire directed to possible racial prejudice where the crime charged was interracial and was a capital offense. Because of the severity and finality of the punishment, the broad discretion entrusted to the jury in sentencing and the risk of racial prejudice infecting the proceeding, the Court acknowledged a right of voir dire on possible racial prejudice of jurors.[89] In a third case from Massachusetts, however, in which the only racial factor was assault by a black on a white security guard, the Court held that a general inquiry into the impartiality of potential jurors was sufficient and no specific questions related to race were required to be asked.[90]

What remedy does a defendant have if a prospective juror admits, or is suspected of having, racial bias?

If a potential juror admits to racial bias that would preclude the rendering of a fair and impartial verdict, then the juror is disqualified from service and must be excused for cause by the court.[91]

Jurors who deny racial bias, or whom the court refuses to excuse for cause, may still be excused by the defendant through exercise of what are called *peremptory challenges*. Peremptory challenges may ordinarily be used for any or no reason at all, but are designed to rid the jury of real or suspected bias and to ensure that jurors will decide cases solely on the basis of evidence before them. There is no constitutional right to peremptory challenges, but their use is provided in all jurisdictions and is deeply rooted in our jury system.

Do both sides get peremptory challenges? How many?

Yes, both sides get them. In federal felony trials, the defendant gets ten and the prosecution six peremptory challenges, while in misdemeanor trials each side is entitled to three peremptory challenges.[92] The practice in state trials may be different, and local rules or statutes should be consulted.

May a prosecutor use peremptory challenges to exclude blacks from service on a particular jury panel?

No. In *Batson v. Kentucky*,[93] decided in 1986, the Court ruled for the first time that it was a violation of the equal protection clause of the Fourteenth Amendment for a prosecutor to exclude minority jurors in a particular case because of their race. Prior to *Batson* a defendant could prevail in a challenge to the misuse of peremptory challenges only by showing a pattern and practice of exclusion of blacks in case after case, whatever the circumstances, whatever the crime, and whomever the defendants or victims may be.[94] This rule had been increasingly criticized by both state and lower federal courts because of the nearly impossible burden of proof it placed on minority defendants and because it tolerated discrimination in jury selection. A new rule was warranted, according to the Supreme Court, to strengthen respect for our system of criminal justice and to ensure that no citizen was disqualified from jury service because of race.

Must the defendant be a member of the excluded group to raise a *Batson*-type claim?

No, provided the claim of exclusion is based on the Four-

teenth Amendment.[95] The answer is otherwise if the basis of
the claim is limited to the Sixth Amendment. A plurality of the
Supreme Court has held that the Sixth Amendment requirement of a fair cross section on the venire was to ensure an
impartial, not a representative, jury and that it did not violate
the amendment for the prosecution to use peremptory challenges to eliminate minority jurors it believed would favor the
defendants.[96] Given the different treatment by the Court of
claims of misuse of peremptory challenges depending upon
whether they were based upon the Sixth or Fourteenth
Amendments, a defendant would obviously be advised to base
any *Batson*-type claim of discrimination on the Fourteenth
Amendment.

**Has the discriminatory use of peremptory challenges by the
prosecution been widespread?**
Yes. According to the Supreme Court the practice of peremptorily eliminating blacks from trial juries in cases with black
defendants has been, and remains, widespread.[97]

**What is a defendant's remedy for the discriminatory use of
peremptory challenges?**
Without expressing a preference, the Supreme Court indicated in *Batson v. Kentucky* that upon a finding of discrimination the trial court should discharge the venire and select a new
jury from a panel not previously associated with the case or
disallow the discriminatory challenges and resume selection
with the improperly challenged jurors reinstated on the venire.

How does a defendant go about raising a *Batson*-type claim?
A defendant should take care to raise any objections to a
prosecutor's discriminatory use of challenges in a timely manner, i.e., as soon as the misuse becomes apparent and certainly
no later than before the jury is sworn.[98] Otherwise, the right
to challenge the discrimination may be deemed waived. Other
than that, because of the variety of jury selection practices used
in the state and federal courts, the Supreme Court has not
imposed any particular procedures for implementing the holding in *Batson*, leaving such procedures to be developed by the
lower courts in subsequent litigation.[99]

How does a defendant prove discrimination in the prosecution's use of peremptory challenges?

To establish a prima facie case of discrimination, the defendant must show that the prosecutor exercised strikes to remove persons of one race or ethnicity from the jury. Proof of these facts and any other relevant circumstances, such as evidence of a pattern of strikes against other minorities or the prosecution's questions and statements during the voir dire examination of jurors, raises an inference of purposeful discrimination and shifts the burden to the prosecution to prove a racially neutral reason related to the particular case to be tried for striking the minority jurors. While the prosecution's explanations need not rise to the level of justifying the excuse of a challenged juror for cause, mere denials of discrimination, or statements that the challenged jurors would be partial to the defendant because of their shared race, would be insufficient to rebut a prima facie case. The trial judge must then determine, based upon all the evidence, if the defendant has established purposeful racial discrimination.

Is a defendant entitled to an adversarial hearing on a *Batson* claim?

Yes, in most cases and provided the defendant has established a prima facie case of discrimination. Adversarial proceedings are the norm in our system of criminal justice and ex parte proceedings are a disfavored exception.[100] Lower courts have generally concluded that a defendant is entitled to an adversarial hearing outside the presence of the jury on a *Batson* claim in all but the most unusual circumstances, as where there might be an overriding need for the court to act quickly or to keep sensitive information from the opposing party.[101] In one case, for instance, the court of appeals held it was proper for the trial court in a drug prosecution case to hold the jury exclusion hearing *in camera*, i.e. in private and without the defendant or defense counsel being present. The trial court's decision of the defendant's *Batson* claim was reviewed by the appellate court based upon the sealed (nonpublic) record of the *in camera* hearing.[102]

What kind of evidence should the court consider in a *Batson* hearing?

The Supreme Court has said that the pattern of strikes against minority jurors and the prosecution's questions and statements during the voir dire examination are examples of relevant evidence of discrimination. Other courts have identified additional factors: whether the prosecution challenged white jurors on grounds similar to those on which minority jurors were challenged;[103] whether the reasons given for striking minority jurors were related to the case;[104] whether the challenged juror was asked meaningful questions; whether the explanation given in fact applied to the challenged juror; and whether the prosecution used fewer than all its peremptory challenges.[105] One court has said that the central question is one of comparability. If blacks are struck for a stated reason but similarly situated whites are not, then the stated reason is racially suspect.[106]

Has it been difficult in practice for the prosecution to meet its burden of rebuttal in *Batson* hearings?

Yes and no, depending on the court in which the claim has been heard. Although the Supreme Court said in *Batson* that the prosecution's explanation of nondiscrimination must be "clear and reasonably specific" and "legitimate,"[107] it later held that "[u]nless a discriminatory intent is inherent in the prosecutor's explanation, the reason offered will be deemed race neutral."[108] In practice some courts have tended to accept any reason offered by the prosecution, provided it was not overtly racial.[109] Others have been more exacting. In one case from Arkansas, for example, the prosecution struck all potential black jurors. In justifying its actions, it said that several of the jurors were unemployed and/or unmarried. In rejecting this as a valid, nonracial explanation for the challenges the court said that "actions sometimes speak louder than words, and any prosecutor who uses all of his peremptory challenges to strike black people better have good reasons available . . . the best answer is for prosecutors to put blacks on juries."[110]

Clearly, if *Batson* is to have any real meaning, a court is obligated to examine available evidence closely to determine if an explanation is in fact bona fide and not merely an excuse contrived after the fact to disguise or rationalize racial discrimination in jury selection.

Is the decision in *Batson* retroactive?

Yes. The rule in *Batson* applies to cases that were pending or were on appeal at the time of the decision. The rule does not apply to convictions that became final before *Batson* was decided.[111]

May a defendant, as opposed to the prosecution, use peremptory challenges to exclude members of a racial group?

No. In a case from Dougherty County, Georgia, in which three whites were charged with assault and battery against two blacks, the defendants indicated that they intended to use their peremptory strikes to exclude blacks from the jury. The prosecution moved for an injunction to prohibit the defendants from exercising their challenges in a racially discriminatory manner but the state courts denied relief. The Supreme Court reversed, holding that if a trial court allows a defendant in a criminal prosecution to exclude jurors on the basis of their race the court "is a willing participant in a scheme that could only undermine the very foundation of our system of justice—our citizens' confidence in it."[112] The Court also held that a defendants' exercise of peremptory challenges was state action for purposes of the Fourteenth Amendment and that the state had standing to raise the jury exclusion issue.

Can a private civil litigant challenge the use of peremptory challenges to exclude persons from jury service on account of race?

Yes. The Supreme Court has held that the action of a private party in a civil action in using peremptory challenges in a racially discriminatory manner is a form of state action in violation of the Fourteenth Amendment because such challenges are authorized by the government and are exercised in the course of a government conducted and regulated trial.[113]

Are there other remedies, in addition to voir dire, for combatting an atmosphere of racial prejudice at trial?

Yes. The courts have recognized that a questioning of potential jurors, no matter how searching and in spite of denials by jurors of prejudice, cannot disclose and neutralize all racial bias jurors might have. Accordingly, defendants may move for a change of venue (place of trial) to a site less affected by prejudice[114] or request postponement of trial until prejudicial feelings may have subsided. The Supreme Court has also indicated that if a conviction is so permeated by racial feelings "that counsel, jury and judge were swept to the fatal end by an irresistible wave of public passion," it violates constitutional standards of due process and cannot be sustained.[115] Very few cases, however, can be expected to meet such a strict standard for reversal or to overcome the problem of waiver inherent in going to trial without having sought to neutralize prejudice through a venue change.

What are the standards for determining whether to grant a change of venue?

In a line of cases beginning in 1959, some of them unrelated to race, the Supreme Court has held that a motion to change venue, based upon the Sixth Amendment's guarantee of an impartial jury and due process, should be granted where there is a "probability" or "reasonable likelihood" of prejudice if the trial is held at the scheduled site.[116]

When must a request for change of venue be made?

In federal trials, Rule 21 of the Federal Rules of Criminal Procedure requires that a motion for change of venue be made before the plea is entered or within such "reasonable time thereafter as permitted by the court." In other trials, local rules will govern and should be scrupulously followed to avoid waiver or by-pass.

How can a defendant prove the likelihood of prejudice to gain a venue change?

A likelihood, or presumption, of prejudice may be shown by evidence of bias in the community;[117] pretrial publicity such as assertions of guilt in the media;[118] and publication of alleged confessions,[119] prior criminal record,[120] allegations of bad character, or evidence in the case.[121] Pretrial publicity emanating from the government or the prosecution is regarded as particularly prejudicial because of the enhanced credibility likely to be attached to it and because of the prosecution's overriding responsibility of providing a fair trial.[122] Evidence of the absence of prejudice in the surrounding jurisdictions should also be developed to assist the court in locating a bias-free alternate site for trial.

Is it easy in practice to show that pretrial publicity might deprive, or has deprived, a defendant of the right to a fair trial before an impartial jury?

No. Not only have the courts held that the burden of showing the likelihood of prejudice from pretrial publicity is an extremely heavy one, but the Supreme Court has ruled that a defendant has no right to question jurors specifically about the contents of publicity they may have read or heard prior to trial.[123] Not surprisingly, cases in which convictions have actually been set aside on the basis of prejudicial pretrial publicity are rare.[124]

Can anything be done to combat prosecutorial bias in a particular case?

Sometimes. If a law is being enforced to discriminate against persons because of their race, the defendant is entitled to have the prosecution dismissed on the grounds of selective enforcement. This doctrine was developed and applied in a famous case decided in 1886, *Yick Wo v. Hopkins*,[125] involving an ordinance of the city of San Francisco that required all laundries to be located in buildings of brick or stone. Two Chinese, Yick Wo and Wo Lee, requested permission to operate their laundries in wooden buildings, were refused, and were subsequently convicted of violating the ordinance. The facts were, however, that two hundred others, all Chinese, had similarly been denied permission to operate laundries in wooden buildings but that eighty others, none of whom were Chinese, had been exempted from compliance with the restriction. Under the circumstances, the Supreme Court held the convictions violated the Fourteenth Amendment and could not stand. According to the Court:

> Though the law itself be fair on its face, and impartial in appliance, yet, if it is applied and administered by public authority with an evil eye and an unequal hand, so as practically to make unjust and illegal discriminations between persons in similar circumstances, material to their rights, the denial of equal justice is still within the prohibition of the Constitution.[126]

Is it difficult to prove selective enforcement of the law?

Yes. The defense of selective enforcement has been exceedingly difficult to establish because of the requirement of proof of intent to discriminate and because the Supreme Court has held that the conscious exercise of "some selectivity" in enforcement of the law by the prosecution does not establish a constitutional violation.[127]

Will the federal courts ever enjoin state court prosecutions or expunge the record of convictions on the grounds of discriminatory, selective enforcement?

Yes, but only in the most limited of circumstances. Generally, federal courts will not interfere with state criminal proceedings because of federal statutory prohibitions[128] and because of the three doctrines of "comity" (respect for state court functions), "equity" (avoiding a duplication of legal proceedings where the defendant has an adequate state court remedy), and "federalism" (a policy of noninterference with legitimate state activities in recognition of the fact that the country is a union of separate state governments).[129]

During the early days of the civil rights movement, federal courts occasionally enjoined state proceedings in extreme cases where the law was clearly being enforced in a discriminatory manner. In one such case, a state prosecution had been brought against a worker with the Student Nonviolent Coordinating Committee (SNNC) who had assisted blacks in registering to vote in Walthall County, Mississippi. The defendant, John Hardy, whose conduct had been entirely peaceful, was assaulted by the voter registrar and charged by the sheriff with "disturbing the peace and bringing an uprising among the people."[130] The court of appeals, relying upon the Civil Rights Act of 1957 prohibiting interference with voting, held that the state proceedings should be enjoined to give the defendant Hardy a chance to prove his allegations that the prosecution was depriving him and other blacks in the county of protected rights.

In a similar case, blacks leaving a voter registration meeting in Dallas County, Alabama, were arrested en masse and charged and prosecuted for improper license-plate lighting. The court of appeals found that the prosecutions had been brought not "to eradicate the sinful practice of driving with burned-out license-plate lights" but solely to harass voting workers and interfere with voter registration, purposes prohibited by the Civil Rights Act of 1957.[131] To remedy the violations, the court ordered county officials to return all fines, expunge from the record all arrests and convictions, and reimburse the defendants for the costs (including reasonable attorneys' fees) incurred in defense of the state criminal prosecutions.

Such cases must be regarded as exceptional, however, for the Supreme Court has more recently indicated that when federal courts are asked to enjoin state proceedings, normally they must refuse. The only exception to the rule is where the state prosecution poses a danger of "irreparable loss" that is "both great and immediate."[132] Such a loss must involve more than prosecution under a law that may be unconstitutional but must include bad faith and harassment or other extraordinary circumstances. Experience has shown that it is very hard, but not impossible, to prove irreparable loss.[133] In a case from DeKalb County, Georgia, the federal district court enjoined a state court prosecution for terroristic threats after finding that the defendants had exercised their First Amendment rights in criticizing county officials, that the prosecutions were brought for harassment and retaliation and would not have been brought but for the improper interference of certain local judges.[134]

Do federal courts have the power to enjoin federal officials from following a deliberate policy of discriminatory investigations and prosecutions?

Yes. Where black voters and elected officials of Alabama's "Black Belt" alleged that the attorney general of the United States and other Department of Justice officials had engaged in a pattern and practice of investigating and prosecuting blacks in an effort to deprive them of their constitutional rights to vote and to associate freely, the court of appeals held it was erroneous for the trial court to dismiss the complaint and prayer for relief without giving the plaintiffs an opportunity to prove their allegations.[135]

Is there any way to remove state prosecutions to the federal courts if it is necessary to protect constitutional rights?

Yes, but the scope of removal has been so narrowed by the Supreme Court as to be almost nonexistent. The present removal statute is a descendant of a portion of the Civil Rights Act of 1866[136] and provides that any civil or criminal action in a state court may be removed by the defendant to the federal district court where the action is pending when the defendant is denied or cannot enforce in the state court a right under any laws providing for the equal civil rights of citizens of the United States. In a series of cases beginning in 1880 and ending in 1906, the Supreme Court established a quite narrow area in which pretrial removal of state prosecutions could be sustained. The cases held essentially that a law providing for equal civil rights referred to in the statute meant a law couched in terms of racial equality, as distinguished from a law of general application such as the due process clause of the Fourteenth Amendment and secondly that the denial or rights protected by such a law must be manifest in a formal expression of state law. Applying this test, removal was proper in a case in which a black defendant was prosecuted in a state court that excluded blacks from jury service.[137]

After 1906 the Supreme Court did not consider the removal statute again until sixty years later, a principal reason being that an order denying removal, or sending the case back to the state court, could not be appealed after the year 1887.[138] As part of the Civil Rights Act of 1964, however, Congress specifically provided for appeals from orders denying removal to give the federal reviewing courts an opportunity to supervise administration of the removal statute.[139] In a pair of cases decided in 1966, the Supreme Court adopted the earlier construction of the removal statute, consigning it once again nearly to the status of dead letter.

The first of the two cases[140] involved black defendants who sought removal of state prosecutions for trespass growing out of sit-in demonstrations at a Georgia restaurant. The Supreme Court held that the prosecutions could be removed, applying the two pronged test developed in the earlier cases. The defendants showed that the law providing for equal civil rights upon which they relied was the Civil Rights Act of 1964 guaranteeing the equal enjoyment of public accommodations and that the right was denied or could not be enforced in the courts of the state because the Civil Rights Act of 1964 granted an absolute right not to be prosecuted for seeking access to public accommodations. The defendants had a right, in other words, not even to be brought to trial on trespass charges in the state court. The case was sent back to the federal district court to establish whether or not the defendants had been ordered to leave the restaurant because of their race or some other reason. If the defendants were correct in their allegation that a racial motivation was present, then their right to removal would be clear.

In the second case, however, the Court denied removal, showing the exceedingly narrow range of cases that could be exempted from state prosecution. The defendants were members of a civil rights group engaged in a Mississippi voter registration drive. They satisfied the law providing for equal civil rights requirement by alleging a denial of equal voting rights under the Civil Rights Acts of 1866 and 1964. The Court concluded, however, that the second requirement, that the right involved would be denied or could not be enforced, was not met since neither of the civil rights acts conferred immunity from state prosecution as did the public accommodations provisions of the Civil Rights Act of 1964, nor did they confer an absolute right for the defendants to engage in the conduct involved, that is, obstructing a public street in connection with voter registration efforts. The Court also held that it was not enough to support removal to prove that the defendants' federal equal civil rights had been illegally and corruptly denied in advance of trial, that the charges were false, or that the defendants would be unable to obtain a fair trial. Removal was proper only in those cases where it could be clearly predicted by reason of the operation of a pervasive and explicit state or federal law, that the protected rights would inevitably be denied by the very act of bringing the defendant to trial in the state court. Such a burden can rarely be carried. The Supreme Court supported the result it reached by observing that federal judges were not permitted "to put their brethren of the state judiciary on trial" and that a contrary holding would revolutionize the relationship of state and federal courts by depriving states of authority to prosecute in certain cases and at the same time dramatically expanding the jurisdiction of the federal courts.[141]

The removal statute was last considered by the court in 1975, when it adhered to its earlier decisions and refused to make any changes in the long-settled interpretation of the provisions of the century-old removal statute.[142]

NOTES

1. 18 Stat. 336, presently codified in 18 U.S.C. § 243.
2. 28 U.S.C. § 1861 *et seq.*
3. 18 U.S.C. § 245.
4. *Strauder v. West Virginia*, 100 U.S. 303, 308 (1880).
5. *Thiel v. Southern Pacific Co.*, 328 U.S. 217 (1946); *Carter v. Jury Commission*, 396 U.S. 320 (1970).
6. *Rose v. Mitchell*, 443 U.S. 545, 555–56 (1979).
7. *Duren v. Missouri*, 439 U.S. 357 (1979).
8. *Id.*, at 364–66.
9. *Holland v. Illinois*, 110 S. Ct. 803, 805 (1990).
10. *Castaneda v. Partida*, 430 U.S. 482 (1977); *Turner v. Fouche*, 396 U.S. 346, 360 (1970); *Alexander v. Louisiana*, 405 U.S. 625, 630 (1972).
11. *Cassell v. Texas*, 339 U.S. 282 (1950). *See also Amadeo v. Zant*, 486 U.S. 214 (1988).
12. *Whitus v. Georgia*, 385 U.S. 545 (1967).
13. *Avery v. Georgia*, 345 U.S. 559 (1953).
14. *Billingsley v. Clayton*, 359 F.2d 13 (5th Cir. 1966).
15. *Smith v. Texas*, 311 U.S. 128 (1940).
16. *United States v. Clifford*, 640 F.2d 150 (8th Cir. 1981); *United States v. Aimone*, 715 F.2d 822 (3d Cir. 1983).
17. 380 U.S. 202 (1965).
18. *Foster v. Sparks*, 506 F.2d 805, 811–37 (5th Cir. 1975)(appendix to the opinion of Judge Walter P. Gewin); *United States v. Rodriguez*, 776 F.2d 1509 (11th Cir. 1985).
19. *Alexander v. Louisiana*, 405 U.S. 625, 629–30 (1972) (using both the absolute and comparative deficiency methods); *Stephens v. Cox*, 449 F.2d 657 (4th Cir. 1971); *Thompson v. Sheppard*, 502 F.2d 1389, 1390 n. 1 (5th Cir. 1974) (Brown, J., dissenting); *Berry v. Cooper*, 577 F.2d 322, 326 n. 11 (5th Cir. 1978); *United States v. Clifford*, 640 F.2d 150 (8th Cir. 1981).
20. *United States v. Suttiswad*, 696 F.2d 645 (9th Cir. 1982); *United States v. Jenkins*, 496 F.2d 57 (2d Cir. 1974).
21. *Castaneda v. Partida*, 430 U.S. 482, 496 n. 17 (1977); *Whitus v. Georgia*, 385 U.S 545, 552 n. 2 (1967); *Alexander v. Louisiana*, 405 U.S. 625, 630 n. 9 (1972).
22. For cases adopting the statistical probability analysis, see *Moultrie v. Martin*, 690 F.2d 1078 (4th Cir. 1982); *Villafane v. Manson*, 504 F. Supp. 78 (D. Conn. 1980).
23. *Cf. United States v. Maskeny*, 609 F.2d 183 (5th Cir. 1980), rejecting comparative and statistical probability disparity in favor of the absolute

disparity approach. For a further discussion of the various techniques for calculating underrepresentation and their use by the courts, see Beale, *Integrating Statistical Evidence and Legal Theory to Challenge the Selection of Grand and Petit Jurors*, 46 Law & Contemp. Probs. 269 (1983).

24. *Alexander v. Louisiana*, 405 U.S. 625, 632 (1972); *Hill v. Texas*, 316 U.S. 400 (1942); *United States v. Zirpolo*, 450 F.2d 424 (3d Cir. 1971).

25. 430 U.S. 482 (1977).

26. *Id.*, at 500.

27. *Strauder v. West Virginia*, 100 U.S. 303 (1880); *Hernandez v. Texas*, 347 U.S. 475 (1954).

28. *United States ex rel. Leguillou v. Davis*, 115 F. Supp. 392 (D.V.I. 1953).

29. *United States v. Fujimoto*, 105 F. Supp. 747 (D. Haw. 1952), *cert. denied*, 344 U.S. 852 (1953).

30. *State v. Plenty Horse*, 184 N.W. 2d 654 (1971).

31. *Montoya v. Colorado*, 141 Colo. 9, 345 P.2d 1062 (1950).

32. *Carter v. Jury Commission*, 396 U.S. 320 (1970); *Turner v. Fouche*, 396 U.S. 346 (1970).

33. *Ballard v. United States*, 329 U.S. 187 (1946); *Labat v. Bennett*, 365 F.2d 698 (5th Cir. 1966), *cert. denied*, 386 U.S. 991 (1967); *Rabinowitz v. United States*, 366 F.2d 34 (5th Cir. 1966).

34. *Brown v. Allen*, 344 U.S. 443 (1953).

35. *Whitus v. Georgia*, 385 U.S. 545 (1967); *Sims v. Georgia*, 389 U.S. 404 (1967).

36. *Simmons v. United States*, 406 F.2d 456 (5th Cir. 1969); *Blackwell v. Thomas*, 476 F.2d 443 (4th Cir. 1973); *Berry v. Cooper*, 577 F.2d 322, 328 n. 16 (5th Cir. 1978).

37. *United States v. Cecil*, 836 F.2d 1431 (4th Cir. 1988)(*en banc*); *United States v. Young*, 822 F.2d 1234 (2d Cir. 1987); *United States v. Gometz*, 730 F.2d 475 (7th Cir. 1984)(*en banc*).

38. *Lockhart v. McCree*, 476 U.S. 162 (1986); *Taylor v. Louisiana*, 419 U.S. 522 (1975). *See also, Teague v. Lane*, 489 U.S. 288 (1989), in which the Court declined to decide whether the fair cross section requirement applied to individual juries.

39. *Carter v. Jury Commission*, 396 U.S. 320 (1970).

40. *Peters v. Kiff*, 407 U.S. 493 (1972); *Taylor v. Louisiana*, 419 U.S. 522 (1975).

41. *Turner v. Fouche*, 396 U.S. 346 (1970); *Carter v. Jury Commission*, 396 U.S. 320 (1970).

42. 42 U.S.C. § 1988.

43. *Whitus v. Georgia*, 385 U.S. 545 (1967).

44. *Hill v. Texas*, 316 U.S. 400 (1942).

45. *Carter v. Jury Commission*, 396 U.S. 320, 340 (1970).
46. *Berry v. Cooper*, 577 F.2d 322 (5th Cir. 1978); *Broadway v. Culpepper*, 439 F.2d 125 (5th Cir. 1971).
47. *Tumey v. Ohio*, 273 U.S. 510 (1927).
48. *Peters v. Kiff*, 407 U.S. 493 (1972).
49. *Rose v. Mitchell*, 443 U.S. 545 (1979); *Vasquez v. Hillery*, 474 U.S. 254 (1986).
50. *Hobby v. United States*, 468 U.S. 339 (1984).
51. *Davis v. United States*, 411 U.S. 233 (1973).
52. *Francis v. Henderson*, 425 U.S. 536 (1976); *Wainwright v. Sykes*, 433 U.S. 72 (1977); *Coleman v. Thompson*, 111 S. Ct. 2546 (1991).
53. *Wainwright v. Sykes*, 433 U.S. 72 (1977); *Reed v. Ross*, 468 U.S. 1 (1984); *Murray v. Carrier*, 477 U.S. 478 (1986); *Coleman v. Thompson*, 111 S. Ct. 2546 (1991); *Sawyer v. Whitley*, 112 S. Ct. 2514 (1992).
54. *Amadeo v. Zant*, 486 U.S. 214, 228 n.6 (1988).
55. *Johnson v. Virginia*, 373 U.S. 61 (1963); *Hamilton v. Alabama*, 376 U.S. 650 (1964). Segregation beyond the courtroom, *i.e.*, in prisons and jails, is also unconstitutional. *Lee v. Washington*, 390 U.S. 333 (1968).
56. *Wayte v. United States*, 470 U.S. 598 (1985).
57. *Plessy v. Ferguson*, 163 U.S. 537 (1896).
58. *Pace v. Alabama*, 106 U.S. 583 (1883).
59. *McLaughlin v. Florida*, 379 U.S. 184 (1964).
60. *Loving v. Virginia*, 388 U.S. 1 (1967).
61. *U.S. Bureau of Prisons, National Prisoner Statistics: Capital Punishment 1930-1970* (Washington, D.C.: U.S. Department of Justice, 1971); *Furman v. Georgia*, 408 U.S. 238, 364 (1972)(Marshall, J., concurring).
62. *Coker v. Georgia*, 433 U.S. 584 (1977).
63. Gross and Mauro, *Death & Discrimination* 17 (1989).
64. *Id.*, at 17–31, 43–94; *Furman v. Georgia*, 408 U.S. 238, 364 (1972)(Marshall, J., concurring).
65. *Moorer v. South Carolina*, 368 F.2d 458 (4th Cir. 1966); *Maxwell v. Bishop*, 398 F.2d 183 (8th Cir. 1968).
66. 481 U.S. 279 (1987).
67. *Id.*, at 344.
68. 18 Stat. 336, presently codified in 18 U.S.C. § 243.
69. 18 U.S.C. § 245(b)(2)(D).
70. *Ex parte Virginia*, 100 U.S. 339 (1880).
71. 28 U.S.C. §§ 1861, 1862, 1863, 1863(a).
72. 28 U.S.C. § 1863(6).
73. 28 U.S.C. § 1866(a).

74. 28 U.S.C. § 1869(h). For a discussion of disclosure of race on state voter registration forms, see chapter 2.

75. *United States v. Kennedy*, 548 F.2d 608 (5th Cir. 1977).

76. *United States v. Pepe*, 747 F.2d 632, 648 n.17 (11th Cir. 1984); *United States v. Herbert*, 698 F.2d 981 (9th Cir. 1983).

77. 28 U.S.C. §§ 1867 and 1867(d).

78. *United States v. Hawkins*, 566 F.2d 1006 (5th Cir. 1978); *United States v. Young*, 822 F.2d 1234 (2d Cir. 1987).

79. *United States v. Davis*, 546 F.2d 583 (5th Cir. 1977); *United States v. Evans*, 529 F.2d 523 (5th Cir. 1976); *United States v. Geelan*, 509 F.2d 737 (8th Cir. 1974).

80. *United States v. Dalton*, 465 F.2d 32 (5th Cir. 1972). *See also United States v. Savides*, 787 F.2d 751 (1st Cir. 1986); *United States v. Gregory*, 730 F.2d 692 (11th Cir. 1984).

81. *United States v. Kennedy*, 548 F.2d 608 (5th Cir. 1977).

82. *United States v. Okiyama*, 521 F.2d 601 (9th Cir. 1975).

83. *Id.; United States v. Coleman*, 429 F. Supp. 792 (E.D. Mich. 1977); *United States v. Armsbury*, 408 F. Supp. 1130, 1143 (D. Or. 1976); *United States v. Kennedy*, 548 F.2d 608 (5th Cir. 1977).

84. 28 U.S.C. § 1867; *United States v. Hyde*, 448 F.2d 815 (5th Cir. 1977).

85. 28 U.S.C. § 1867(d).

86. 28 U.S.C. § 1867(e); *United States v. Kennedy*, 548 F.2d 608 (5th Cir. 1977).

87. *Duncan v. Louisiana*, 391 U.S. 145 (1968); *Irvin v. Dowd*, 366 U.S. 717 (1961).

88. *Ham v. South Carolina*, 409 U.S. 524 (1973).

89. *Turner v. Murray*, 476 U.S. 28 (1986).

90. *Ristaino v. Ross*, 424 U.S. 589 (1976).

91. *Aldridge v. United States*, 283 U.S. 308 (1931).

92. Rule 24(b), Fed. R. Crim. P. In federal cases in which the death penalty is authorized, each side is entitled to twenty peremptory challenges.

93. 476 U.S. 79 (1986).

94. *Swain v. Alabama*, 390 U.S. 202 (1965).

95. *Powers v. Ohio*, 111 S. Ct 1364 (1991).

96. *Holland v. Illinois*, 110 S. Ct. 803 (1990).

97. *Batson v. Kentucky*, 476 U.S. 79, 99, 101–2 (1986).

98. *United States v. Thompson*, 827 F.2d 1254 (9th Cir. 1987); *State v. Jones*, 293 S.C. 54, 358 S.E.2d 701 (1987).

99. *Ford v. Georgia*, 111 S. Ct. 850 (1991).

100. *United States v. Bagley*, 473 U.S. 667 (1985).

101. *United States v. Thompson*, 827 F.2d 1254 (9th Cir. 1987); *United States v. Tucker*, 836 F.2d 334 (7th Cir. 1988); *United States v. Garrison*, 849 F.2d 103 (4th Cir. 1988); *United States v. Rogers*, 850 F.2d 435 (8th Cir. 1988).
102. *United States v. Davis*, 809 F.2d 1194 (6th Cir. 1987).
103. *Garnett v. Morris*, 815 F.2d 509 (8th Cir. 1987); *Gamble v. State*, 257 Ga. 325, 357 S.E.2d 792 (1987).
104. *People v. Hall*, 35 Cal.3d 161, 672 P.2d 854, 197 Cal. Rptr. 71 (1983).
105. *Ex parte Branch*, 526 So. 2d 609 (Ala. 1987).
106. *United States v. Wilson*, 853 F.2d 606 (8th Cir. 1988).
107. *Batson v. Kentucky*, 476 U.S. 79, 98 and n. 20 (1986).
108. *Hernandez v. New York*, 111 S. Ct. 1859, 1866 (1991).
109. *State v. Martinez*, 294 S.C. 72, 362 S.E.2d 641 (1987).
110. *Ward v. State*, 293 Ark. 88, 94, 733 S.W. 2d 728 (1987).
111. *Allen v. Hardy*, 478 U.S. 255 (1986); *Griffith v. Kentucky*, 479 U.S. 314 (1987).
112. *Georgia v. McCollum*, 112 S. Ct. 2348, 2354 (1992).
113. *Edmonson v. Leesville Concrete Co.*, 111 S. Ct. 2077 (1991).
114. *Irvin v. Dowd*, 366 U.S. 717 (1961); *Rideau v. Louisiana*, 373 U.S. 723 (1963); *Groppi v. Wisconsin*, 400 U.S. 505 (1971).
115. *Moore v. Dempsey*, 251 U.S. 86, 91 (1923); *Shepherd v. Florida*, 341 U.S. 50 (1951).
116. *Marshall v. United States*, 360 U.S. 310 (1959); *Estes v. Texas*, 381 U.S. 532 (1965); *Sheppard v. Maxwell*, 384 U.S. 333 (1966).
117. *Johnson v. Beto*, 469 F.2d 1396 (5th Cir. 1972).
118. *Sheppard v. Maxwell*, 384 U.S. 333 (1966); *Coleman v. Kemp*, 778 F.2d 1487 (11th Cir. 1985).
119. *Rideau v. Louisiana*, 373 U.S. 723 (1963).
120. *Marshall v. United States*, 360 U.S. 310 (1959).
121. *Sheppard v. Maxwell*, 384 U.S. 333 (1966).
122. *Henslee v. United States*, 246 F.2d 190 (5th Cir. 1957).
123. *Mu'Min v. Virginia*, 111 S. Ct. 1899 (1991).
124. *Coleman v. Kemp*, 778 F.2d 1487 (11th Cir. 1985).
125. 118 U.S. 356 (1886).
126. *Id.*, at 373–74.
127. *Wayte v. United States*, 470 U.S. 598 (1985); *Oyler v. Boles*, 368 U.S. 448, 456 (1962). *See also United States v. Falk*, 479 F.2d 616 (7th Cir. 1973); *United States v. Steele*, 461 F.2d 1148 (9th Cir. 1972).
128. *E.g.*, 28 U.S.C. § 2283 forbidding injunctions against proceedings in a state court and 28 U.S.C. § 2254, forbidding the issuance of habeas corpus unless the petitioner has exhausted state remedies. Civil rights suits under 42 U.S.C. § 1983, however, are an exception to

the anti-injunction provisions of 28 U.S.C. § 2283. *Mitchum v. Foster*, 407 U.S. 225 (1972).

129. *Younger v. Harris*, 401 U.S. 37 (1971).

130. *United States v. Wood*, 295 F.2d 772, 776 (5th Cir. 1961).

131. *United States v. McLeod*, 385 F.2d 734, 742, 744 (5th Cir. 1967).

132. *Younger v. Harris*, 401 U.S. 37, 46, 54 (1971).

133. *Allee v. Medrano*, 416 U.S. 802 (1974); *Huffman v. Pursue, Ltd.*, 420 U.S. 592 (1975).

134. *Fitzgerald v. Peck*, 636 F.2d 944 (5th Cir. 1981). *See also Lewellen v. Raff*, 843 F.2d 1103 (8th Cir. 1988).

135. *Smith v. Meese*, 821 F.2d 1484 (11th Cir. 1987).

136. 14 Stat. 27, now codified in 28 U.S.C. § 1443(1).

137. *Strauder v. West Virginia*, 100 U.S. 303 (1880); *Kentucky v. Powers*, 201 U.S. 1 (1906).

138. *Georgia v. Rachel*, 384 U.S. 780, 786 (1966).

139. 28 U.S.C. § 1447(d).

140. *Georgia v. Rachel*, 384 U.S. 780 (1966).

141. *Greenwood v. Peacock*, 384 U.S. 808, 828 (1966).

142. *Johnson v. Mississippi*, 421 U.S. 213 (1975).

IX

Federal Criminal Statutes Protecting the Rights of Minorities

One of the most melancholy chapters in the history of race relations in the United States involves the failure of criminal law to protect the lives and property of minorities. That failure was a predictable consequence of racial exclusion in the justice system discussed earlier, as well as the entire way of life that placed a different valuation on people according to the color of their skin. The law, no matter what its theory, in practice worked first and always to protect the rights of whites and only thereafter, if at all, to protect the rights of minorities.

Racial violence and terrorism, the ultimate forms of discrimination, have been rampant and often unobstructed by the normal operation of state laws prohibiting criminal misconduct. During the 1880s and 1890s, for example, there were about 100 reported lynchings of blacks every year in the United States. In 1892 there were 155. Lynchings continued briskly over the next twenty years. There were 75 in 1909, 80 in 1910, 63 in 1911, and rarely less than 50 per year from then until 1923.[1] During the height of the civil rights movement from 1956 to 1965, there were 80 race-related killings of blacks and their white sympathizers.[2] In Mississippi during the summer of 1964 alone there were reports of racial violence involving 35 shootings, 30 bombings, 35 church burnings, and at least 6 murders.[3]

A lynching in 1922 in Moultrie, Georgia, was all too typical of the times. A black man named Will Anderson was suspected of having attempted a criminal attack on a white woman. Before he could be tried, Anderson was seized by a mob, handcuffed, taken to the scene of the crime, shot, and then dragged behind an automobile. A grand jury was hurriedly convened the next day to investigate the lynching, but the panel adjourned after a few hours because it was unable, it said, to get any evidence upon which to base indictments. The Moultrie *Observer*, the town's only newspaper, soft-pedaled the affair and speculated that the lynch mob was small: "It was pointed out that he was not swung to a tree and that he was shot less than twenty-five times. . . . It was hardly believed that this would have been the way the body would have been found if the crowd that participated had been of the proportion mobs usually assume on such occasions."[4] A local judge condemned the violence, but no person was ever charged or tried for Anderson's death.

There are criminal laws, however, enacted by Congress specifically to meet the problem of racial violence and related discrimination against minorities. These laws and their enforcement will be discussed in the following pages.

RECONSTRUCTION-ERA CRIMINAL STATUTES

Have any federal criminal statutes been enacted to give minorities general protection against racial violence and other forms of discrimination?

Yes. Although under our federal system the states are regarded as having primary responsibility for prosecuting criminal offenses, including those that are racially motivated, Congress enacted two laws during the Reconstruction period to give minorities general protection against violence and discrimination. 18 U.S.C. § 242, enacted in 1866, makes it a crime for any person acting "under color of law" willfully to deprive another of any right protected by the Constitution or laws of the United States "by reason of his color, or race."[5] Those convicted may be punished by fine of not more than $1,000 or imprisonment for not more than one year or both. If bodily injury results, the offender may be fined or imprisoned not more than ten years or both; and if death results, the offender may be imprisoned for any term of years or for life.

Four years later, in 1870, Congress enacted a companion statute, 18 U.S.C. § 241, to curb the terrorist activities of organizations such as the Ku Klux Klan and the Knights of the White Camellia, which were becoming increasingly active during the post-Civil War years.[6] Section 241 prohibits conspiracies by two or more persons to injure or intimidate any citizen in the exercise of any right protected by the Constitution or laws of the United States. The section also applies if two or more persons go in disguise on the highway or onto the premises of another with the intent to prevent or hinder the free exercise of protected rights. Those convicted may be punished by a fine or not more than $10,000 or imprisoned for not more than ten years or both. If death results, the offender may be imprisoned for any term of years or for life.

What does "under color of law" mean in section 242?

"Under color of law" refers to a misuse of power possessed by virtue of state or federal law and made possible because the wrongdoer is clothed with the authority of law.[7] Acts are deemed done under color of law even though they may be themselves violations of the law. Thus, a law enforcement officer who beats a prisoner or turns him over to a lynch mob or intentionally fails to protect him from such a mob acts under color of law.[8]

Are private individuals ever subject to prosecution under section 242?

Yes, if they act under color of law, or if they engage in criminal conduct with others who act under color of law. In one case, for instance, several private individuals conspired during the summer of 1964 with the sheriff and deputy sheriff of Neshoba County, Mississippi, to murder three young men, Michael Schwerner, James Chaney, and Andrew Goodman, who had been taken into custody because of their civil rights activities.[9] As part of the conspiracy, the young men were released at night from the jail in Philadelphia, Mississippi, then later intercepted by eighteen people (including the sheriff, the deputy, and the private individuals), taken from their car, and murdered; their bodies were buried in an earthen dam five miles southwest of the city. All eighteen of the conspirators were indicted and found to be acting under color of law for purpose of prosecution under section 242. The deputy, Cecil Ray Price, and six others were eventually convicted in federal court and sentenced to six years in prison for depriving the youths of their civil rights. There were never any state convictions, however, for murder or any other state crime.[10]

Is state action also required for prosecution of conspiracies under section 241?

No. In two cases in 1966, a majority of the Supreme Court indicated, without expressly deciding the question, that Congress had the power to punish all conspiracies that interfere with constitutional rights under section 241—with or without state action.[11] As one of the justices pointed out, Senator Pool of North Carolina, who introduced section 241 into Congress, intended the section to apply to the acts of individuals whether they acted as "officers or whether they are acting upon their own responsibility."[12] Then, in a case decided two years later in 1968, the Court simply assumed without lengthy discussion that section 241 applied to private conspiracies and reversed a trial court that had dismissed indictments against several people who had assaulted blacks seeking to exercise their right to receive service at a restaurant.[13]

What kind of offenses are generally punishable under sections 241 and 242?

The Supreme Court has made it clear that sections 241 and 242 do not make all wrongful acts of racial discrimination federal crimes. Only those acts that are "willful" and deprive a person of some right made specific either by the express terms of the Constitution or laws of the United States or by decisions interpreting them are indictable. The requirement of willfulness was elaborated upon in a 1945 case in which a Georgia sheriff bludgeoned a Negro prisoner to death.[14] The sheriff was indicted for violating section 242 by depriving the prisoner of due process, of a trial by jury, and of the right to be punished in accordance with the law. The indicted sheriff argued that section 242 contained no ascertainable standard for guilt since the definition of constitutional rights, especially the right to due process, was fluid and subject to interpretation by the judiciary. The Supreme Court ruled that the problem of vagueness was cured by requiring the prosecution to prove willfulness—that is, that the sheriff acted with "the purpose to deprive the prisoner of a constitutional right, e.g., the right to be tried by a court rather than by ordeal."[15]

In addition to prosecutions brought against persons who engaged in police brutality and denied due process, prosecutions have been brought under sections 241 and 242 for interference with the right to vote,[16] with the right to perfect a homestead,[17] with the right of federal officers to perform their duties,[18] with the right to be free from involuntary servitude and slavery,[19] with the right to attend school without regard to race or color,[20] with the right to participate in a civil rights protest march,[21] with equal protection under the Fourteenth Amendment, with the full enjoyment of public accommodations, and with the right to interstate travel.[22]

Has the requirement of proving willfulness for violations of sections 241 and 242 proved to be an insurmountable barrier to successful prosecution for denial of constitutional rights?

No. Proof of willfulness has not been as difficult to present as it originally appeared. In a subsequent case involving assault of a black prisoner by state law enforcement officers, the Supreme Court held that willfulness could be inferred from the circumstances of the attack and the relationship between the victim and the officers.[23] The fact remains, however, that requiring proof that a defendant acted willfully to deprive someone of a specific constitutional right, as opposed to showing that the defendant acted in general with a bad purpose, the standard for most criminal prosecutions, has hampered enforcement of sections 241 and 242.[24]

Have sections 241 and 242 been effectively enforced?

Generally, no. Immediately after the Civil War the federal government made a concerted effort to enforce sections 241 and 242 as well as other civil rights laws enacted for the protection of minorities. A number of prosecutions were brought against persons interfering with the rights of blacks to vote in congressional elections and to be secure in their persons and property.[25] However, only about 20 percent of all prosecutions resulted in convictions, while some major decisions severely limited the application of the statutes.[26]

From the turn of the century until 1939, the enforcement of sections 241 and 242 declined dramatically. Only four cases involving section 241 reached the Supreme Court during this period, and none involving section 242.[27]

In 1939, however, a civil rights section was established in the Department of Justice charged with the duty "to pursue a program of vigilant action in the prosecution of infringement" of civil liberties.[28] More prosecutions were brought under sections 241 and 242 than during prior years, and the Supreme Court upheld indictments against election officials who made a fraudulent ballot count[29] and who stuffed ballot boxes in federal elections.[30] But the federal policy of enforcement was for the most part cautious and restrained. Indeed, in one of the first of the modern cases arising under section 242 to reach the Supreme Court, the Justice Department's policy of enforcement was noted to be one of "strict self-limitation" to avoid unnecessary interference by the federal government with the administration of local criminal laws by the states.[31]

CRIMINAL STATUTES PROHIBITING SLAVERY, INVOLUNTARY SERVITUDE, AND PEONAGE

Has Congress made slavery, involuntary servitude, and peonage criminal activities?

Yes. In addition to sections 241 and 242, which are general prohibitions on unconstitutional conduct, Congress enacted a variety of criminal statutes during Reconstruction prohibiting such specific discriminatory practices as slavery,[32] involuntary servitude (compulsory service of one person to another),[33] and peonage (involuntary servitude with the additional factor of indebtedness of one person to another).[34]

Punishments for violations of these statutes range from fines of $2,000 to $10,000 and imprisonment for up to five years.[35]

Are slavery, involuntary servitude, and peonage widespread practices today?

Slavery and involuntary servitude, except in a few isolated cases, no longer exist in this country.[36] Peonage in the form of holding and forcing a person to work to pay off a debt is more common, though admittedly not as widespread as it was during the years following the Civil War, when debt labor was often little more than a substitute for slavery.[37]

The federal peonage statute, though enacted in 1867, lay dormant throughout the nineteenth century, while many states enacted and strictly enforced laws making it a crime for a person to quit work if he owed money to his employer. As a consequence of federal inaction and state enforcement of debt law, the Immigration Commission in 1910 reported that cases of probable peonage had been found in all but two states in the Union.[38] Maine was said to have had the most complete system of peonage in the entire country in its lumber camps.

In 1905 the first case under the antipeonage statute reached the Supreme Court and the statute was held constitutional.[39] A series of subsequent cases struck down state laws in Alabama, Georgia, and Florida that made it a crime for a person to fail to perform work for which he had been paid.[40] In the last of these cases, decided in 1944, the Court reversed the state court conviction of a black laborer who had received a five dollar advance but failed to perform promised work. The states are free to punish fraud, the Court held, but "no state can make the quitting of work a component of a crime, or make criminal sanctions available for holding unwilling persons to labor."[41] The employer's remedy for failure to perform work for which he has paid was said to be a suit for breach of contract.

With the demise of state debt labor statutes and the establishment of the Civil Rights Section of the Department of Justice in 1939, peonage has steadily declined. Many of the modern cases involving peonage and the included offense of involuntary servitude have been brought against labor camp operators who used physical force or the threat of force to hold migrant agricultural workers in a state of virtual slavery.[42]

Are there forms of compulsory service that are constitutional?

Yes. Neither the draft,[43] compulsory civilian labor as an alternative to military service,[44] jury duty,[45] nor hard labor pursuant to a lawful prison sentence[46] violate the Thirteenth Amendment's ban on slavery and involuntary servitude.[47]

MODERN CRIMINAL STATUTES

Has there been any modern federal legislation imposing criminal penalties for interference with minority rights?

Yes. Congress enacted 18 U.S.C. § 245 as part of the Civil Rights Act of 1968[48] providing for criminal penalties for willful interference by force or threat with certain enumerated rights and activities. The statute prohibits anyone, whether or not acting under color of law, from injuring or interfering with one who has voted, campaigned for office, or qualified as an election official; participated in any federal program; applied for or secured federal employment; served as a grand or trial juror;

or participated in any program receiving federal assistance. The statute also proscribes racial discrimination in public schools and colleges; in state programs; in employment by states, private individuals, or labor unions; in jury duty; in interstate commerce; and in public accommodations. Persons who interfere with interstate commerce during riot or civil disorder are also subject to prosecution, as are those who intimidate others participating in speech and assembly opposing racial discrimination. The penalties for violation of the statute are a fine of not more than $1,000 or imprisonment for not more than one year or both. If bodily injury occurs the fine may be up to $10,000 or imprisonment for not more than ten years or both while if death results, imprisonment may be for any term of years or for life.

Has section 245 been effectively enforced?

Only partially. The sweep of section 245 appears to be great, but a number of provisions considerably restrict its application. In an obvious attempt to minimize friction resulting from federal prosecution of civil rights offenders, the statute provides that no prosecution may be undertaken except upon the certification in writing of the attorney general, the deputy attorney general, the associate attorney general, or any assistant attorney general specially designated by the attorney general that prosecution "is in the public interest and necessary to secure substantial justice."[49] The function of certification may not be delegated.

The statute also makes clear that state prosecution of offenses is not preempted and that no law enforcement officer shall be considered to be in violation of the statute for lawfully carrying out official duties or enforcing the laws of the United States or any state. Finally, the statute places the heavy burden upon the government of proving willfulness and the use of force or threat of force.

Given these strictures and the comity—or respect for state functions—that the federal government normally pays to state law enforcement, it is not surprising that there have been relatively few reported prosecutions for violations of section 245. Successful prosecutions under the statute, however, have been brought against those who interfered with civil rights demonstrators,[50] denied minorities the use and enjoyment of public accommodations,[51] blocked efforts by a civil rights organization to promote employment and housing opportunities for blacks,[52] and impeded the ability of blacks to attend desegregated schools.[53]

Has Congress taken any other action in response to acts of discrimination and intimidation against racial and other minority groups?

Yes. Congress enacted the Hate Crime Statistics Act of 1990[54] to establish a national data collection system for the compilation of statistics concerning bias-related crimes. The act requires the attorney general to publish an annual summary of the findings to be used for research and statistical purposes.[55]

What should a person do who believes that someone has committed an act made a crime by federal laws prohibiting racial discrimination?

Notify the Department of Justice, Washington, D.C., or the department's nearest local office, and request that it investigate the incident for possible violations of federal law. The state prosecutor should also be notified, since the incident may involve violations of state law as well.

STATE LAWS PROHIBITING RACIAL DISCRIMINATION

Do the states also have criminal laws prohibiting discrimination based upon race?

Yes. Every state, except Alaska, Utah, and Wyoming, has enacted some form of law making it a crime to discriminate against persons because of their race. These laws are frequently referred to as *hate crime laws*. The older laws generally prohibited wearing a mask, burning a cross, "Kukluxing," i.e. making intimidating and threatening statements, or desecrating a religious place of worship and were aimed at terrorist groups such as the Ku Klux Klan. More recent laws have been enacted in response to a general upsurge in bias-motivated crimes, including hate crimes committed against lesbians and gay men and foreign immigrants, or to increased paramilitary training by white supremacist groups. These laws make specific acts of racial discrimination unlawful, such as conspiring to deprive someone of their civil rights, or increasing the punishment for already existing crimes (such as assault and battery) committed out of bigotry or with a racially discriminatory intent. For further information about the specific hate crime laws of a particular state contact the state attorney general or one of the organizations listed in appendix B.

Have state hate crime laws been held constitutional?

Yes and no. The supreme court of Georgia ruled that its antimasking law was constitutional that made it a crime to wear a "mask, hood, or device . . . to conceal the identity of the wearer" but that provided exceptions for persons wearing a traditional holiday costume on the occasion of the holiday, a person wearing a gas mask in a fire drill, and so forth.[56] The supreme court of Wisconsin, however, invalidated its state law that increased the maximum penalty for aggravated battery from two to seven years where the defendant intentionally selected his victim because of the victim's race.[57] The court held that a defendant's intent to commit a criminal act could be punished, but that his motive could not. Thus, the maximum penalty for aggravated battery was two years.

The legal status of hate crime laws was thrown into considerable doubt by the 1992 decision of the Supreme Court in *R.A.V. v. City of St. Paul, Minnesota*.[58] In *R.A.V.* a white teenager burned a cross in the yard of a black family and was convicted of violating a city ordinance making it a crime to place an object, including a burning cross, on public or private property that "arouses anger, alarm or resentment in others on the basis of race, color, creed, religion or gender." While acknowledging that the defendant might have violated other state laws, e.g., those prohibiting arson and damage to property, a unanimous Court invalidated the city's hate crime ordinance. The majority found the ordinance unconstitutional because it only prohibited the use of symbols that aroused anger or resentment on the basis of race, color, creed, religion, or gender, and was therefore impermissibly based on the content of expressive conduct. In the words of the majority, "[t]he First Amendment does not permit St. Paul to impose special prohibitions on those speakers who express views on disfavored subjects."[59] The minority of the Court were of the view that the ordinance was overbroad in that "[a]lthough [it] reaches conduct that is unprotected, it also makes criminal expressive conduct that causes only hurt feelings, offense, or resentment, and is protected by the First Amendment."[60] The minority sharply disagreed with the majority that the ordinance was too narrowly drawn and charged that the reasoning of the majority would confuse the law in the area of the First Amendment and prohibit a jurisdiction from enacting laws aimed specifically at bias-motivated crimes.

Cases such as *R.A.V.* are controversial because they present the courts with fundamental but competing interests—a state's compelling interest in regulating racially discriminatory conduct with its enormous potential for individual and social harm and the right of free speech that lies at the heart of our democratic system. Reconciling these interests has proven to be an extremely difficult task.[61]

If an act is a violation of both federal and state criminal laws, may it be prosecuted by both governments?

Yes. The Supreme Court has held that when an act is made a crime by both federal and state governments, it is a separate offense to the peace and dignity of each and may be punished as such.[62] However, the Department of Justice has adopted a policy of not prosecuting individuals previously tried in a state court for offenses involving the same acts, unless there exists "most compelling reasons" and then only after the specific approval of the appropriate assistant attorney general has been obtained.[63]

NOTES

1. 2 T. Emerson, D. Haber, and N. Dorsen, *Political and Civil Rights in the United States* 1356-65 (3d ed. Little, Brown & Co., Boston, 1967) and sources cited therein. Between 1881 and 1960 some 3,441 blacks were lynched in the United States. U. S. Comm'n on Civil Rights, *Law Enforcement: A Report on Equal Protection in the South 11* (1965).
2. Civil Liberties, Mar. 1966, at 6.
3. U.S. Commission on Civil Rights, *Law Enforcement: A Report on Equal Protection in the South 13* (1965).
4. Moultrie Observer, July 28, 1922.
5. 14 Stat. 27, enacted as part of the Civil Rights Act of 1866.

6. 16 Stat. 141, enacted as part of the Enforcement Act of 1870.
7. *United States v. Price*, 383 U.S. 787 (1966); *United States v. Classic*, 313 U.S. 299 (1941); *Screws v. United States*, 325 U.S. 91 (1945).
8. *Screws v. United States*, 325 U.S. 91 (1945); *Lynch v. United States*, 189 F.2d 476 (5th Cir. 1951).
9. *United States v. Price*, 383 U.S. 787 (1966).
10. *See also, Williams v. United States*, 341 U.S. 97 (1951), holding that a private detective, who held a special police card and who used brutal methods to extract confessions from suspects, acted under color of law and was subject to prosecution under § 242.
11. *United States v. Guest*, 383 U.S 745, 762, 781–84 (1966); *United States v. Price*, 383 U.S. 787 (1966).
12. *United States v. Price*, 383 U.S. 787, 805 (1966).
13. *United States v. Johnson*, 390 U.S. 563 (1968).
14. *Screws v. United States*, 325 U.S. 91 (1945).
15. *Id.*, at 107.
16. *United States v. Classic*, 313 U.S. 299 (1941).
17. *United States v. Waddell*, 112 U.S. 76 (1884).
18. *United States v. Mason*, 213 U.S. 115 (1909).
19. *United States v. Harris*, 701 F.2d 1095 (4th Cir. 1983); *United States v. King*, 840 F.2d 1276 (6th Cir. 1988).
20. *United States v. Hayes*, 444 F.2d 472 (5th Cir. 1971).
21. *Wilkins v. United States*, 376 F.2d 552 (5th Cir. 1967).
22. *United States v. Guest*, 383 U.S. 745 (1966).
23. *Williams v. United States*, 341 U.S. 97 (1951).
24. *Pullen v. United States*, 164 F.2d 756 (5th Cir. 1947).
25. *Ex parte Yarbrough*, 110 U.S. 651 (1884); *ex parte Siebold*, 100 U.S. 371 (1880); *United States v. Waddell*, 112 U.S. 76 (1884); *Logan v. United States*, 144 U.S. 263 (1892).
26. *United States v. Cruikshank*, 92 U.S. 542 (1876).
27. *United States v. Mosley*, 238 U.S. 383 (1915); *United States v. Gradwell*, 243 U.S. 476 (1917); *United States v. Bathgate*, 246 U.S. 220 (1918); *United States v. Wheeler*, 254 U.S. 281 (1920).
28. 2 T. Emerson, D. Haber, and N. Dorsen, *Political and Civil Rights in the United States* 104 (3d ed. Little, Brown & Co., Boston, 1967).
29. *United States v. Classic*, 313 U.S. 299 (1941).
30. *United States v. Saylor*, 322 U.S. 385 (1944).
31. *Screws v. United States*, 325 U.S. 91, 159–61 (1945).
32. 18 U.S.C. § 1582 (using vessels for slave trade); 18 U.S.C. § 1583 (enticing a person into slavery); 18 U.S.C. § 1585 (selling, transporting, or detaining slaves); 18 U.S.C. § 1586 (serving on a slave ship); 18 U.S.C. § 1587 (possessing slaves on such a ship); and 18 U.S.C. § 1588 (transporting slaves from the United States).

33. 18 U.S.C. § 1584 (holding, selling, or bringing into the country a person in involuntary servitude); *United States v. Kozminski*, 487 U.S. 931 (1988).

34. 18 U.S.C. § 1582 (holding, arresting, or returning anyone to a condition of peonage).

35. In addition to criminal laws, Congress has enacted a civil statute abolishing peonage and declaring void any law, regulation, or usage that maintains a system of peonage. 42 U.S.C. § 1994. The statute has been held to create a cause of action for damages against one who has held another in such involuntary servitude. *Bryant v. Donnell*, 239 F. Supp. 681 (W.D. Tenn. 1965).

36. *See, e.g., United States v. Ingalls*, 73 F. Supp. 76 (S.D. Cal. 1947); *United States v. Shackney*, 333 F.2d 475 (3d Cir. 1964); *United States v. Booker*, 655 F.2d 562 (4th Cir. 1981); *United States v. Bibbs*, 564 F.2d 1165 (5th Cir. 1977); *United States v. Harris*, 701 F.2d 1095 (4th Cir. 1983); *United States v. King*, 840 F.2d 1276 (6th Cir. 1988); *United States v. Warren*, 722 F.2d 827 (4th Cir. 1985); *United States v. Mussry*, 726 F.2d 1448 (9th Cir. 1984).

37. For a discussion of the subject, see P. Daniel, *The Shadow of Slavery: Peonage in the South, 1901–1969* (Urbana: University of Illinois Press, 1972).

38. *Pollock v. Williams*, 322 U.S. 4 (1944).

39. *Clyatt v. United States*, 197 U.S. 207 (1905).

40. *Bailey v. Alabama*, 219 U.S. 219 (1911); *United States v. Reynolds*, 235 U.S. 133 (1914); *Taylor v. Georgia*, 315 U.S. 25 (1942); *Pollock v. Williams*, 322 U.S. 4 (1944).

41. *Pollock v. Williams*, 322 U.S. 4, 18 (1944).

42. *See* note 36, *supra*.

43. *Selective Draft Law Cases*, 245 U.S. 366 (1918).

44. *Badger v. United States*, 322 F.2d 902 (9th Cir. 1963).

45. *United States v. Kozminski*, 487 U.S. 931 (1988).

46. *Linsey v. Leavy*, 149 F.2d 899 (9th Cir. 1945).

47. Curt Flood's argument that professional baseball's reserve system was a form of involuntary servitude was also rejected by the courts. *Flood v. Kuhn*, 407 U.S. 258 (1972), *aff'g*, 443 F.2d 264 (2d Cir. 1971).

48. 82 Stat. 73.

49. 18 U.S.C. § 245(a)(1).

50. *United States v. White*, 846 F.2d 678 (11th Cir. 1988) (§ 245(b)(2)(B)).

51. *United States v. Ebens*, 800 F.2d 1422 (6th Cir. 1986) (§ 245(b)(2)(F)); *United States v. Bledsoe*, 728 F.2d 1094 (8th Cir. 1984)(§ 245(b)(2)(B)).

52. *United States v. Johns*, 615 F.2d 672 (5th Cir. 1980) (§ 245(b)(5)).

53. *United States v. Griffin*, 525 F.2d 710 (1st Cir. 1975) (§ 245(b)(4)(A)).

54. 28 U.S.C. § 534 nt.

55. For a discussion of the act, *see* J. Fernandez, *Bringing Hate Crimes into Focus—The Hate Crimes Statistics Act of 1990, Pub. L. No. 101-275*, 26 Harv. Civ. Rights-Civ. Lib. L. Rev. 261 (1991).
56. *State v. Williams*, 260 Ga. 669, 398 S.E.2d 547 (1990).
57. *State v. Mitchell*, 485 N.W.2d 807 (Wis. 1992).
58. 112 S. Ct. 2538 (1992).
59. *Id.*, at 2547.
60. *Id.*, at 2560.
61. For a discussion of the subject, *see* S. Gellman, *Sticks and Stones Can Put You in Jail, but Can Words Increase Your Sentence? Constitutional and Policy Dilemmas of Ethnic Intimidation Laws*, 39 U.C.L.A. Law Rev. 333 (1991).
62. *Bartkus v. Illinois*, 359 U.S. 121 (1959); *Abbate v. United States*, 359 U.S. 187 (1959).
63. *Watts v. United States*, 422 U.S. 1032, 1033 (1975).

X

Race Conscious Remedies

A "profound moral and constitutional challenge" for this nation is to remedy the "lingering effects of racial discrimination."[1] And the "American public, acting through democratic and representative processes" of the United States government, "has concluded time and again that serious remedial efforts sometimes require race conscious programs."[2] Race conscious programs enable members of minority groups to enter various areas—in employment or education, for example—from which they have been excluded previously through discrimination. Such measures are attempts to ensure that all Americans are treated as equal citizens and to achieve equal opportunity that is truly open to all.

What are race conscious strategies?

In the broadest sense, whenever race is specifically used to design or implement a program, there is a race conscious strategy. In the effort to overcome racial discrimination and to achieve cultural diversity, many schools, employers, and other institutions have used programs designed to bring more minorities into the classroom and the workplace. These race conscious strategies recognize that for generations minorities have been denied an opportunity to participate as equals in the political, social, cultural, and economic life of this country. These strategies also realize that although formal state enforcement of segregation and other legal barriers to equal opportunity have been abandoned in the past thirty years, the legacy of discrimination is all too evident today.

What are some examples of race conscious strategies?

Some of the strategies that are most familiar in our society are school desegregation plans, voting redistricting to increase minority participation, affirmative action, and set-asides.[3]

How are race conscious strategies used?

There are different models for race conscious programs. Most, however, adopt two main strategies. First, an attempt is made to expand the pool of applicants from the group that is underrepresented. Second, is to give the underrepresented group special consideration in the allocation of benefits.[4]

Can the problem of excluding minorities be entirely addressed by removing the legal barrier that excluded minorities?

No. While this is an important part of overcoming the past practice of discrimination and exclusion, it is not enough. Eliminating the law will often maintain the status quo.[5] As Justice Powell noted on a number of occasions, we cannot undo the legacy of race discrimination simply by repealing laws. Race must be taken into account affirmatively, in order to overcome racism.[6]

Who benefits from affirmative action programs?

We all do. A society that is free of invidious racial discrimination or the effects of such discrimination celebrates our diversity and benefits the entire society.

Why is it necessary to consider race? Isn't the best way to overcome racism to ignore race as a factor?

In order to remedy the effects of past discrimination, race must be taken into account.[7] Properly tailored remedial measures are efforts to achieve a social situation in which individuals are evaluated on their individual merit, rather than as a product of their race.[8] In addition, after carefully considering other, race neutral alternatives, Congress found the race conscious measure actually adopted to be the most effective in promoting and protecting diversity in our society, as for example in the broadcasting industry. Because the industry is owned and controlled almost exclusively by white males, the Court found a lack of diversity, which Congress has a legitimate interest in correcting.[9]

In many areas where there was invidious racial discrimination, minorities remain significantly underrepresented and face disproportionately difficult challenges in achieving success. First, many employers who used discriminatory practices in the past maintain a biased candidate profile that they use in making hiring decisions. Second, these employers have discriminatory reputations in minority communities that deter minorities from applying for jobs with them. Third, most employers, despite protestations of nondiscrimination, continue to recruit potential employees by word of mouth. This practice works to the advantage of friends and relatives of most employers' predominantly white work forces and thus to the disadvantage of minorities who are not yet inside this word-of-mouth system. In order to place disfavored persons in a position of equal footing, institutions seek, or may be required, to affirm minority applicants.

Do some race conscious programs, like affirmative action, require unqualified minority persons to be employed or promoted?

No. Affirmative action has never meant that a minority person who is not qualified must be given a job. Instead, affirmative action means that qualified minority persons must be recruited and fully considered for employment and promotion.

At the same time, affirmative action requires employers to look at how "qualifications" are used and what the word means. First, employers have been forced to realize that, regardless of the advent of affirmative action, many persons have been hired or promoted not on the basis of job qualifications but on the basis of appearance, personality, club membership, and even friendship. Since the applicant who is theoretically best qualified is not necessarily the one who wins the job or the promotion, affirmative action simply requires that minority applicants, too, be fully considered even though they are not the best friends of employers. Second, and more importantly, employers have been forced to realize that many so-called qualifications are discriminatory devices unrelated to job performance. For example, many employers use culturally biased written tests, which are not only discriminatory but are also unable to predict job performance. Affirmative action requires employers to reexamine required qualifications, to recognize that many minority members who do not possess these are in fact qualified for employment and promotion, and thereby to include minority persons in the pool of qualified applicants.

An appropriate preference program does not abandon qualifications but tries to ensure that qualifications used are related to performance. For these programs, race becomes a factor only when an employer is choosing between highly qualified candidates. Therefore, when institutions use quotas or set-asides, there is normally a provision that requires that the quota be waived if qualified applicants cannot be identified within a given time period.[10]

Are government programs that classify and treat people differently based on race a violation of the Fourteenth Amendment?

Not necessarily. There is a vast difference between governmental measures that classify persons according to their race to exclude them from opportunities accorded to all citizens, and governmental measures that take race into account to correct the effects of such past discrimination. The former pushes disfavored persons from a position of equality to a position of second class citizenship, and the latter strives to return disfavored persons to a position of equal footing. Race must be taken into account in order to achieve the latter objective.[11]

Likewise, there is a vast difference between governmental classifications that use race "to advance debilitating stereotypes and the perpetuation of racial exclusion"[12] and governmental distinctions based on race to promote a few identified compelling interests such as diversity. People of various ethnic and racial backgrounds in our heterogeneous society can contribute to a diversity of viewpoints in the broadcast industry, for example.[13] Simple recognition of racial differences to provide the public with such diversity is neither based on debilitating stereotypes nor geared to exclude on racial grounds.[14]

What interests are compelling enough for a governmental body to enact race conscious measures?

The Supreme Court has held that the desire to achieve racial diversity in certain public forums is important enough to be the sole constitutional basis for race conscious preference policies enacted by Congress.[15] *Metro Broadcasting* involved two policies of the Federal Communications Commission, adopted with specific Congressional approval, that gave certain preferences to minority-controlled broadcasting firms to enable them to operate radio and television stations in the United States.[16] The policies were adopted after a congressional finding that past racial and ethnic discrimination in the broadcast industry had resulted in severe underrepresentation of minorities.[17] However, Congress and the Commission did not justify their "policies strictly as remedies for victims of past discrimination."[18] Rather, they justified them as measures to promote diversity in the broadcast industry.[19]

The Court held that even though the measures were not "remedial in the sense of being designed to compensate victims of past governmental or societal discrimination," such "benign race conscious measures mandated by Congress . . . are constitutionally permissible" if "they serve important governmental objectives within the power of Congress and are substantially related to the achievement of those objectives."[20] Diversity in the airwaves involved the important First Amendment value of the public's right to receive varied information reflecting the amalgam of racial and ethnic cultures in the United States.

On another occasion, the Court recognized a governmental interest, other than that of remedying the effects of discrimination, as important enough for the government to consider race in its policies.[21] The Court concluded in the *Bakke* case, discussed in chapter 4, that although race could not be the basis for a rigid quota, race could be considered as a factor in a university's admission process.[22] The diversity of a student body "contributing to a robust exchange of ideas" implicating First Amendment values, like diversity in the airwaves, was an important governmental interest justifying consideration—though not to set a quota—of race in the admission process.[23] Presently, diversity in the two foregoing settings are the only nonremedial governmental interests recognized by the Court as important enough to allow governmental consideration of race in its policies. The Court rejected, in *Wygant*, the asserted interest of providing students with a diverse, integrated school faculty as a basis for a race conscious plan.[24]

Has the Supreme Court ruled on the constitutionality of affirmative action programs or in any way limited their use?

The Supreme Court has not found that affirmative action programs per se are unconstitutional. In a recent important case, *City of Richmond v. Croson*,[25] the Supreme Court narrowed the use of race conscious programs by government entities other than Congress. As a result, states and local governments are more limited in their use of affirmative action programs. *Croson* did not limit nongovernment programs or federal programs.

How have affirmative action programs been narrowed for state and local governmental bodies?

The Court will examine race conscious programs adopted by state and local government bodies under a standard called "strict scrutiny."[26] *Croson* was the first case in which a majority used this standard to examine a race conscious program designed to help minorities. Under strict scrutiny, a governmental program that takes race into account to benefit certain groups must be for a "compelling," or very important, interest and must be "narrowly tailored" to advance that interest. This standard is difficult but not impossible to meet.[27] Moreover, the language used in *Croson* seems to indicate that the Court may define the strict scrutiny standard in the context of affirmative action in a slightly more relaxed way.

Does the use of a strict scrutiny standard mean that states and local governmental bodies will not be able to have race conscious affirmative action programs?

No. Strictly scrutinizing race conscious measures does not mean that all such measures violate equal protection guarantees. The purpose of strict scrutiny is to separate "benign" or "remedial" racial classifications from those "motivated by illegitimate notions of racial inferiority or simple racial politics."[28] There is thus an implicit recognition that benign and remedial racial classifications can be constitutional and indeed further the guarantee of equal protection by remedying the effects of past discrimination. The race conscious measure in *Croson*, however, did not pass the test of strict scrutiny.

Croson involved a set-aside plan in a city ordinance that required nonminority-owned prime contractors awarded city construction contracts to subcontract at least 30 percent of the amount of the contract to minority business enterprises.[29] First, the majority of the Court concluded that the city did not show that it had a compelling interest in adopting the plan because there was insufficient identifiable evidence of past discrimination by anyone in the city's construction industry, and general societal discrimination by itself was not enough to justify "rigid racial preferences."[30] Similarly, the generalized assertion of past discrimination in the construction industry was not enough to justify the race based measure because it does not give the legislature sufficient guidance as to the scope of the injury that needs to be remedied.[31]

So, in determining whether a race conscious program is constitutional, can the identity of the governmental body enacting the program make a difference for the Court's decision?

Yes. The Supreme Court will apply only intermediate scrutiny to race conscious plans adopted by or pursuant to federal authority. In other words, the Court gives substantial (although not complete) deference to Congress when it adopts a race conscious strategy.[32] In *Fullilove v. Klutznick*,[33] the Supreme Court held that the minority business enterprise provision of the Public Works Employment Act, requiring a 10 percent set-aside of federal funds for minority businesses on local public works projects, did not violate the equal protection clause. In reviewing the federal program, the Court explicitly rejected the application of strict scrutiny analysis, which would have decreased the chances of the plan to pass constitutional muster.[34]

Why has the Court adopted a standard for federal race conscious programs that is different from state and local programs?

In *Metro Broadcasting*, the Supreme Court decided that strict scrutiny does not apply to a "benign racial classification employed by Congress."[35] The Court reasoned that when an administrative agency adopts a "program employing a benign racial classification at the explicit direction of Congress," the Court should give proper deference to the judgment of Congress: Congress is "a co-equal branch" of the United States government that is given the power under the Constitution to enforce the equal protection guarantees of Constitution.[36] Furthermore, the federal government was less likely to be captured by ethnic and racial minorities to be used as an instrument of discrimination.[37]

Similarly, in *Johnson v. Transportation Agency, Santa Clara County*,[38] a case involving a challenge to a county's affirmative action promotion plan, the Court granted deference to Congress's enactment of Title VII pursuant to when the plan had been adopted and utilized a lower level of scrutiny.[39] The Santa Clara County plan was reviewed only with regard to whether it was consistent with the requirements and goals of Title VII.[40] The Court upheld the plan as consistent with Title VII.[41]

Thus, under *Fullilove*, *Metro Broadcasting*, and *Johnson*, strict scrutiny is not applied to affirmative action programs promulgated pursuant to federal civil rights legislation like Title VII.[42] Such programs must be treated with the same deference as other benign race conscious measures mandated by Congress. When Congress has targeted an area of discrimination and expressed the intent to remedy it, the courts' only duty is to assure that such remedial plans "serve important governmental objectives within the power of Congress and are substantially related to achievement of those objectives."[43]

What happens when a state or local government implements a federally funded project?

When federal programs are being implemented by state or local governmental bodies, the federal standard should be used. Lower federal courts have eschewed the application of strict scrutiny to affirmative action programs that are "implementations of federal programs" or "primarily federally funded."[44] For example, in *Milwaukee County Pavers Assoc. v. Fiedler*,[45] the Seventh Circuit held that *Croson* did not apply to the portion of Wisconsin's set-aside plan implementing the federal Surface Transportation Act. Affirming the district court's finding that the Wisconsin plan was a "mere elaboration" of the federal program, the Court held that in this regard the state was acting as an agent of the federal government. It went on to state that "[t]he joint lesson of *Fullilove* and *Croson* is that the federal government can, by virtue of the enforcement clause of the Fourteenth Amendment, engage in affirmative action with a freer hand than states and municipalities can do."[46]

Therefore, when a state explicitly implements a federal affirmative action plan, it need not make findings of past discrimination, as *Croson* requires.[47] In addition, projects that are "primarily federally funded" may also be beyond the reach of *Croson*, as such projects will be considered part of the federal legislation. The *Milwaukee County Pavers* court did not address what percentage of the funding must be federal but held that projects receiving 70 to 75 percent of funding from a federal source must meet the requirement.[48]

The lower court in *Milwaukee County Pavers* also held that where the federal law dictates that a project must be partially funded by the state, such expenditure of state funds does not cause the program to lose its character as a federal program.[49] Moreover, the state is permitted to set minority participation goals based on the total project costs (as opposed to the federal share only) and remain within the bounds of the federal authority.[50]

Is remedying past discrimination a "compelling" state interest that can justify a state or local government's adoption of an affirmative action hiring plan?

Yes. The Court indicated in *Croson*[51] that the goal of remedying past discrimination would be considered "compelling" in order to justify a minority set-aside. However, the evidence of prior discrimination must be based on precise legislative findings and should at least approach a prima facie case of constitutional or statutory violation.[52] The following factors would be enough to justify a set-aside:

1. Where the government can prove the existence of discrimination by specific individuals or groups. The best possibility of satisfying this threshold question is where the governmental body that adopted the preference program is itself responsible for the past discrimination.[53] Preferably, assertions of such discrimination should be backed up with written or oral descriptions by several people evidencing specific examples of the discrimination. Evidence of specific acts that form a pattern may be required.[54]

2. Where a governmental body can prove by inference that discrimination against a minority exists. Thus, if the government can show that qualified minority firms are getting a substantially smaller percentage of work than their numbers would indicate, a valid statistical inference of discrimination can be made. For example, a relevant statistic would be how many minority business enterprises (MBEs) in the relevant market (city, county, state) are qualified to undertake prime or subcontracting

work in public construction projects. Similarly, the percentage of total city construction dollars that minority firms are receiving as subcontractors compared to the total dollars awarded would also be relevant.

3. Where the government has become a "passive participant" in a system of racial exclusion. For instance, a government's spending practices may compound discrimination by other governmental or private bodies.[55] In this case, the government would have the authority to "take affirmative steps to dismantle such a system."[56]

What interests are *not* "compelling" enough to justify a set-aside?

The majority opinion in *Croson* implies that the following justifications for affirmative action by a state or local government are not compelling:

1. A set-aside designed to remedy the effects of general societal discrimination. The history of private and public discrimination that has contributed to a lack of opportunities for minorities, alone, is "too amorphous a basis" for employing a racially based remedy.[57]

2. Generalized assertions that there has been past discrimination in an entire industry. Such assertions will not suffice because they provide no guidance in determining the precise scope of the injury, and the remedy on which they are based has no logical stopping point.[58]

3. A state or local legislature's mere recitation of a "benign" or legitimate purpose for the racial classification. This justification will be given "little or no weight," as will individual legislators' views that there has been past discrimination in the industry.[59]

4. Statistical comparisons between the actual percentage of minorities receiving contracts and the percentage of minorities in the general population where special qualifications are necessary to fill particular jobs. The Supreme Court has held that "the relevant statistical pool for purposes of demonstrating discriminatory exclusion must be the number of minorities qualified to undertake the particular task."[60] In *Croson*, the city of Richmond argued that MBE membership in local contractor associations was extremely low. The Court found that this statistic standing alone was not probative of any discrimination. For low minority membership in these associations to be relevant,

the city would have to link it to the number of local MBEs eligible for membership.[61]

5. U.S. Congressional findings of nationwide discrimination in the construction industry. This evidence was deemed extremely limited as a justification for a state/local government set-aside plan. The Court reasoned that Congress, when making such findings, was exercising its powers under section 5 of the Fourteenth Amendment, a power that states do not possess.[62]

6. The inclusion of minority groups in a set-aside program, where there has been no evidence that those groups have been disadvantaged. Such a justification may necessitate a finding that the city's compelling interest is not in fact the remedying of past discrimination.[63] The issue left open by the Court, however, was whether a state or local government could have a compelling interest in preventing future discrimination. If so, an affirmative action plan that identified groups who had not been subject to past discrimination (but were likely to be discriminated against) could be found constitutional.

7. The goal of achieving diversity in the workplace. Such a goal has been considered "important" but not a "compelling interest."[64] Seeking diversity on university campuses and in the broadcast industry is an "important" interest that warrants affirmative action in these limited arenas.[65]

A state or local government that wants to adopt a race conscious program must have a compelling interest in doing so. Once it has satisfied this requirement, will its program be constitutional?

Not necessarily. There is a second requirement that the program be narrowly tailored to achieve the intended results.

In the context of the *Croson* case, what would be required to meet the second requirement in a state or local set-aside program?

The second prong of the test can be met by a government showing that:

1. The government exhausted race neutral means (financing programs, nondiscriminatory hiring plans) to increase minority participation in the industry.[66] Thus, if the MBEs' only problem is that they disproportionately lack capital or cannot meet bond-

ing requirements, a race neutral program of city financing for small firms could adequately solve the problem.

2. The MBE set-aside goal is tied to the proper statistical finding used to justify the plan and that the racial preference program does not follow a rigid quota.[67] Rather than a quota, an acceptable program would "tailor remedial relief to those who truly have suffered the effects of prior discrimination."[68]

3. There is a sufficient waiver provision. For example, the Court contrasted Richmond's plan, which granted a waiver of the requirements where a contractor could demonstrate that sufficient qualified MBEs were unavailable or unwilling to participate in the contract, to the plan approved in *Fullilove*. The *Fullilove* plan allowed for a waiver of the set-aside provision where an MBE's higher price was not attributable to the effects of past discrimination.[69] Because the Richmond plan focused solely on the availability of MBEs, without inquiry into whether or not the particular MBE seeking a racial preference had suffered from the effects of past discrimination by the city or prime contractors, the Court found the plan not "narrowly tailored."[70]

How have the lower federal courts dealt with state and local set-aside programs since *Croson*?

A number of lower court cases following *Croson* have found affirmative action plans to pass constitutional analysis. For example, in *Coral Construction Co. v. King County*,[71] the District Court for the Western District of Washington, applying the *Croson* strict scrutiny analysis, upheld a county set-aside plan challenged on equal protection grounds. Similarly, in *Cone Corp. v. Hillsborough County*,[72] the Eleventh Circuit found that the county minority set-aside plan survived constitutional scrutiny.[73]

The guidance given by these two cases should be followed by state and local governments promulgating or reviewing set-aside plans in the wake of *Croson*. To be constitutionally valid, such plans must meet four basic requirements: (1) sufficient factual evidence is presented to justify the set-aside plan; (2) evidence is presented that the state or local government has considered race neutral plans as alternatives to the set-aside plan; (3) the percentage preference contained in the set-aside plan is tied to the availability of qualified minority contractors as opposed to the existence of minority persons in the general population; and (4) the set-aside plan contains a provision whereby the minority preference may be waived or reduced if qualified MBEs are not available or if a bidding MBE's higher price is not attributable to the effects of past discrimination.[74]

The precise evidence presented in these cases provides a good example of the type of examination a county should undertake to survive a constitutional attack. Specifically, the evidence presented by King County for justification of its set-aside plan consisted of written or oral descriptions by several dozen people evidencing past discrimination in the King County construction industry, including numerous specific examples of such discrimination. Nearly all the evidence applied directly to the construction industry within King County's jurisdiction,[75] as opposed to evidence concerning general "societal discrimination."[76] Similarly, Hillsborough County presented an analysis of statistical data on minority businesses, which included a review of contracts awarded by the county over a three-year period and which indicated that blacks and women were significantly underrepresented in such awards. In addition, anecdotal evidence was presented by persons who had received a number of complaints alleging discrimination in county construction and procurement.[77]

The evidence presented in support of a narrowly tailored remedy was equally sufficient under the *Croson* standard. In King County, it consisted of language in the statute itself that no effective race neutral alternatives appeared to be presently available.[78] In addition, deposition testimony was posited showing that many race neutral alternatives were in fact considered. Notably, the Court found that "*Croson* does not compel the county to consider every imaginable race neutral alternative, nor to try alternatives that would be plainly ineffective."[79] Likewise, in Hillsborough County, evidence was presented that the county tried for six years to implement a race neutral program in which contractors would list their minority subcontractors and thereby become more aware and accountable regarding MBEs. It was only when this program failed that the county adopted a set-aside plan.[80]

With regard to the statistical evidence, King County tied its MBE utilization requirements to the availability of qualified MBE contractors, not to the percentage of minorities or women in the population in general. The Court found that the remedy was narrowly tailored in this respect since it conformed to the appropriate statistical disparities.[81] The Hillsborough County plan was also upheld as narrowly tailored, partially because the plan set goals for each individual project based on the number of qualified MBE subcontractors in each subcontractable area.[82]

Finally, both courts were impressed by the waiver provisions of each county's plan. King County was permitted to waive or reduce the MBE preferences if qualified MBEs were not available or if a bidding MBE's higher price was not attributable to the effects of past discrimination. In addition, the plan contained another waiver provision permitting the denial of benefits if the group in question had not been discriminated against.[83] The Hillsborough County plan also contained a waiver provision whereby a low bidder who did not meet the plan goals could still obtain a contract simply by demonstrating a good faith effort to find MBE contractors. In addition, the Hillsborough plan contained a cap prohibiting MBE participation goals to be set at greater than 50 percent.[84]

Another example of useful evidence that may be presented to justify and show narrow tailoring of a state or local government's set-aside plan is the recent study undertaken by the city of Atlanta to document racial discrimination in an effort to meet the *Croson* test.[85] The Atlanta study used anecdotal, statistical, and historical evidence to disclose discrimination in bonding, customer/end-user discrimination, exclusion from the "good old boy" network in subcontracting, bid shopping, bid manipulation, price discrimination by suppliers, financing discrimination, employment discrimination, double standards in performance and qualifications, limited access to private sector markets, slow payment and nonpayment, and stereotypical attitudes by customers and professional buyers.[86]

To what extent are court-ordered affirmative action plans affected by the Court's decision in *Croson*?

With respect to court-ordered affirmative action plans, at least one federal court has rejected the application of *Croson* to judicial remedies imposed after a finding of illegal employment discrimination under Title VII.[87] In *U.S. v. City of Buffalo*, the question was whether *Croson* strict scrutiny would apply to court-ordered affirmative action remedies that included hiring goals and selection procedures subsequent to a finding of Title VII violations. In rejecting the application of *Croson*, the Court stated:

> Unlike the present case, *City of Croson v. J. A. Croson Co.* did not involve a judicially imposed remedial decree issued following a finding, after trial, of illegal employment discrimination. Furthermore, neither that case [*Croson*] nor *Wards Cove Packing Co. v. Atonio* altered the broad power of federal district courts to implement relief that operates both retrospectively to redress past discrimination and prospectively to ensure that it does not recur. . . . As the Second Circuit noted in reaffirming the propriety of the relief granted by this court, "[s]uch broad discriminatory conduct" as that found here "demands equally broad prospective equitable relief. Otherwise the wrong will not be remedied."[88]

How have the courts dealt with affirmative action plans under Title VI and Title VIII of the Civil Rights Act, which prohibit discrimination in federally assisted programs in housing?

The courts have rejected the application of *Croson* to such plans insofar as the remedies stayed within the broad discretionary powers granted to housing authorities under these statutes.[89] For instance, in *S. J. Groves and Sons Company v. Fulton County*, the Eleventh Circuit applied intermediate scrutiny to review a county's minority set-aside program that was adopted pursuant to the Airport and Airway Development Act of 1970 and the Department of Transportation's implementing regulations.[90] In upholding the state's program, the court noted that the federal statute endorses rules similar to the nondiscrimination rules under Title VI, which "condon[e], and in some cases requir[e], race conscious regulations and/or action."[91]

How have the courts dealt with affirmative action in the area of education?

Determining what standard to apply to affirmative action educational plans has proven to be a difficult task. For plans adopted pursuant to school desegregation litigation, it seems clear that *Croson* should not apply because of the court's broad remedial power in these cases[92] and the existence of federal legislation, such as Title VI, in this area.[93]

The more difficult issue in education arises where a school (or school district or state) has based its affirmative action plan on a congressional mandate or its interest in something other than remedying the effects of past discrimination.[94] Under the Supreme Court's decision in *Metro Broadcasting*, it is clear that an affirmative action plan may be justified on grounds other than the remedying of past discrimination. In *Metro Broadcasting*, the Court held that equal protection was not violated when the federal government fashioned an affirmative action plan "primarily to promote programming diversity."[95] Similarly, in the *Bakke* case,[96] the Court held that a "diverse student body" contributing to a "robust exchange of ideas" is a constitutionally permissible goal on which race conscious university admissions programs may be based.[97]

Whether such "nonremedial" objectives will be sufficient for state and local governments to bring their educational affirmative action programs outside the reach of *Croson* is unclear at this time. Under *Croson*, a purely state or local government plan may be in jeopardy, but if such plans can be tied to federal legislation or the broad remedial powers of courts, a lesser level of scrutiny should apply.[98]

To what extent can a governmental program that considers race as a factor in giving preferential treatment for certain groups burden nonbenefited groups, without encroaching on equal protection guarantees of the Constitution?

Justice Powell stated in *Wygant* that, "[a]s a part of this Nation's dedication to eradicating racial discrimination, innocent persons may be called upon to bear some of the burden of the remedy."[99] However, the remedy cannot *unduly* burden innocent persons and the layoff plan in *Wygant* unduly burdened nonminority teachers.[100] In contrast to "hiring goals [which] impose only a diffuse burden" because the goals "foreclos[e] only one of several opportunities" for nonminority individuals, "layoffs impose the entire burden of achieving racial equality on particular individuals, often resulting in serious disruptions of their lives."[101] As a result, the Court held that the layoffs were "too intrusive" and were "not sufficiently narrowly tailored" to accomplish "purposes that otherwise may be legitimate."[102] Less burdensome means, such as hiring goals, were available.[103]

Likewise, the Court's determination of whether the minority preference policies in *Metro Broadcasting* were constitutional rested in part on whether the policies unduly burdened nonminority groups. The benign race conscious program was consistent with equal protection principles if it did not unduly burden nonbenefited groups.[104] This time, the Court concluded that the policies were not unduly burdensome.[105]

Can race conscious numerical measures be adopted voluntarily by private employers without regard to past discrimination?

Yes. This issue is precisely what was addressed and approved by the Supreme Court in *United Steelworkers of America v. Weber*.[106] At issue in *Weber* was a race conscious on-the-job training program for skilled-craft workers. In order to increase minority representation in its work force, the private company voluntarily set a goal of 39 percent minority representation (the minority representation in the surrounding labor force), adopted a hiring ratio of one minority for every white (so that 50 percent of the new skilled-craft employees would be minority workers), and estimated that its goal would be reached under a thirty-year timetable. A white employee challenged this numerically based program as discriminatory under Title VII of the Civil Rights Act of 1964. The Supreme Court rejected the challenge. In its view, the spirit and intent of Title VII was to open job opportunities for minority workers. Since the company's race conscious numerical plan served that purpose without excluding whites, the plan was held lawful under Title VII.[107]

NOTES

1. *Constitutional Scholars' Statement on Affirmative Action after* City of Richmond v. J. A. Croson Co., 98 Yale L.J. 1711, (1989).
2. *Id.* In broad terms, a race conscious program can be any program where race is a deliberate consideration in design, implementation, or purpose of the program. Under this definition, a program to exclude

blacks because of race, as well as a program to include blacks, would be a race conscious program. In this book, we will use the term only to refer to programs that are designed to benefit racial minorities, as when race is used to include or in some way as a plus factor for racial minorities.

3. For a further discussion of affirmative action in the schools, see chapter 4.

4. When there has been a history of past discrimination by an employer or a school, quotas are an appropriate remedy. *City of Richmond v. J. A. Croson*, 488 U.S. 469, 491 (1989). Programs that utilize quotas set aside a certain number of positions that can only be filled by the group to be affirmed. The opponents of affirmative action accuse all affirmative action programs of utilizing this plan even though very few institutions adopt quotas. These opponents argue that affirmative action (quotas) are unfair for two reasons: 1) they take positions away from innocent white males; and 2) they place unqualified minorities in these positions. In fact, very few institutions adopt quotas, and even when quotas are adopted, they do not involve the placement of unqualified people.

5. See discussion of housing and education in chapters 4 and 5. For a good general discussion of the limits of only removing the legal barrier see, Michel Rosenfeld, *Affirmative Action and Justice: A Philosophical and Constitutional Inquiry* (Yale University Press, 1991).

6. *University of California Regents v. Bakke*, 438 U.S. 265 (1978); *Wygant v. Jackson Board of Education*, 476 U.S. 267, 280 (1986) (Powell, J., opinion).

7. *Wygant v. Jackson Board of Education*, 476 U.S. 267, 280 (1986).

8. It is also important to recognize that many scholars feel that a color blind society is not the ideal. All too often, integration of a society requires minorities to assimilate into the dominant culture.

9. *Metro Broadcasting v. FCC*, 110 S. Ct. 2997, 3022 (1990).

10. *See Fullilove v. Klutznick*, 448 U.S. 448, 472 (1980). The *Fullilove* plan allowed for a waiver of the set-aside provision where a Minority Business Enterprise's (MBE) higher bid for a construction project was not attributable to the effects of past discrimination.

11. *Wygant v. Jackson Board of Education*, 476 U.S. 267, 280 (1986) (Powell, J., opinion).

12. *Constitutional Scholars' Statement on Affirmative Action after* City of Richmond v. J. A. Croson Co., 98 Yale L.J., 1711, 1713 (1989).

13. *See Metro Broadcasting v. FCC*, 110 S. Ct. 2997 (1990).

14. *See Id.*, at 3016–17.

15. *Id.*, at 3010.

16. *Id.*, at 3002.

17. *Id.*, at 3009–10.
18. *Id.*
19. *Id.*
20. *Id.*, at 3008–9.
21. *University of California Regents v. Bakke*, 438 U.S. 265 (1978).
22. *Id.*, at 320.
23. *Metro Broadcasting v. FCC*, 110 S. Ct. 2997, 3010 (citing *Bakke*, 438 U.S. at 311–13).
24. 476 U.S. 267, 275 (1986).
25. 488 U.S. 469 (1989).
26. *Id.*, 493–98.
27. *See infra* notes 74 and 75 and accompanying text for disussion of a case in which the Court held that a city had met the strict scrutiny test.
28. *City of Richmond v. J.A. Croson*, 488 U.S. 469, 493 (1989).
29. *Id.*, at 477.
30. *Id.*, at 500.
31. *Id.*, at 498.
32. Section 5 of the Fourteenth Amendment gives Congress the power to enact laws to enforce the provisions of the Fourteenth amendment.
33. 448 U.S. 448 (1980).
34. *Id.* at 490–92 (Burger, C.J. joined by White, J. and Powell, J.)(rejecting the application of traditional equal protection analysis to acts of Congress); *id.* at 519 (Marshall, J., dissenting joined by Brennan, J., and Blackmun, J.)(applying midlevel scrutiny to racial classifications designed for remedial purposes).
35. *Metro Broadcasting v. FCC*, 110 S. Ct. 2997, 3009 (1990).
36. *Id.*, at 3008.
37. *Id.*, at 3009.
38. 480 U.S. 616 (1987).
39. The fact that *Johnson* involved gender discrimination, as opposed to race discrimination, was not relevant to the level of scrutiny applied to the affirmative action plan.
40. Congressional intent with regard to the goals of Title VII, however, has been a subject of debate among the justices. *See e.g.*, *Price Waterhouse v. Hopkins*, 109 S. Ct. 1775 (1989) (O'Connor, J., concurring). Deciphering congressional intent will surely be critical to the extent an employer is arguing that its affirmative action plan comports with the goals and intent of Title VII. But the exact parameters of Congress's intent regarding permissible affirmative action programs should not dictate the level of scrutiny applied to such programs under the Fourteenth Amendment.

41. *Johnson v. Transportation Agency, Santa Clara County,* 480 U.S. 616, 632 (1987). No constitutional claims were raised in *Johnson.*

42. Another indication that *Croson* is not intended to cover affirmative action plans under Title VII is the double standard it would create for public and private employers adopting such plans. Public employers who voluntarily adopt such plans would be subject to the Fourteenth Amendment's strict scrutiny standard while private employers would only have to comply with the less restrictive standards of Title VII. *See* Dixon, *The Dismantling of Affirmative Action Programs: Evaluating* City of Richmond v. J. A. Croson Co., VII Symp. N.Y.L. Sch. J. Hum. Rts. 35, 54–55 (1990).

43. *Metro Broadcasting v. FCC,* 110 S. Ct. 2997, 3009 (1990). *See also City of Richmond v. J.A. Croson,* 488 U.S. 469, 490 (1989) ("Congress, unlike any State or political subdivision, has a specific constitutional mandate to enforce the dictates of the Fourteenth Amendment.").

44. *See Milwaukee County Pavers Ass'n. v. Fiedler,* 731 F. Supp. 1395, 1411–12 (W.D. Wis. 1990), *aff'd,* 922 F.2d 419 (7th Cir. 1991); *see also Harrison & Burrowes Bridge Constructors v. Cuomo,* 743 F. Supp. 977, 1003–4 (N.D.N.Y. 1990)(upholding state minority set-aside program created pursuant to federal statute).

45. 731 F. Supp. 1395 (W.D. Wis. 1990), *aff'd,* 922 F.2d 419 (7th Cir. 1991).

46. *Milwaukee County Pavers Ass'n v. Fiedler,* 922 F.2d 419, 423–24 (7th Cir. 1991).

47. *Id.,* 731 F. Supp. at 1408-10, *aff'd,* 922 F.2d 419 (7th Cir. 1991). The Court rejected plaintiffs' argument that *Fullilove* did not control this case because it was a facial challenge and therefore inapposite to Wisconsin's *implementation* of a federal statute; plaintiffs argued that *Fullilove* still required state and local governments to make specific findings of past discrimination in order to ensure that their implementation of the federal program was "narrowly tailored." The Court attached no significance to the implementation distinction finding that states do not have to make separate findings of past discrimination and may rely on congressional findings under the federal legislation when implementing such legislation. *Id.,* at 1409-10.

48. *Id.,* 731 F. Supp. at 1411.

49. *Id.,* at 1412.

50. *Id.*

51. For a more complete discussion of *Croson, see Constitutional Scholars' Statement on Affirmative Action after* City of Richmond v. J. A. Croson Co., 98 Yale L.J. 1711 (1989) and June 10, 1991 ACLU memo by john a. powell, The Law Since *Croson.*

52. *City of Richmond v. J.A. Croson*, 488 U.S. 469, 500 (1989), *citing Wygant v. Jackson Board of Education*, 476 U.S. 267, 274–75 (1986) (O'Conner, J., concurring).
53. *Id.*, at 500, 507.
54. *Id.*, at 509.
55. *Id.*, at 504.
56. *Id.*, at 492.
57. *Wygant v. Jackson Board of Education*, 476 U.S. 267, 276 (1986); *See also City of Richmond v. J.A. Croson*, 488 U.S. 469, 499, 503 (1989). The majority opinion in *Croson* leaves open the issue of whether the history of such discrimination may be a factor in justifying a more flexible program than the quota utilized in Richmond. See below for a further discussion of *Wygant*.
58. *Id.*, 488 U.S. at 498.
59. *Id.*, at 500.
60. *Id.*, at 501–2.
61. *Id.*, at 502–3.
62. *Id.*, at 504.
63. *Id.*, at 506.
64. *Wygant v. Jackson Board of Education*, 476 U.S. 267, 275 (1986). *Cf. Bakke* and *FCC* where achieving diversity was held to be a compelling state interest.
65. *See* discussion below.
66. *City of Richmond v. J.A. Croson*, 488 U.S. 469, 507 (1989).
67. *Id.*, at 507–8.
68. *Id.*, at 508.
69. The *Fullilove* plan was subject to federal regulations and guidelines requiring that MBE applicants identify "with the disadvantages of his or her racial group generally, and that such disadvantages must have personally affected the applicant's ability to enter into the mainstream of the business system." The sufficiency of the disadvantaged showing was to be determined on a case-by-case basis with membership alone in any group not being conclusive. *See* 448 U.S. at 463–65, 464 n.44.
70. *City of Richmond v. J.A. Croson*, 488 U.S. 469, 508 (1989).
71. 729 F. Supp. 734 (W.D. Wash. 1989).
72. 908 F.2d 908 (11th Cir. 1990).
73. *Also See Milwaukee County Pavers Ass'n v. Fiedler*, 710 F. Supp. 1532 (W.D. Wis. 1989) (modifying and lifting previous preliminary injunction order re: federal set-aside plan and retaining injunction for state set-aside plan), 731 F. Supp. 1395 (W.D. Wis. 1990)(summary judgment), *aff'd*, 922 F.2d 419 (7th Cir. 1991), *cert. denied*, 111 S. Ct. 2261 (1991). *See also Cone Corp. v. Florida Dept. of Trans.*, 921

F.2d 1190 (11th Cir. 1991)(holding that plaintiffs lacked standing to challenge state minority set-aside plan because they did not show past injury or likelihood of future injury).

But see Contractors Ass'n v. City of Philadelphia, 735 F. Supp. 1274 (E.D. Pa. 1990)(MBE set-aside plan stricken), 739 F. Supp. 227 (E.D. Pa. 1990)(denying motion for injunction pending appeal); *Main Line Paving v. Board of Educ.*, 725 F. Supp. 1349 (E.D. Pa. 1989)(MBE set-aside plan stricken); *Ohio Contractors Ass'n v. City of Columbus, Ohio*, 733 F. Supp. 1156 (S.D. Ohio 1990)(MBE set-aside plan permanently enjoined). In each of these cases, the courts struck down the set-aside plans primarily because the defendants failed to present specific evidence of discrimination against the intended beneficiaries of the plans. Instead, the defendants relied on generalized assertions of discrimination. In addition, the Court in *Contractors Ass'n v. City of Philadelphia* found that the city's presentation of evidence of the type found impermissible in *Croson* had tainted the permissible evidence the city did present.

74. *Coral Construction Co. v. King County*, 729 F. Supp. 734 (W.D. Wash. 1989) involved King County's set-aside plan, whereby contractors whose bids were within 5 percent of the lowest bid were given preference if they were MBEs or planned to use MBEs in the project. In addition, for contracts greater than $10,000, the set-aside plan required that MBEs be used for a certain percentage of the work that was tied to the availability of qualified MBE contractors. The Court in *Cone Corp. v. Hillsborough County*, 908 F.2d 908 (11th Cir. 1990) analyzed Hillsborough County's set-aside plan which provided for a Goal Setting Committee to set MBE participation goals for each project based on the available and eligible MBE contractors in the subcontractable area.

75. *Id.*, 729 F. Supp. at 737. The Court permitted the county to rely on evidence of other local jurisdictions with inclusive or common geographic borders. The Court also permitted the county to rely on evidence showing discrimination in the private sector. The Court rejected the argument that the evidence must show discrimination by the county itself. Instead, the Court found that six justices in *Croson* supported the finding that "passive participation" (in private discrimination) by the local government is sufficient to justify remedial action. *Id.* at 737–38.

76. *See City of Richmond v. J.A. Croson*, 488 U.S. 469, 499, 503 (1989).

77. *Cone Corp. v. Hillsborough County*, 908 F.2d 908, 914–15 (11th Cir. 1990).

78. *Coral Construction Co. v. King County*, 729 F. Supp. 734, 739 (W.D.

Wash. 1989) (citing King County, Wash. Code § 4.18.005(E) which found that "no effective [race neutral] alternatives appear to be presently available"). The race neutral alternatives were considered unavailable in part because they were barred by state law.

79. *Id.*

80. *Cone Corp. v. Hillsborough County,* 908 F.2d 908, 916 (11th Cir. 1990).

81. *Coral Construction Co. v. King County,* 729 F. Supp. 734, 739 (W.D. Wash. 1989).

82. *Cone Corp. v. Hillsborough County,* 908 F.2d 908, 917 (11th Cir. 1990).

83. *Coral Construction Co. v. King County,* 729 F. Supp. 734, 739–40 (W.D. Wash. 1989).

84. *Cone Corp. v. Hillsborough County,* 908 F.2d 908, 917 (11th Cir. 1990).

85. This study was prompted by a recent Georgia Supreme Court case holding Atlanta's MBE set-aside program unconstitutional. *See American Subcontractors Ass'n, Georgia Chapter v. City of Atlanta,* 376 S.E. 2d 662 (1989).

86. *See Public Policy and Promotion of Minority Economic Development,* Hearings on *Richmond v. Croson:* Assessing Its Impact on Minority Business Development Programs, Before the Senate Subcomm. on Urban and Minority-Owned Business Development (Aug. 1, 1990) (statement of Andrew F. Brimmer) at 4–5.

87. *See U.S. v. City of Buffalo,* 721 F. Supp. 463 (W.D.N.Y. 1989). *But see Davis v. City and County of San Francisco,* 890 F.2d 1438 (9th Cir. 1989), *cert. denied sub nom. San Francisco Firefighters Local 798 v. City and County of San Francisco,* 111 S. Ct. 248 (1990) (decided before *Metro Broadcasting,* applying *Croson*-strict scrutiny, but upholding the affirmative action plan); *Chicago Firefighters v. Washington,* 736 F. Supp. 923 (N.D. Ill. 1990)(decided before *Metro Broadcasting,* applying *Croson*-strict scrutiny, but upholding the affirmative action plan); *Krupa v. New Castle County,* 732 F. Supp. 497 (D. Del. 1990)(decided before *Metro Broadcasting,* applying *Croson*-strict scrutiny).

88. *City of Buffalo,* 721 F. Supp. at 467 (citations omitted). Although courts have broad remedial powers to eliminate the discriminatory effects of past discrimination, *see Swann v. Charlotte-Mecklenburg Bd. of Educ.,* 402 U.S. 1 (1971); *Louisiana v. U.S.,* 380 U.S. 145 (1965), *City of Buffalo* should not be distinguished from *Davis* and *Chicago Fire Fighters, supra* on the grounds that the Court fully adjudicated the Title VII claims in *City of Buffalo.* Such distinction is inappropriate given Justice O'Connor's warning in *Wygant:*

The imposition of a requirement that public employers [or the Court] make findings that they have engaged in illegal discrimination before they engage in affirmative action programs would severely undermine public employers' incentive to meet voluntarily their civil rights obligations. This result would clearly be at odds with this Court's and Congress' consistent emphasis on "the voluntary efforts to further the objectives of the law."

See also *Chicago Fire Fighters v. Washington*, 736 F. Supp. 923, 928–29 (A.D. Ill. 1990) ("it warrants reiteration that a formal judicial finding of past discrimination is not a constitutional prerequisite to voluntary agreement to an affirmative action program").

89. See *McGrath v. Dept. of Housing and Urban Devel.*, 722 F. Supp. 902 (D. Mass. 1989).

90. 920 F.2d 752, 767 (11th Cir.), *cert. denied*, 111 S. Ct. 2274 (1991).

91. *Id.*, at 753.

92. See *Swann v. Charlotte-Mecklenburg Bd. of Educ.*, 402 U.S. 1 (1971); *Louisiana v. U.S.*, 380 U.S. 145 (1965).

93. But see *U.S. v. State of La.*, 718 F. Supp. 525 (E.D. La. 1989) (applying *Croson* to school's affirmative action plan in admissions, but upholding the plan). See also *Covington v. Beaumont Independent School District*, 714 F. Supp. 1402 (E.D. Tex. 1989)(applying *Croson* to school's transfer of white coaches after the school had achieved "unitary status").

94. This chapter is not intended to be exhaustive on the issue of affirmative action in education. Pursuant to the Bush administration's announcement of its policy against minority scholarships, the ACLU is currently participating in the drafting of a more detailed memorandum on this issue.

95. 110 S. Ct. 2997, 3010 (1990).

96. 438 U.S. 265 (1978).

97. *Id.*, at 311–13.

98. In *Clark v. Arizona Interscholastic Ass'n*, 886 F.2d 1191 (9th Cir. 1989), the Ninth Circuit held that *Croson* did not apply to a state restriction on interscholastic volleyball limiting competition to single-sex teams where a male student was precluded from playing interscholastic volleyball because the only team at his school was a female team. The Court applied midlevel scrutiny and held that the rule was "substantially related to the goal of redressing past discrimination and promoting equality of the sexes." *Id.*, at 1194.

99. 476 U.S. 267, 280–81 (1986).

100. *Id.*, at 282–83.

101. *Id.*, at 283.

102. *Id.*
103. *Id.*, at 283–84.
104. 110 S. Ct. 2997, 3025–26 (1990).
105. *Id.*
106. 443 U.S. 193 (1979).
107. *Id.*

XI

The Legal System

For many persons, law appears to be magic—an obscure domain that can be fathomed only by the professionals initiated into its mysteries. People who might be able to use the law to their advantage sometimes avoid the effort out of awe for its intricacies. But the main lines of the legal system, and of the law in a particular area, can be explained in terms clear to the layperson.

What does a lawyer mean by saying that a person has a legal right?

Having a right means that society has given a person permission—through the legal system—to secure some action or to act in some way that she or he desires. For example, a woman might have a right to an abortion, a job applicant the right to employment free from discrimination, or a person accused of a crime the right to an attorney.

How does one enforce a legal right?

The concept of enforcing a right gives meaning to the concept of the right itself. While the abstract right may be significant because it carries some connotation of morality and justice, enforcing the right yields something concrete—the abortion, the job, the attorney.

A person enforces a right by going to some appropriate authority—often, a judge—who has the power to take certain action. The judge can order the people who are refusing to grant the right to start doing so, on pain of a fine or jail if they disobey.

The problem with the enforcement process is that it will often be lengthy, time-consuming, expensive, frustrating, and may arouse hostility in others—in short, it may not be worth the effort. On the other hand, in some cases it is not necessary to go to an enforcement authority in order to implement a right. The officials may not realize that a right exists and may voluntarily change their actions once the situation is explained to them. Further, the officials may not want to go through the legal process either—it may be expensive and frustrating for them also.

Where are legal rights defined?

There are several sources. Rights are defined in the statutes or laws passed by the United States Congress and by state and city legislatures. They are also set forth in the written decisions of federal and state judges. Congress and state and local legislatures have also created institutions called administrative agencies to enforce certain laws, and these agencies interpret the laws in decisions and rules that further define people's rights.

Are rights always clearly defined and evenly applied to all people?

Not at all. Because so many different sources define people's rights and because persons of diverse backgrounds and beliefs implement and enforce the law, there is virtually no way to uniformity. Nor do statutes that set forth rights always do so with clarity or specificity. It remains for courts or administrative agencies to interpret and to flesh out the details. In the process of doing so, many of the interpreters differ. Sometimes, two courts will give different answers to the same question. Whether or not a person has a particular right may depend on which state or city he or she lives in.

The more times a particular issue is decided, the more guidance there is in predicting what other judges or administrative personnel will decide. Similarly, the importance of the court or agency that decides a case and the persuasiveness of its reasoning will help determine the impact of the decision. A judge who states thoughtful reasons will have more influence than one who offers poor reasons.

In sum, law is not a preordained set of doctrines, applied rigidly and unswervingly in every situation. Rather, law is molded from the arguments and decisions of thousands of persons. It is very much a human process, of trying to convince others—a judge, a jury, an administrator, the lawyer for the other side—that one view of what the law requires is correct.

What is a decision or case?

Lawyers often use these words interchangeably, although technically they do not mean the same thing. A *case* means the lawsuit started by one person against another, and it can refer to that lawsuit at any time from the moment it is begun until the final result. A *decision* means the written opinion in which the judge declares who wins the lawsuit and why.

What is meant by precedent?

Precedent means past decisions. Lawyers use precedent to influence new decisions. If the facts involved in a prior decision are close to the facts in a new case, a judge will be strongly tempted to follow the former decision. She is not, however, bound to do so and, if persuasive reasons are presented to show that the prior decision was wrong or ill-suited to changed conditions in society, the judge may not follow precedent.

What is the relationship between decisions and statutes?

In our legal system, most legal concepts originally were defined in the decisions of judges. In deciding what legal doctrine to apply to a case, each judge kept building on what other judges had done. The body of legal doctrines created in this way is called the *common law*.

The common law still applies in many situations, but increasingly state legislatures and the Congress pass laws (statutes) to define the legal concepts that judges or agencies should use in deciding cases. The written decisions of individual judges are still important even where there is a statute because statutes are generally not specific enough to cover every set of facts. Judges have to interpret their meaning, apply them to the facts at hand, and write a decision; that decision will then be considered by other judges when they deal with these statutes in other cases. Thus it is generally not enough to know what a relevant statute defines as illegal; you also have to know how judges have interpreted the statute in specific situations.

What different kinds of courts are there?

The United States is unique for its variety of courts. Broadly speaking, there are two distinct court systems: federal and state. Both are located throughout the country; each is limited to certain kinds of cases, with substantial areas of overlap. Most crimes are prosecuted in state courts, for instance, although a number of federal crimes are prosecuted in federal courts. People generally use state courts to get a divorce, but they must sue in federal court to establish rights under certain federal laws.

In both federal and state court systems one starts at the *trial* or *lower court* level, where the facts are "tried." This means that a judge or jury listens and watches as the lawyers present evidence of the facts that each side seeks to prove. Evidence can take many forms: written documents, the testimony of a witness on the stand, photographs, charts. Once a judge or jury has listened to or observed all the evidence presented by each side, it will choose the version of the facts it believes, apply the applicable legal doctrine to these facts, and decide which side has won. If either side is unhappy with the result, it may be able to take the case to the next, higher-level court and argue that the judge or the jury applied the wrong legal concept to the facts or that no reasonable jury or judge could have found the facts as they were found in the trial court and that the result was therefore wrong.

What are plaintiffs and defendants?

The *plaintiff* is the person who sues—that is, who complains that someone has wronged him or her and asks the court to remedy this situation. The *defendant* is the person sued—the one who defends against the charges of the plaintiff. The legal writing in which the plaintiff articulates her or his basic grievance is the *complaint*, and a lawsuit is generally commenced by filing this document with a clerk at a courthouse. The defendant then responds to these charges in a document appropriately named an *answer*.

One refers to a particular lawsuit by giving the names of the plaintiff and defendant. If Mary Jones sues Smith Corporation for refusing to hire her because she is a woman, her case will be called *Jones v. Smith Corporation* (v. stands for versus, or against).

What is an administrative agency?

Agencies are institutions established by either state or federal legislatures to administer or enforce a particular law or series of laws and are distinct from both courts and legislature. They often regulate a particular industry. For example, the Federal Communications Commission regulates the broadcasting industry (radio and television stations and networks) and the telephone and telegraph industry, in accordance with the legal standards set forth in the Federal Communications Act.

Agencies establish legal principles, embodied in rules, regulations, or guidelines. *Rules* are interpretations of a statute and are designed to function in the same way as a statute—to define people's rights and obligations in a general way but in a more detailed fashion than the statute itself. Agencies also issue specific decisions in cases, like a judge, that apply a broad law or rule to a factual dispute between particular parties.

How does one find court decisions, statutes, and agency rules and decisions?

All these materials are published and can be found in law libraries. In order to find a desired item, one should understand the system lawyers use for referring to, or citing, these materials. For example, a case might be cited as *Watson v. Limbach Company*, 333 F. Supp. 754 (S.D. Ohio 1971); a statute, as 42 U.S.C. § 1983; a regulation, as 29 C.F.R. § 1604.10(b). The unifying factor in all three citations is that the first number denotes the particular volume in a series of books with the same title; the words or the letters that follow represent the name of the book; and the second number represents either the page or the section in the identified volume. In the examples above, the *Watson* case is found in the 333rd volume of the series of books called *Federal Supplement* at page 754; the statute is found in volume 42 of the series called the *United States Code* at Section 1983; the regulation is in volume 29 of the *Code of Federal Regulations* at section 1604.10(b).

There are similar systems for state court decision. Once the system is understood, a librarian can point out where a particular series of books is kept so that the proper volume and page or section can be looked up. It is also important to check the same page or section in material sometimes inserted at the back of a book, since many legal materials are periodically updated with "pocket parts." A librarian will explain what any abbreviations stand for that are unclear.

Given this basic information, anyone can locate and read important cases, statutes, and regulations. Throughout this book, such materials have been cited when deemed important. Although lawyers often use technical language, the references cited usually can be comprehended without serious difficulty, and reading the original legal materials gives people self-confidence and a deeper understanding of their rights.

What is the role of the lawyer in the legal system?

A lawyer understands the intricacies and technicalities of the legal system and can maneuver within it. Thus lawyers know where to find out about the leading legal doctrines in a given area and often how to predict the outcome of a case based on a knowledge of those doctrines. A lawyer can advise a client what to do: forget about the case; take it to an administrative agency; sue in court; make a will; and so on. A lawyer also helps take the legal actions that the client wants.

How are legal costs determined and how do they affect people's rights?

The cost of using the legal system is predominantly the cost of paying the lawyer for his or her time. Since the cost has become prohibitive even for middle-class individuals, many people are not able to assert their rights, even though they might ultimately win if they had the money to pay a lawyer for doing the job.

Is legal action the only way to win one's legal rights?

By no means. Negotiation, education, consciousness raising, publicity, demonstrations, organization, and lobbying are all ways to achieve rights, often more effectively than through the standard but costly and time-consuming resort to the courts. In all these areas, it helps to have secure knowledge of the legal underpinnings of your rights. One has a great deal more authority if one is protesting illegal action. The refrain "That's illegal" may move some people in and of itself; or it may convince those with whom a person is dealing that he or she is serious enough to do something about the situation—by starting a lawsuit, for instance.

Appendix A

Federal Agencies Responsible for Enforcing the Rights of Racial Minorities

Under the hundred-year-old Reconstruction constitutional amendments and civil rights acts, little power of enforcement was delegated to federal agencies. Instead, the rights of racial minorities were enforced and obtained almost exclusively through lawsuits filed by racial minorities themselves.

Modern civil rights legislation has supplemented reliance on private enforcement by authorizing and sometimes requiring federal agencies to enforce the rights of racial minorities. The impact of this authorization is twofold. First, the authorization usually means that federal agencies will receive administrative charges of discrimination, will negotiate informally with alleged discriminators, and ultimately may sue the discriminators, thereby making private lawsuits by racial minorities unnecessary. Second, the authorization means that administrative charges of discrimination (e.g., a letter to the federal agency describing the discrimination) should and sometimes *must* be filed with the federal agencies before racial minorities are permitted to file private lawsuits.

The authorization of civil rights enforcement by federal agencies does not mean that the federal agencies adequately perform their enforcement obligations. Nonetheless, when those obligations are performed, it always is helpful to have the power of the federal government on one's side.

The names and addresses of the specific federal agencies responsible for enforcement of a particular area of law are set out in this appendix. Most of the federal agencies mentioned in this book maintain their central offices in Washington, D. C. Most of them also have regional offices in the ten federal regions centered in the following cities:

Boston	Region I
New York	Region II
Philadelphia	Region III
Atlanta	Region IV

Chicago	Region V
Dallas	Region VI
Kansas City, MO	Region VII
Denver	Region VIII
San Francisco	Region IX
Seattle	Region X

In addition to their regional offices, some federal agencies maintain district offices in nearly every city in the United States.

A person who needs information about the rights of racial minorities, about the filing of administrative charges of discrimination, or about the nature and extent of federal agency enforcement should contact the appropriate federal agency. This can be accomplished by contacting the agency either at its main office, *or at any of the regional or district offices throughout the United States.* The addresses and phone numbers of the latter offices are not listed in this book but are readily available through local telephone directories.

The one federal agency that has been delegated the broadest responsibility for civil rights enforcement is the Department of Justice.

Department of Justice
10th and Constitution
Washington, D. C. 20530
202/514-2151

It maintains at least one office and sometimes more than one in each of our fifty states. These offices, usually referred to as offices of the United States Attorney, are located in or near the federal court buildings in the major city or cities of each state. A person who needs information about the rights of racial minorities, about how to file an administrative charge of discrimination with the Department of Justice, or about the nature and extent of civil rights enforcement by the Department of Justice should contact the Department of Justice in Washington, D.C., or a nearby office of the United States Attorney.

As we have indicated in this book, the Department of Justice is not the only federal agency responsible for federal civil rights enforcement. The various agencies, with their addresses and phone numbers, are listed below.

Voting, Chapter 2

The federal agency with responsibility for ensuring nondiscrimination in voting is the Department of Justice. The department has the duty to preclear changes in voting procedures submitted under section 5 of the Voting Rights Act of 1965; to register voters and assign poll watchers where necessary to guarantee equal voting rights; to ensure that language minorities are provided with bilingual voting information and instructions; to file lawsuits against jurisdictions that continue to discriminate against minorities in the elective process; and to defend lawsuits brought by jurisdictions seeking exemption from Voting Rights Act coverage. The address of the Department of Justice is given above.

Employment, Chapter 3

The primary federal agency responsible for enforcing the rights of racial minorities to nondiscrimination in employment is the Equal Employment Opportunity Commission (EEOC). It is responsible under Title VII of the Civil Rights Act of 1964, as amended, for receiving and investigating administrative charges of discrimination, for issuing right to sue letters to persons who intend to sue private employers and unions, for suing private employers and unions, and for resolving appeals involving discrimination in federal employment.

Equal Employment Opportunity Commission
1801 L Street, N.W.
Washington, D. C. 20507
202/663-4110

Another federal agency with civil rights enforcement powers in employment is the Department of Justice. The Department of Justice is responsible, under Title VII, for issuing right-to-sue letters to persons who intend to sue state and local government employers, and for filing pattern-or-practice lawsuits against discriminatory employers. The address of the Department of Justice is given above.

A special federal agency with civil rights enforcement responsibilities in employment relating to state and local law enforcement agencies is the Office of Justice Programs (OJP) within the Department of Justice. The OJP has the duty of ensuring that the recipients of federal funding to state and local law enforcement agencies under the Justice System Improvement Act of 1984 do not engage in discrimination.

Department of Justice
Office of Justice Programs
633 Indiana Avenue, N.W.
Washington, D.C. 20531
202/307-0690

Education, Chapter 4

The federal agency responsible for receiving administrative charges of discrimination and for filing lawsuits against discriminatory school systems is the Department of Justice (address above).

Another federal agency responsible for ensuring nondiscrimination in education is the Department of Education. The department both provides extensive federal funding to educational institutions and is responsible, under Title VI of the Civil Rights Act of 1964, for ensuring that recipients of that funding do not engage in discrimination. Specifically, the department is responsible for receiving, investigating, and attempting to resolve administrative charges of discrimination and for suspending funding to educational institutions that do engage in discrimination.

Department of Education
Civil Rights Office
330 C Street, S.W.
Washington, D.C. 20202
202/732-1213

Housing, Chapter 5

The federal agency responsible, under Title VIII of the Civil Rights Act of 1968, for receiving and investigating administrative charges of discrimination and for suing persons, companies, and state and local governments that engage in discriminatory housing practices is the Department of Housing and Urban Development (HUD). HUD also is responsible, under Title VI of the Civil Rights Act of 1964, for receiving and investigating administrative charges of discrimination filed against recipients of federal housing funding, and for suspending the funding to those recipients that do engage in discrimination.

Department of Housing and Urban Development
Office of Fair Housing and Equal Opportunity
451 7th Street, S.W.
Washington, D.C. 20410
202/708-4252

Public Accommodations, Chapter 6

Three federal agencies have basic responsibility for ensuring equal access to and use of public accommodations.

The Department of Justice has the duty under Titles II and III of the Civil Rights Act of 1964 to investigate complaints and bring (or intervene in) lawsuits against discrimination in public accommodations. The address is given at the beginning of this appendix.

The Community Relations Service (CRS) is a special agency established under Title VIII of the Civil Rights Act of 1964 and has the general responsibility of receiving complaints and assisting communities in resolving disputes relating to racial discrimination. After a lawsuit has been filed to enforce Title II, the federal court has authority to refer the matter to the CRS to seek a voluntary resolution of the discrimination.

Department of Justice
Community Relations Service
5550 Friendship Boulevard
Chevy Chase, MD 20815
301/492-5929

The Interstate Commerce Commission (ICC), established under the Interstate Commerce Act of 1887, has the duty to hear and resolve administrative complaints of discrimination in interstate commerce. The ICC is also authorized to file lawsuits in the federal courts against common carriers who discriminate in the provision of services and accommodations.

Interstate Commerce Commission
12th and Constitution Avenue, N.W.
Washington, D.C. 20423
202/275-7582

Federally Assisted Discrimination, Chapter 7

There are approximately thirty agencies that distribute federal funds to state, local, and private entities and that therefore are required to ensure nondiscrimination in the use of those funds by Title VI of the Civil Rights Act of 1964. Each agency is responsible for receiving and investigating administrative charges of discrimination filed against recipients and for suspending federal funding to recipients engaging in discrimination. The regulations adopted by each agency to administer Title VI are also listed.

Action
1100 Vermont Avenue, N.W.
Washington, D.C. 20525
202/606-4880
45 C.F.R. pt. 1203

Department of Agriculture
Office of Equal Opportunity and Civil Rights
12th and C Streets, S.W.
Washington, D.C. 20250
202/205-0743
7 C.F.R. §§ 15.1-.12, .60-.143

Department of Commerce
Civil Rights Office
14th and Constitution Avenue, N.W.
Washington, D.C. 20230
202/377-0625
15 C.F.R. pt. 8

Department of Defense
The Pentagon
Washington, D.C. 20301
703/695-5261
32 C.F.R. pt. 300

Department of Education
Civil Rights Office
330 C. Street, S.W.
Washington, D.C. 20202
202/732-1213
34 C.F.R. pt. 100

Department of Energy
1000 Independence Avenue, S.W.
Washington, D.C. 20585
202/586-6210
10 C.F.R. pt. 1040

Department of Health and Human Services
200 Independence Avenue, S.W.
Washington, D.C. 20201
202/245-7000
45 C.F.R. pt. 80

Department of the Interior
1849 C Street, N.W.
Washington, D.C. 20240
202/208-7351
43 C.F.R. pt. 17

Department of Justice
10th and Constitution
Washington, D.C. 20530
202/514-2151
28 C.F.R. §§ 42.101-.112

Department of Labor
200 Constitution Avenue, N.W.
Washington, D.C. 20210
202/523-8271
29 C.F.R. pt. 31

Department of State
2201 C Street, N.W.
Washington, D.C. 20520
202/647-5291
22 C.F.R. pt. 141

Department of Transportation
Civil Rights
800 Independence Avenue, S.W.
Washington, D.C. 20591
202/267-3254
49 C.F.R. pt. 21
14 C.F.R. pt. 379

Department of the Treasury
15th and Pennsylvania Avenue, N.W.
Washington, D.C. 20220
202/566-2533
31 C.F.R. pt. 51
12 C.F.R. pt. 529

Department of Veterans' Affairs
810 Vermont Avenue, N.W.
Washington, D.C. 20420
202/535-8900
38 C.F.R. §§ 19.1-.13

Environmental Protection Agency
401 M Street, S.W.
Washington, D.C. 20460
202/260-4700
40 C.F.R. pt. 7

Federal Emergency Management Agency
500 C Street, S.W.
Washington, D.C. 20472
202/646-3923
44 C.F.R. pt. 7

General Services Administration
18th and F Streets, N.W.
Washington, D.C. 20405
202/501-0800
41 C.F.R. §§ 10106.2

International Development Cooperation Agency/
Agency for International Development
320 21st Street, N.W.
Washington, D.C. 20523
202/647-9620
22 C.F.R. pt. 209

National Aeronautics and Space Administration
400 Maryland Avenue, S.W.
Washington, D.C. 20546
202/453-1010
14 C.F.R. pt. 1250

National Endowment for the Arts
1100 Pennsylvania Avenue, N.W.
Washington, D.C. 20506
202/682-5414
45 C.F.R. pt. 1110

National Endowment for the Humanities
1100 Pennsylvania Avenue, N.W.
Washington, D.C. 20506
202/786-0310
45 C.F.R. pt. 1110

National Science Foundation
1800 G Street, N.W.
Washington, D.C. 20550
202/357-7748
45 C.F.R. pt. 611

Nuclear Regulatory Commission
Washington, D.C. 20555
301/492-7000
10 C.F.R. §§ 4.11-.93

Office of Personnel Management
1900 E. Street, N.W.
Washington, D.C. 20415
202/606-1000
5 C.F.R. §§ 900.401-.412

Small Business Administration
409 Third Street, S.W.
Washington, D.C. 20416
202/205-6605
13 C.F.R. pt. 112

Tennessee Valley Authority
400 W. Summit Hill Drive
Knoxville, TN 37902
615/632-3554
18 C.F.R. pt. 1302

Department of Housing and Urban Development
451 7th Street, N.W.
Washington, D.C. 20410
202/708-0417
24 C.F.R. pt. 1

United States Information Agency
301 4th Street, S.W.
Washington, D.C. 20547
202/619-4742
22 C.F.R. pt. 141

Jury Selection and Trials, Chapter 8

As a practical matter, the enforcement of nondiscrimination in jury selection and trials is implemented by defendants in criminal cases and private individuals in affirmative civil lawsuits. There is no federal agency with general supervisory authority over the courts as, for example, the Department of Justice has over changes in voting practices by state and local governments.

Federal Criminal Statutes Protecting the Rights of Minorities, Chapter 9

The President has the duty under article II, section 3 of the Constitution to "take Care that the Laws be faithfully executed." This prerogative of the executive branch of government of enforcing the criminal laws has been implemented by Congress by giving the exclusive power to prosecute federal offenses, including violations of federal statutes protecting racial minorities, to the Department of Justice and the offices of the United States Attorney in the various federal districts. The address of the Department of Justice is given at the beginning of this appendix.

Appendix B
Legal Resources for Racial Minorities
Who Need Legal Assistance

Most of the civil rights laws guaranteeing the rights of minorities are, as we have seen, enforced by the federal government. Thus, in most instances, information about your rights and about enforcement of those rights can and should be obtained from the federal agencies listed in appendix A.

There will be occasions, however, wherein you may need information more quickly, help against the federal government, or representation in a lawsuit you intend to file to obtain your rights. In these and other instances you may need a lawyer.

Finding a lawyer is easier than you might think. Finding the right lawyer for you is sometimes more difficult.

In looking for a lawyer you should be aware of four sources of legal assistance: (1) lawyers in private practice; (2) federally and/or locally supported legal services organizations; (3) national civil liberties and civil rights organizations with local offices; and (4) regional, local, or specialized civil liberties and civil rights organizations. When looking for a lawyer, you should contact the lawyer or organization you think is most appropriate for you. You need not, of course, limit yourself to only one source.

1. *Lawyers in Private Practice.* There simply are not enough lawyers on the staffs of civil liberties and civil rights organizations to assist, much less to represent in lawsuits, all of the people who have had their rights to nondiscrimination violated. Accordingly, much of the advice and representation provided to such people is supplied by lawyers who practice law in private law firms. Many of these lawyers, incidentally, have worked with and remain affiliated with one or more of the civil liberties and civil rights organizations listed below.

There are two ways to find a lawyer in private practice to assist you. The first method is basically by word of mouth. Ask your friends and colleagues about their lawyers. Find out about lawyers in your area who have assisted persons in positions similar to yours. And look in the telephone book for the names of local groups of lawyers (such as the local bar association's lawyers' referral service). Once you find an attorney, you should briefly interview him or her to assure yourself that you feel comfortable with the person and that he or she appears capable and has at least some knowledge about civil rights law.

A second way to find a lawyer in private practice is through the civil liberties and civil rights organizations listed below. Although the organizations themselves might not be able to assist you, they usually will be able to refer you to private lawyers who will. If you are having difficulty finding an attorney, you should contact such an organization for a referral.

Before you obtain your own private lawyer, you should be aware that lawyers, like doctors, have fees you will have to pay. Remember, though, that if you have a good case and have to go to court, you may be able to recover your attorney's fees from your opponent if you win. To recover fees, you must be the "prevailing party," which means you received some of the relief you sought as a result of bringing the case.

2. *Legal Services Organizations.* If you are poor or unemployed, you may be eligible for free legal assistance from a local legal services organization supported by federal and local funding. These organizations, usually referred to as Legal Aid Societies or Legal Services Organizations, employ from a handful to dozens of lawyers who provide legal assistance to poor people in all areas of law, including discrimination law. These organizations exist in nearly every city and county in the country.

In order to find the nearest legal services organization, you should look through the phone book or call your local government for advice. If you have difficulty finding the appropriate local organizations, there are several national organizations that can help.

National Legal Aid and Defender Association
1625 K Street, N.W.
Washington, D.C. 20006
202/452-0620

Most legal services lawyers or their organizations are members of the NLADA. The NLADA might be able to refer you to the appropriate legal services office in your area.

Legal Service Corporation
400 Virginia Avenue, S.W.
Washington, D.C. 20024
202/863-1820

The Legal Services Corporation is an independent agency that provides federal funding to most legal services organizations. It should be able to refer you to an appropriate legal services office in your area.

3. *National Civil Liberties and Civil Rights Organizations.* There are several national civil liberties and civil rights organizations that have state and local offices (usually called chapters or affiliates) throughout the United States. Generally, the national offices will not be able to assist you directly but will refer you to one of their local offices, which may be able to assist you.

The local offices of the following major organizations are listed in your telephone directory. If you can't find them, you should write to the national offices for referrals.

American Civil Liberties Union
132 West 43d Street
New York, New York 10036
212/944-9800

The ACLU specializes in civil liberties/civil rights law. There are state affiliates and local chapters of the ACLU in nearly every state.

Lawyers Committee for Civil Rights under Law
1400 I Street, N.W.
Washington, D.C. 20005
202/371-1212

The Lawyers Committee concentrates on all aspects of racial discrimination law, primarily on behalf of black persons. It maintains a number of regional and local offices, and it widely uses the volunteer services of lawyers in private law firms.

Mexican American Legal Defense and Educational Fund
634 S. Spring Street
Los Angeles, California 90014
213/629-2512

MALDEF specializes in discrimination law and represents Mexican Americans almost exclusively. Its offices are located primarily in the Midwest, the Southwest, and the West.

National Association for the Advancement of Colored
    People
4805 Mount Hope Drive
Baltimore, Maryland 21215
301/358-8900

The NAACP, the oldest and largest of the civil rights organizations, specializes in racial discrimination law on behalf of black persons. It has state and local chapters throughout the United States.

National Lawyers Guild
55 Avenue of the Americas
New York, New York 10003
212/966-5000

The Guild, a membership organization of civil rights lawyers, focuses upon unpopular legal causes, including the rights of dissenters and minorities. It maintains offices in most major cities and has over 110 chapters throughout the country.

National Urban League
1111 14th Street, N.W.
Washington, D.C. 20005
202/898-1604

Like the NAACP, the National Urban League specializes in racial discrimination law on behalf of black people and has offices throughout the United States.

Puerto Rican Legal Defense and Education Fund
99 Hudson Street
New York, New York 10013
212/219-3360

The PRLDEF specializes in discrimination law and particularly in bilingual education law. It maintains several offices, primarily in the Northeast.

4. *Regional, Local, and Specialized Civil Liberties and Civil Rights Organizations.* There are numerous regional, local, and